A

BOOK
IS A PRESENT

YOU CAN OPEN
AGAIN
and
AGAIN

This Book Belongs To

Karen S. Campbell

© Mary Engelbreit

An Illustrated
Guide to
Composers of
Opera

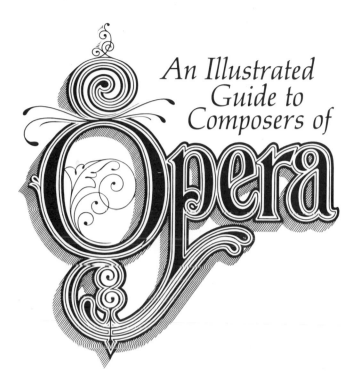

*An Illustrated
Guide to
Composers of*

Opera

a Salamander book

Published by Arco Publishing, Inc.
NEW YORK

A SALAMANDER BOOK

Published by
Arco Publishing, Inc.,
219 Park Avenue South,
New York,
N.Y. 10003,
United States of America

© 1980 by Salamander Books Ltd.,
27 Old Gloucester Street,
London WC1N 3AF,
United Kingdom.

Library of Congress catalog card number 81-66319

ISBN 0-668-05317-8

All correspondence concerning the content of this volume
should be addressed to Salamander Books Ltd.

CONTENTS

CREDITS

Compiler: Peter Gammond, former
Music Editor of the monthly British magazine
Hi-Fi News. Since 1960 he has worked in a
freelance capacity for various periodicals and
newspapers and on BBC radio and television.
He is the author of 25 books on music.

Editor: Marita Westberg

Designer: Rod Teasdale

Printed in Belgium by
Henri Proost et Cie.

Publisher's Note: A cross-reference symbol » is
used throughout the book after the names of those
composers who have their own main entry.

The biographies in this book have previously
appeared in *The Illustrated Encyclopedia of
Recorded Opera*.

FOREWORD

Opera, to its devotees, is the most fascinating and diverse kind of music-making ever devised, and because of its immense variety it has something to offer all tastes. The music reflects the fashions and tastes of its audiences throughout its history perhaps more clearly than any other musical activity, for opera, by its very nature, was always written for public appreciation and acclaim. But opera is more than just music; it is basically song—the magical blending of words and music that immediately adds another dimension of interest. It is also drama and has all the added human involvement of the theatre. In some music-making, chamber music for instance, it is almost desirable that its exponents shall intrude their personalities as little as possible. But opera is written to spotlight personalities and characters and takes us into a literary as well as a musical world.

It has been said many times, and with some justification, that opera is the most nonsensical of all art forms; an artificial entertainment where characters sing what might as well be spoken, or, at times, might even be better spoken. Even an opera fanatic can

sense the precarious nature of the art. Yet each time we experience a great opera production, the magic happens; song becomes as natural as speech, music heightens emotion and the theatrical atmosphere of the opera house ensnares us. It is a glorious artistic juggling act when everything goes right—but how easily it could go wrong if it were not for the skill and dedication of its performers, who not only have to act a part but also perform difficult and demanding music for a whole evening.

Because of its fascinating history and its intriguing nature, there will never be an end to the books on opera. For many, a convenient and satisfying way of getting to know the operatic repertoire is through the superb recordings that exist, covering almost every worthwhile work and often performed by a cast of star performers that only the top opera houses could afford. For the newcomers to opera, who wish to be guided into this magical world, this book is a brief factual guide to opera composers and their works; an introduction to much potential enjoyment and satisfaction.

ADOLPHE ADAM
(b. Paris 24.7.1803; d. Paris 3.5.1856)

Adam's father, a musician, was reluctant to encourage him to enter the profession. Eventually he relented and the young Adam entered the Paris Conservatoire, where he studied under Boieldieu ». In his spare time he played in theatre orchestras and wrote some pieces for the music-halls, then in 1825 Boieldieu asked him to help with the orchestration of *La Dame Blanche*. This brought Adam to the attention of the Opéra-Comique, where his *Pierre et Catherine* was produced in 1829. Although Adam's music was mainly facile and only occasionally inspired, he nevertheless remains important as one of the few composers who bridged the gap between the opéra-comique and the operettas of Offenbach » and his successors. Berlioz » described Adam's music as "admirably suited to the requirements of the Opéra-Comique, for it is stylish, fluent, undistinguished and full of catchy little tunes which one can whistle on the way home". His light, vaudeville style was first seen in *Le Châlet* (1834) and his first full-length work, *Le Postillon de Longjumeau* (1836), has some excellent ensembles and one memorable aria which has remained popular with tenors. He was a prolific writer, eventually producing 24 operas, most of which are remembered today mainly for their catchy overtures. Ironically, his most popular work is not operatic, but the ballet *Giselle* (1841). In 1847 Adam founded the Théâtre National, and in 1849 became Professor of Composition at the Paris Conservatoire.

Le Postillon de Longjumeau
Opéra-comique in 3 Acts.
Text by Adolphe de Leuven and Léon Lévy Brunswick.
First performance: Paris (Opéra-Comique) October 13, 1836.

Le Toréador
Opéra-comique in 2 Acts.
Text by Thomas Sauvage.
First performance: Paris (Opéra-Comique) May 18, 1849.

Giralda
Opéra-comique in 3 Acts.
Text by Eugène Scribe.
First performance: Paris (Opéra-Comique) July 20, 1850.

La Poupée de Nuremburg
Opéra-comique in 1 Act.
Text by Adolphe de Leuven and Arthur de Beauplan.
First performance: Paris (Opéra-National) February 21, 1852.

Si j'etais roi
Opéra-comique in 3 Acts.
Text by Adolphe d'Ennery.
First performance: Paris (Théâtre-Lyrique) September 4, 1852.

Above: *Adolphe Adam, composer of 24 operas in the light French* opéra-comique *vein, and of the ballet* Giselle.

Pierre et Catherine (1829)
Danilowa (1830)
Le Châlet (1834)
Le Fidèle Berger (1838)
Le Brasseur de Preston (1838)
Régine, ou Les Deux Nuits (1839)
La Reine d'un jour (1839)
La Rose de Péronne (1840)
Le Roi d'Yvetot (1842)
Lambert Simnel (1843)

Cagliostro (1844)
Richard in Palestine (1844)
Le Farfadet (1852)
Le Sourd, ou L'Auberge pleine
  (1853)
Le Roi des Halles (1853)
Le Bijou perdu (1853)
Le Muletier de Tolède (1854)
Falstaff (1856)
Les Pantins de Violette (1856)

THOMAS ARNE

(b. London 12.3.1710; d. London 5.3.1778)

Intended for a legal career, Arne was educated at Eton and then apprenticed to a lawyer; but his inclinations were musical and he spent most of this time composing. He soon made his mark with a distinct vein of Englishness at a time when British music was submerged under the influence of Handel » and Italian opera. His writing has been described as having "an agreeable straight-forwardness and honourable simplicity". His reputation as a composer was established with the masque *Comus*, a setting of Milton's words written in 1738; and he achieved wide popularity with the masque *Alfred*, which contained the immortal song 'Rule, Britannia'. He was appointed resident composer at Drury Lane and started to produce his best operas after 1760 when he collaborated with Isaac Bickerstaffe on *Thomas and Sally*, followed by the ballad opera *Love in a Village* (1762). His most substantial and lasting opera was *Artaxerxes* (1762), which remained in the Covent Garden repertoire until the 19th century.

Thomas and Sally
Dramatic pastoral in 2 Acts.
Text by Isaac Bickerstaffe.
First performance: London (Covent Garden) November 28, 1760

Notes:
Interesting as the first English opera to use clarinets in its scoring: an innovation probably due to the helping hand of J. C. Bach. It also used recitative instead of dialogue — unusual at the time in English opera. The work once enjoyed great popularity.

Artaxerxes
Opera in 2 Acts.
Text by Thomas Arne, translated from Metastasio's 'Artaserse'.
First performance: London (Covent Garden) February 2, 1762.

The Cooper
Opera in 1 Act.
Text by Thomas Arne, based on 'Le Tonnelier' by Audinot and Quétant.
First performance: London (Haymarket) June 9, 1772.

Rosamond (1733)
The Opera of Operas, or
*   Tom Thumb (1733)*
The Temple of Dullness (1745)
Eliza (1755)
Love in a Village (1762)
L'Olimpiade (1764)
etc.

Left: *The eccentric but much-loved Thomas Arne.*

Above: *A caricature by André Gill of composer Daniel Auber.*

DANIEL AUBER
(b. Caen 29.1.1782; d. Paris 12.5.1871)

Auber composed early in life, but for some years he followed a commercial career in London. He won attention as a composer by some attractive songs and his Cello and Violin Concertos (1804). His first opera, *L'Erreur d'un moment*, appeared in Paris in 1805, but he had little success in this field until 1820 when *La Bergère Châtelaine* was well received at the Opéra-Comique. In 1842 he became the Director of the Paris Conservatoire. He wrote 43 operas, now mainly remembered for their overtures and an occasional aria. He had a good technique and, like so many of the best French opéra-comique composers, wrote in a decidedly Mozartian vein. His most sparkling opera was *Fra Diavolo* (1830), while his *La Muette de Portici* (1828, also known as *Masaniello*) was his grandest, remaining popular till the end of the 19th century.

La Muette de Portici (Masaniello)
Opera in 5 Acts.
Text by Eugène Scribe and Germain Delavigne.
First performance: Paris (Opéra) February 29, 1828.

Fra Diavolo
Opéra-comique in 3 Acts.
Text by Eugène Scribe.
First performance: Paris (Opéra-Comique) January 28, 1830.

Lestocq
Opéra-comique in 4 Acts.
Text by Eugène Scribe.
First performance: Paris (Opéra-Comique) May 24, 1834.

Le Cheval de Bronze
Opéra-féerique in 3 Acts.
Text by Eugène Scribe.
First performance: Paris (Opéra-Comique) March 23, 1835; revised as an opera-ballet, Paris (Opéra) September 21, 1857.

Le Domino Noir
Opéra-comique in 3 Acts.
Text by Eugène Scribe.
First performance: Paris (Opéra-Comique) December 2, 1837.

Les Diamants de la Couronne
Opéra-comique in 3 Acts.
Text by Eugène Scribe and Vernoy de Saint-Georges.
First performance: Paris (Opéra-Comique) March 6, 1841.

Marco Spada
Opéra-comique in 3 Acts.
Text by Eugène Scribe and Germain Delavigne.
First performance: Paris (Opéra-Comique) December 21, 1852; revised as a ballet in 1857.

Manon Lescaut
Opéra-comique in 3 Acts.
Text by Eugène Scribe, based on the novel by Provost.
First performance: Paris (Opéra-Comique) February 23, 1856.

L'Erreur d'un Moment (1805)
Couvin (1812)
Le Séjour militaire (1813)
Le Testament et les billets-doux (1819)
La Bergère châtelaine (1820)
Emma (1821)
Leicester (1823)
La Neige (1823)
Vendome en Espagne (1823)
Le Concert à la cour (1824)
Léocadie (1824)
Le Macon (1825)
Le Timide (1826)
Fiorella (1826)
La Fiancée (1829)
Le Philtre (1831)
Le Serment (1832)
Gustave III (1833)

Actéon (1836)
Les Chaperons blancs (1836)
L'Ambassadrice (1836)
Le Lac des fées (1839)
Zanetta (1840)
Le Duc d'Olonne (1842)
La Part du Diable (1843)
La Sirène (1844)
La Barcarolle (1845)
Haydée (1847)
L'Enfant prodigue (1850)
Zerline (1851)
Jenny Bell (1855)
La Circassienne (1861)
La Fiancée du Roi de Garbe (1864)
Le Premier Jour de bonheur (1868)
Rêve d'amour (1869)
etc.

~~MI~~CHAEL BALFE

(~~D~~ublin 15.5.1808; d. Rowney Abbey, Herts 20.10.1870)

~~So~~n of a dancing master, he lived in Wexford, Ireland from ~~1~~810 where he studied the violin. In 1823 he went to London to study under C. E. Horn and played in the Drury Lane orchestra. He studied singing and composition, first appearing as a singer in Weber's » *Der Freischütz* at Norwich in 1824. After further singing studies in Rome and Milan, he went to Paris where he met Rossini » and in 1827 he appeared in *Il Barbiere di Siviglia*. His own first opera was produced in Palermo in 1830 and his first English opera, *The Siege of Rochelle*, at Drury Lane in 1835. In 1836 Malibran sang in his *The Maid of Artois*. He worked in Paris for several years, returning to London to produce his most popular work, *The Bohemian Girl*, in 1843. Achieved great popularity both as an opera-singer and composer, writing 29 operas in all before retiring to spend his last years farming in Hertfordshire.

Left: *Michael Balfe, Irish composer and singer. He was so popular and admired in his day that, when he died, a statue of him was placed in the entrance hall of Drury Lane Theatre alongside those of Garrick, Kean and Shakespeare. Although his operas, and those of his contemporaries, are at present neglected, there may well come a day when the simple tunefulness of his music will again be admired.*

The Bohemian Girl
Opera in 3 Acts.
Text by Alfred Bunn, based on a story by Cervantes as used in the ballet 'La Gypsy' by Vernoy de Saint-Georges.
First performance: London (Drury Lane) November 27, 1843.

Notes:
The lilting, memorable melodies and a generally uncomplicated score pleased the opera-going public of the day. Drawing-room piano stools were full of such songs by Balfe and others, who had evolved a popular English style based on Italian opera. The first night audience went mad with enthusiasm and the opera continued to run to packed audiences, creating a current craze for gypsy songs, novels and art. Balfe was paid £500 by Chappell & Co for the right to print and publish the opera's songs.

The Daughter of St Mark
Opera Seria in 3 Acts.
Text by Alfred Bunn.
First performance: London (Drury Lane) November 27, 1844.

Notes:

A typically involved plot used by Halévy in *La Reine de Chypre*, Donizetti » in *Catarina Cornaro*, and others. Even in those days the story was criticised for its complicated absurdities, but Balfe's music and reputation made the work palatable.

Satanella, or The Power of Love

Opera in 4 Acts.
Text by Edmund Falconer and Augustus Harris.
First performance: London (Covent Garden) May 14, 1858.

Notes:

In spite of its even greater absurdities, the opera became almost as popular as *The Bohemian Girl* and was played at Covent Garden until 1884 and by the Carl Rosa Opera as late as 1930. Again, Balfe's approachable music came to the rescue and the song 'The power of love' had astonishing popularity, remaining a favourite orchestral piece well into this century.

The Siege of Rochelle (1835)
The Maid of Artois (1836)
Catherine Grey (1837)
Joan of Arc (1837)
Diadeste (1838)
Falstaff (1838)
Këolanthe (1841)
Geraldine (1843)
The Castle of Aymon (1844)
The Enchantress (1845)
L'Etoile de Séville (1845)
The Bondman (1846)

The Maid of Honour (1847)
The Sicilian Bride (1852)
The Devil's in It (1852)
The Rose of Castille (1857)
Bianca (1860)
The Puritan's Daughter (1861)
The Armourer of Nantes (1863)
Blanche de Nevers (1863)
The Sleeping Queen (1864)
Il Talismano (1874)
etc.

Below: *One of the 'hits' of the day was 'The power of love'.*

SAMUEL BARBER
b. West Chester, Pa, USA 9.3.1910)

Leading American composer who studied at the Curtis Institute of Music in Philadelphia; graduated in 1932. A thoughtful, not particularly prolific composer, his style is a kind of 'moderate modernism'. He has written symphonies and other orchestral music, chamber music and songs, and is perhaps best known for his *Adagio for Strings*. He has been a close collaborator of Gian-Carlo Menotti ≫ , the librettist of his best-known opera *Vanessa*, and co-author of the mini-opera *A Hand of Bridge* (1960). For a third opera, *Antony and Cleopatra* (1966), Barber turned to a text based on Shakespeare.

Vanessa
Opera in 4 Acts.
Text by Gian-Carlo Menotti.
First performance: New York
(Metropolitan Opera) January 15,
1958. Salzburg 1958.

A Hand of Bridge
Mini-opera.
Co-author Gian-Carlo Menotti.
First performance: New York 1960.

Antony and Cleopatra
First performance: New York
(Metropolitan) 1966.

BÉLA BARTÓK
(b. Nagyszentmiklós, Hungary 25.3.1881; d. New York 26.9.1945)

Many of Bartók's compositions are among the central masterpieces of modern music, notably the six string quartets, the piano concertos, the *Music for strings, percussion and celeste*, the second *Violin concerto*, the *Concerto for Orchestra*. He was a dedicated collector of folk music, and in association with his friend and compatriot Zoltan Kodály ≫ gathered an invaluable collection of Magyar folk songs and dances, the spirit of which infuses much of his own music. He wrote only one opera, but that one is full of his tough, uncompromising attitude and style, and though wanting in conventional 'action' is remarkable for its evocation of mood.

Duke Bluebeard's Castle (A Kékszakállú Herceg Vára)
Opera in 1 Act.
Text by Béla Balázs.
First performance: Budapest, May 24, 1918. Berlin 1929; New York 1952; London (Sadler's Wells) 1954.

JACK BEESON
(b. Muncie, Indiana, 15.7.1921)

Beeson studied at the Eastman School of Music from 1939 to 1944 and with Béla Bartók » in New York 1944-5. He joined the Columbia University opera workshop in 1945 and the musical department soon after, becoming the MacDowell Professor of Music in 1967. He has been the recipient of various distinguished awards and is a prominent figure in various American musical organisations. Although not heard much outside the USA, his operatic output has been considerable, showing a strong dramatic sense and an ability to write expressively and attractively. He has been particularly successful in bringing American background and stories into his operas with strong characterisation of interesting figures. They include *Jonah* (1950), *Hello Out There* (1953), *The Sweet Bye and Bye* (1957), *Lizze Borden* (1965), *My Heart's in the Highlands* (1970) and *Captain Jinks of the Horse Marines* (1975).

Hello Out There
Chamber Opera in 1 Act.
Text by William Saroyan.
First performance: New York (Columbia University Opera Workshop) 1953.

The Sweet Bye and Bye
Opera in 2 Acts.
Text by Kenward Elmslie.
First performance: New York (Juilliard School of Music) November 1957.

Lizzie Borden
Opera in 3 Acts and an Epilogue.
Text by Kenward Elmslie, based on a scenario by Richard Plant.
First performance: New York (City Opera) March 25, 1965.

Captain Jinks of the Horse Marines
Romantic Comedy in 3 Acts.
Text by Sheldon Harnick, based on the play by Clyde Fitch.
First performance: Kansas City (Lyric Theatre) September 20, 1975.

Jonah (1950)
My Heart's in the Highlands (1970)
etc.

Below: *Jack Beeson's* Lizzie Borden; *its world premiere by the New York City Opera.*

LUDWIG VAN BEETHOVEN

(b. Bonn 16.12.1770; d. Vienna 26.3.1827)

Beethoven wrote only one opera, but that one occupied a great deal of his creative energies. It took nearly ten years of frustration and several versions before the masterpiece we know as *Fidelio* emerged. It was commissioned by Emanuel Schikaneder, the subject of Mozart's *Der Schauspieldirektor* and librettist of *The Magic Flute*, who was then a Viennese theatre manager. Opera was a fresh departure for Beethoven and he approached the project with misgiving. His models were, in the beginning, Méhul and Cherubini », but as the work progressed it soon passed out of the reach of such influences and became pure Beethoven, structurally and ethically. Beethoven was always on the lookout for the chance to write another opera, but he never found a suitable libretto. His demands were high: nothing frivolous or immoral, always something 'elevating'. Some ideas did inspire him—Goethe's *Faust*, *Macbeth*, even Alexander the Great—but apart from the occasional start nothing ever came from them.

Fidelio

Opera in 2 Acts.
Text by J. and G. Sonnleithner and G. F. Treitschke, after J. N. Bouilly.
First performance: Vienna (Kärntnertor) May 23, 1814.

Notes:

In its original form, under the title *Leonora* (which Beethoven himself always preferred) it was in three acts. On its first appearance in 1805 it suffered from the fact that Vienna was in occupation by Napoleon's troops and the consequent attentions of the censor, but it was also felt that the opera was not satisfactory; despite magnificent parts, it was too long and diffuse. After much haggling and resistance by Beethoven it was revised and reduced to two acts in 1806, but that failed too, making an almost total rewrite necessary. This was accomplished in 1814, producing the *Fidelio* we know and honour today. In all its forms it is basically a mixture of German *Singspiel*, retaining a certain amount of spoken dialogue, and *opera seria* (especially in the finely constructed second part).

Right: *Rene Kollo and Gundula Janowitz were Florestan and Leonora in the 1978* Fidelio *recording, based on the Vienna State Opera production.*

VINCENZO BELLINI

(b. Catania, Sicily 3.11.1801; d. Puteaux, France 23.9.1835)

With Donizetti » and Rossini », Bellini was one of the founders of modern Italian opera. His delicate, sensitive style was in complete contrast to Donizetti's easy-going facility and Rossini's muscular brilliance. It evolved out of the three central forces within him—Sicilian ancestry, delicate health, and short life. His ancestry undoubtedly had a major effect upon the development of his genius. His melody, subtly supported by extended harmony, was a true continuation of the Italian *bel canto* style. The element of *morbidezza* (a term derived from painting and signifying delicacy and gentleness rather than 'morbidity') is not only distinctive but exercised an important influence on several later instrumental composers, notably Chopin. There is nothing of the jocularity of Italian *opera buffa* in Bellini; still less the patriotic fervour found in most Italian composers, especially Giuseppe Verdi ». In many ways, though not in this, Bellini was the true precursor of Verdi in Italian opera, his integration of violent passion with lyric tenderness unquestionably anticipates his great successor. The generosity of a Sicilian nobleman enabled Bellini to study at the Naples Conservatoire, where he met Donizetti. Thereafter he produced a successful series of 11 operas, visiting several towns in Italy and also London and Paris for the occasions. It was after visiting London for a performance of *I Puritani*, his last work, that he went to Puteaux outside Paris, where he was taken fatally ill. His later operas were sung by some of the legendary singers in Italian opera, notably tenor Giovanni Battista Rubini, sopranos Giuditta Pasta and Giulia Grisi, baritone Antonio Tamburini and bass Luigi Lablache. He was unusually fortunate in having for all but three of his operas the collaboration of the outstanding librettist Felice Romani. In modern times, the two leading exponents of Bellini's music in the theatre and on record are the late Maria Callas and Joan Sutherland.

Adelson e Salvini

Opera in 3 Acts.
Text by Andrea Leone Tottola.
First performance: Naples (Teatrino del Collegio San Sebastiano) January 12, 1825.

Il Pirata

Opera in 2 Acts.
Text by Felice Romani.
First performance: Milan (La Scala) October 27, 1827. London (King's Theatre) 1830; Paris 1832; New York 1832.

Notes:
Romani's libretto is 'topped and tailed' by matter which does not appear in the opera. In the introductory material it is revealed that Gualtiero and Ernesto were on opposite sides in the

struggle between Manfred and Charles of Anjou. After Charles's victory Gualtiero became a pirate, but his ships were defeated by Ernesto. At the end of the tale, the pirates try to rescue Gualtiero but when Imogene appears he sends them off and kills himself.

La Straniera
Opera in 2 Acts.
Text by Felice Romani after a novel by C. V. P. d'Arlincourt.
First performance: Milan (La Scala) February 14, 1829.

I Capuleti e i Montecchi
Opera in 2 Acts.
Text by Felice Romani after Matteo Bandello (c. 1480-1562) and, loosely, Shakespeare.
First performance: Venice (Teatro La Fenice) March 11, 1830. London 1833.

La Sonnambula
Opera in 2 Acts.
Text by Felice Romani after Eugène Scribe.
First performance: Milan (Teatro Carcano) March 6, 1831. London (Haymarket) 1831; New York 1835; London (Covent Garden) 1910; New York (Met) 1932.

Norma
Opera in 2 Acts.
Text by Felice Romani after Louis Alexandre Soumet & Louis Belmontet.
First performance: Milan (La Scala) December 26, 1831. London (Haymarket) 1833; New York 1841; New York (Met) 1891 & 1927; London (Covent Garden) 1929.

Beatrice di Tenda
Opera in 2 Acts.
Text by Felice Romani.
First performance: Venice (Teatro la Fenice) March 16, 1833. London 1836. New York 1844.

I Puritani (di Scozia)
Opera in 3 Acts.
Text by Count Carlo Pepoli after Francois Ancelot and Xavier Boniface Saintine, based on the play 'Old Mortality' by Sir Walter Scott.
First performance: Paris (Théâtre des Italiens), January 25, 1835. London (King's) 1835; New York 1844.

Bianca e Gernando (1826)
Zaira (1829)
Il fù ed il sarà (1832)

Left: *Vincenzo Bellini, one of the founders of modern Italian opera.*

19

ALBAN BERG
(b. Vienna 9.2.1885; d. Vienna 24.12.1935)

Of the two most famous pupils of Arnold Schoenberg » (the other was Anton Webern, who wrote no opera), Berg showed more inclination to bridge the gap between the former tonal system and atonality leading to seriality. Berg was by nature an eminently warm and emotionally generous man; qualities which come through in his music, alongside and interwoven with the intellectual severity. His last completed work, the marvellous Violin Concerto, shows both aspects of his genius at their most creative. Of his two operas, the first, *Wozzeck*, is built on a form of extended tonality with clearly atonal passages, some in strict serial form; the second, *Lulu*, unfinished at his death, is more strictly serial, though still modified to Berg's expressive requirements. In both operas, individual sections are deliberately constructed to traditional absolute forms—*sonata, rondo, fugue, passacaglia, scherzo* etc. In *Wozzeck* the music is dedicated to the evocation of a great variety of moods, from the tenderest to the most violent and horrifying; in *Lulu* the effect is achieved by setting strictly formal music alongside passages which parody modern dance forms and idioms. Berg, a man greatly loved and admired by all who knew him, died after a short but agonising illness on Christmas Eve, 1935, aged only 50. His loss to modern music remains incalculable.

Wozzeck
Opera in 3 Acts (of 5 scenes each).
Text by Alban Berg, based on the play by Georg Büchner
First performance: Berlin (State Opera) December 14, 1925. Prague 1926; Philadelphia 1931; London (Covent Garden) 1952.

Notes:
Following in the footsteps of Schoenberg, Berg was less revolutionary and kept a more traditional musical feeling in his use of atonal and 12-note methods. In the case of *Wozzeck* there was immediate recognition of a masterpiece, and the work may be said to be the first major vindication of the whole school of atonal composition.

Lulu
Opera in Prologue and 3 Acts (unfinished).
Text by Alban Berg based on dramas by Franz Wedekind.
First performance: Zurich, June 2, 1937. Venice 1949; Essen 1953.

Notes:
Berg left *Lulu* unfinished at his death, having broken off to write his fine Violin Concerto. Acts 1 and 2 were complete and sketches for Act 3 existed, but not in sufficient detail to allow performances in the form Berg intended. After his death his widow asked Schoenberg » to complete the score but he refused, and thereafter she would allow no one to touch it. It was not until her death in 1976 that the work could be carried

out and Berg's embryonic wishes realised, by the Austrian composer Friedrich Cerha; and this final version of the opera was given complete in Paris in March, 1979. Until then the last Act had been given in the form of the Lulu Symphony, as substitute (the text always existed; it was the music that was incomplete). Now that we have at last heard the whole, some perspectives are adjusted, and the impression is reinforced that this is one of the major masterpieces of 20th century music. A recording was made from the Paris production under Pierre Boulez.

Above: *A Royal Opera House production of Berg's* Wozzeck, *with Sir Geraint Evans.*
Left: *Berg, the most approachable of the 'twelve-tone' composers.*

HECTOR BERLIOZ

(b. Côte-Saint-André, Isère 11.12.1803; d. Paris 8.3.1869)

France's foremost composer was the son of a doctor who instilled in his son a lifelong enthusiasm for the Latin classics of literature, especially Virgil. Berlioz possessed a vivid dramatic imagination and a high order of original genius; yet he never made the best of either quality, and for many years Berlioz's genius was slenderly appreciated and little understood. Much of his work for the stage, and his many choral compositions, show Berlioz as an apostle of 19th century giganticism, fired by exalted visions of his vocation. He was also a gifted author and his criticisms and autobiographical writings are of permanent value. A master of orchestration (on which he wrote a famous treatise), Berlioz was also a master of a unique type of melody and a leading figure of the French Romantic movement. Yet his ingrained classicism resulted in an underlying purity of style that did much to counteract the natural excesses of romanticsm. He composed three operas, contrasted in style and subject matter, and two vocal/orchestral works that are sometimes admitted into the operatic canon though they were designed primarily as concert pieces and are nearer to cantata than opera, even though both have been adapted for the stage. The cause of all these compositions has been greatly advanced by high class modern recordings and the advocacy and insight of conductor Colin Davis. His orchestral music, notably the *Symphonie fantastique*, *Harold in Italy* and many overtures, and a number of choral/orchestral works (*Te Deum*, *Grand messe des morts*, *Symphonie funèbre et triomphale*) as well as the song cycle *Nuits d'été* are essential to a full understanding of his genuis.

Below: Benvenuto Cellini *with Nicolai Gedda in the title role.*

Left: *Hector Berlioz.*

Benvenuto Cellini
Opera in 2 (3) Acts.
Text by Léon de Wailly and August Barbier after the 'Memoirs of Benvenuto Cellini'.
First performance: Paris (Opéra) September 10, 1838. Weimar (Court Theatre) 1852; London (Covent Garden) 1853.

Béatrice et Bénédict
Opera in 2 Acts.
Text by Berlioz, based on Shakespeare's 'Much Ado About Nothing'.
First performance: Baden-Baden August 9, 1862. Paris (Opéra-Comique) 1890. Glasgow (in English) 1936 New York (concert performance) 1960.

Notes:
The 15 scenes and 5 Acts are drawn mainly from the comic side of Shakespeare's play, the darker and more sinister elements largely by-passed.

Les Troyens
Opera in 2 Parts, 5 Acts.
Text by Hector Berlioz after Virgil's 'Aeneid'.
First performance: Part 1—Carlsruhe (in German) December 6, 1890; Part 2—Paris (Théâtre-Lyrique) November 4, 1863; complete—Carlsruhe December 5/6, 1890.

La Damnation de Faust
Dramatic legend in 4 Parts.
Text by Berlioz and Almire Gandonnière after Gérard de Nerval's translation of Goethe's 'Faust', incorporating material from Berlioz's earlier 'Huit Scènes de Faust (1828).
First performance: Paris 1846. Stage version Monte Carlo 1893; Liverpool (in English) 1894; New Orleans and New York 1894.

Notes:
La Damnation de Faust is not, strictly speaking, an opera but a dramatic cantata; it was, however, arranged for the stage by Raoul Gunsbourg and given at Monte Carlo in 1893. Although as a stage work it contravenes, in some respects, Berlioz's intentions, we include it since it contains some of his most popular music.

23

GEORGES BIZET
(b. Paris 23.10.1838; d. Bougival 3.6.1875)

Above: *The immortal* Carmen. *Shirley Verrett is seen in this most demanding and criticised of roles.*

Bizet first learnt music from his parents: his singing-teacher father Adolphe Armand Bizet and his pianist mother, Aimée Léopoldine Joséphine Delsarte. Admitted to the Paris Conservatoire in 1848, he won second prize in the Marmontel piano class in 1851 and shared first prize the next year. His exceptional talents were widely recognised and he studied composition with Halévy. He won the coveted Prix de Rome in 1857 after his operetta, *Le Docteur Miracle*, had been successful in a competition sponsored by Offenbach », tying with one by Lecocq. Both works were performed alternately at the Théâtre des Bouffes-Parisiens. After a visit to Rome in 1860 Bizet produced a series of works including operas, beginning with *Les Pêcheurs de perles* (1863). Another opera, *Ivan le Terrible*, written in 1865, was thought to have been destroyed by Bizet until its rediscovery in 1944. It was eventually produced in Germany (Württemberg) in 1946. (Bizet's engaging Symphony in C, written when he was still a student, was also thought to have been lost, but it was discovered in 1935, premiered the following year and has since become popular.) Other operas followed, including *La jolie fille de Perth* (after Sir Walter Scott) and *Djamileh* which failed when it was produced in 1872 — despite Bizet's high hopes. In 1875 he produced the masterpiece upon which his fame most solidly rests: *Carmen*. At first, it received a mixed reception, but nowhere near the romantic legend that it was such a total failure it hastened Bizet's early death. That is pure sentimental imagination. Certainly Bizet died before his great opera had achieved world popularity; but from the beginning it had as many champions as detractors.

Les Pêcheurs de Perles

Opera in 3 Acts.
Text by Michel Carré and Eugène Cormon.
First performance: Paris (Théâtre-Lyrique) September 30, 1863. Milan (in Italian) 1886; London (Covent Garden) 1887; Philadelphia (Italian) 1893.

Notes:

This, Bizet's first full-scale opera, is lyrical in style, owing something to Offenbach and the French operetta tradition. He had not yet discovered the note of realism and the stylistic innovations which made *Carmen* so artistically important.

La Jolie Fille de Perth

Opera in 4 Acts.
Text by J. H. Vernay de St Georges and Jules Adenis after Scott.
First performance: Paris (Théâtre-Lyrique) December 26, 1867.

Djamileh

Opera in 1 Act.
Text by Louis Gallet.
First performance: Paris (Opéra-Comique) May 22, 1872. London (Covent Garden) 1893; Boston 1913.

Carmen

Opera in 4 Acts.
Text by Henri Meilhac and Ludovic Halévy after the novel by Prosper Merimée.
First performance: Paris (Opéra-Comique) March 3, 1875. Vienna (Court Opera) (in German) 1875; London (His Majesty's) (in Italian) 1878; New York (Italian) 1878.

Notes:

Carmen has been damned as pseudo or bogus Spanish music. It is no such thing, and was never intended as such. It is French music evocative of Spain; and succeeds triumphantly. Many of the individual numbers, vocal and orchestral, such as the 'Habanera', the 'Seguidilla', the 'Toreador's Song, the 'Flower Song', the 'March of changing of the guard', and the Prelude, have gained universal currency outside the opera itself. There are also the two orchestral suites which are everlastingly popular. The problem of editions of *Carmen* is severe. Bizet wrote it with spoken dialogue; but later this was altered to sung recitatives by his friend Ernest Guiraud. This was the current version for a long time (except in Paris); but nowadays the spoken dialogue is, advantageously, usually restored. There are various editions and versions of this (notably by Oeser and by Choudens), and often a mixture of several. Of the many recordings, Sir Georg Solti's (Decca) seems to reach the most satisfactory solution, the way to it lucidly explained by Sir Georg in the accompanying booklet. Beecham and von Karajan use the Guiraud edition; Abbado and Bernstein, one with spoken dialogue.

Le Docteur Miracle (1857)   Sol-si-ré-pif-pan (1872)
Malbrough s'en va-t-en guerre (1867)   etc.

25

JOHN BLOW

(b. Newark, Nottinghamshire ?.2.1649; d. London 1.10.1708)

The teacher of Henry Purcell ≫, Dr Blow was the composer of what may justly be called the first English opera, an honour frequently accorded to Purcell's *Dido and Aeneas*. Blow was probably educated first at the Magnus Song School in Newark. On the reconstitution of the Royal Chapel with the Restoration of Charles II, Blow became a chorister under Henry Cooke. He later became organist at Westminster Abbey, rejoined the royal service in 1669, being sworn as a Gentleman of the Royal Chapel in 1674 when he was also appointed Master of the Children of the Royal Chapel on the death of Pelham Humfrey. The same year Blow married the daughter of the Master of the Children of Westminster Abbey, Edward Braddock. His numerous compositions include many anthems, English and Latin services, various Welcome and other occasional songs and choral Odes, plus a few songs for theatrical productions.

Venus and Adonis
Masque for the Entertainment of the King. Prologue and 3 Acts.
Text by unknown author.
First performance: London (at Court), c. 1684 (date of composition uncertain, but after 1680).

Notes:
Venus and Adonis is described as a masque, but in every significant respect it is a mini-opera. It is not merely an important precursor of Purcell's masterpiece, but an original and memorable work in its own right.

Left: *Plaque commemorating John Blow in Westminster Abbey, where he was organist for 15 years. He was buried close to Purcell, who was his pupil.*

Below: *John Blow, English composer whose only opera,* Venus and Adonis, *remains the work for which he is best known.*

FRANÇOIS ADRIEN BOÏELDIEU
(b. Rouen 16.12.1775; d. Jarcy 8.10.1834)

After studying with the organist at Rouen, and producing his first opera there (libretto by his father, who was secretary to the Archbishop), he then went to the Paris Conservatoire where he became professor of piano and began to present a series of successful light operas, beginning with *La Famille Suisse*. He studied for a while with Cherubini », who chided him with winning a too easy success. In 1803 he went to St Petersburg as conductor of the Imperial Opera and wrote more operas himself. He returned to Paris in 1811 and repeated, even increased, his earlier triumphs. He was a master of the French *opéra comique* who never achieved, nor sought, the profounder regions of creative art; but his works are admirably written and gave enormous pleasure. Boïeldieu collaborated with various others (including Cherubini) on operas, but his best and most famous he did on his own. His best known and most durable opera is *La Dame blanche*, but *Le Calife de Bagdad*, *Jean de Paris* and others made him famous within and outside France.

Zoraime et Zulnar
Opera in 3 Acts.
Text by Claude Godard d'Aucour de Saint-Just.
First performance: Paris (Théâtre Favart) May 11, 1798.

Le Calife de Bagdad
Opera in 1 Act.
Text by Claude Godard d'Aucour de Saint-Just.
First performance: Paris (Théâtre Favart) September 16, 1800.

Ma Tante Aurore
Opera in 3 Acts.
Text by Charles de Longchamps.
First performance: Paris (Opéra-Comique) January 13, 1803.

Angéla
Opera in 1 Act.
Text by G. Montcloux d'Epinay.
First performance: Paris (Opéra-Comique) June 13, 1814.

La Dame Blanche
Opera in 3 Acts.
Text by Eugène Scribe after Sir Walter Scott's 'The Monastery' and 'Guy Mannering'.
First performance: Paris (Opéra-Comique) December 10, 1825. Liège 1826; London (Drury Lane) (in English) 1826; New York 1927.

Notes:
The score contains traditional Scots tunes.

La Fille coupable (1793)
Rosalie et Myrza (1795)
La Famille suisse (1797)
L'Heureuse Nouvelle (1797)
Le Pari (1797)
La Dot de Suzette (1798)
Les Meprises espagnoles (1799)
Béniowski (1800)
Aline (1804)
Abderkhan (1804)
La Jeune Femme colère (1805)

Amour et Mystère (1806)
Un Tour de soubrette (1806)
Télémaque (1806)
La Dame invisible (1806)
Jean de Paris (1812)
Le Nouveau Seigneur de village (1813)
La Fête du village voisin (1816)
Charles de France (1816)
Le Petit Chaperon rouge (1818)
Les Deux Nuits (1829)
etc.

ARRIGO BOITO
(b. Padua 24.2.1842; d. Milan 10.6.1918)

A versatile man of the theatre, Boito is famous above all for his libretti, from Shakespeare, for Verdi's » two last masterpieces, Otello and Falstaff. (He also wrote a libretto from Hamlet for Franco Faccio (1840-1891). But he was also a composer in his own right, as well as a gifted conductor. His own operas make an oddly incongruous pair; they have little in common and the second, Nerone, was not produced until after his death and is little heard today. But the first, Mefistofele, based on Goethe's Faust, has remained popular.

Left: *Arrigo Boito was the son of an Italian painter and a Polish countess and the friend of Victor Hugo, Berlioz, Rossini and Verdi, amongst many. Always involved in the operatic world, he wrote librettos for Ponchielli and Verdi.*

Mefistofele
Opera in Prologue, 4 Acts, and Epilogue.
Text by Arrigo Boito.
First performance: Milan (La Scala) March 5, 1868. London (Her Majesty's) 1880; Boston (in English) 1880.

Notes:
The music of *Mefistofele* is complex, frequently contrapuntal, more intellectual than Italian audiences were accustomed to; there is little of *bel canto* style. It was a failure at first (partly through hostility to its composer) but was later revised and became successful. The Prologue and several of the individual numbers have gained great popularity, even though the opera as a whole is not quite so convincing. Oddly, the libretto is partly to blame; it shows little of the sure skill and theatrical aptitude of those he wrote for Verdi. All the same, it is an effective stage piece, several times recorded.

Nerone
Opera in 4 Acts.
Text by Arrigo Boito.
First performance: Milan (La Scala) May 1, 1924. Rome 1928; Buenos Aires 1926.

ALEXANDER BORODIN
(b. St Petersburg 11.11.1833; d. St Petersburg 28.2.1887)

The illegitimate son of a nobleman, Borodin was a scientist (chemist) as well as a musician. He studied in St Petersburg at the Academy of Medicine; then went to Germany where he met and married pianist Ektarina Protopopova. Studied composition with Balakirev and lectured at School of Medicine for Women. He composed three symphonies (the third unfinished), a number of orchestral and instrumental works, and one great opera, *Prince Igor*, (also unfinished at his death; completed by Rimsky-Korsakov » and Glazunov).

Prince Igor
Opera in Prologue and 4 Acts.
Text by Borodin from a draft by Vladimir Stassov.
First performance: St Petersburg November 4, 1890. Prague (in Czech) 1899; London (Drury Lane) 1914; New York (in Italian) 1915.

BENJAMIN BRITTEN

(b. Lowestoft 22.11.1913; d. Aldeburgh 4.12.1976)

After piano studies with Harold Samuel and composition with Frank Bridge, Britten won a scholarship to London's Royal College of Music. Prior to the Second World War some of his music was heard at various festivals, and during the early years of the war, while in America, he wrote his first opera, a light work with text by W. H. Auden on the subject of *Paul Bunyan* (this has recently been revived with great success and a recording is expected). His first notable success was with *Variations on a theme of Frank Bridge* which was heard at the Salzburg Festival in 1937 and astonished everyone with its novel sounds. The *Sinfonia da Requiem* (1940) and the *Serenade for Tenor, Horn and Strings* (1943) confirmed his reputation as one of the leading British composers of his time. Although he continued to write some orchestral, chamber and instrumental music, his reputation was chiefly to be founded on his special flair for setting words to music. He wrote many songs and song-cycles, and many choral works, but it is as a writer of opera that

Inset: *Benjamin Britten.* **Below:** *Jon Vickers as Peter Grimes at Covent Garden, a role he has sung in New York and Milan.*

he will always be thought of first; not only the leading writer of English opera in his day, but arguably the greatest and most consistent composer in this field that we have produced. Major choral works and operas appeared regularly throughout his composing career and each one was eagerly awaited and rapturously received: *Peter Grimes* (1945); *The Rape of Lucretia* (1947); *Albert Herring* (1947); *Let's Make an Opera* (1949); *Billy Budd* (1951); *Gloriana* (1953); *The Turn of the Screw* (1954); *A Midsummer Night's Dream* (1960); *Owen Wingrave* (1970); *Death in Venice* (1973). In between came the Chester miracle play *Noye's Fludde* (1958); the church parables *Curlew River* (1964), *The Burning Fiery Furnace* (1966) and *The Prodigal Son* (1968); and the *War Requiem* (1962).

Peter Grimes
Opera in Prologue and 3 Acts.
Text by Montagu Slater, based on a poem by George Crabbe.
First performance: London (Sadler's Wells) June 7, 1945. New York (Met) 1948.

Notes:
Few works have made a greater impact than *Peter Grimes*, either on stage or on record, with its stark realism and the power of its music in keeping with its grim setting. Outstanding features are the fine orchestral interludes, which are frequently played as individual items.

The Rape of Lucretia
Opera in 2 Acts.
Text by Ronald Duncan from the play by André Obey.
First performance: England (Glyndebourne) July 12, 1946. Basle 1947; New York 1949.

Albert Herring
Comic Opera in 3 Acts.
Text by Eric Crozier.
First performance: Glyndebourne June 20, 1947. Hanover 1950; New York 1952.

The Little Sweep
The second part, being the actual opera which the cast write, compose and rehearse (involving the audience) in the first part of 'Let's Make an Opera'.
Text by Eric Crozier.
First performance: Aldeburgh (Jubilee Hall) April 14, 1949.

Billy Budd
Opera in 4 Acts.
Text by E. M. Forster and Eric Crozier, adapted from the story by Herman Melville.
First performance: (original version in 4 Acts) London (Covent Garden) December 1, 1951; revised in 2 Acts and heard on BBC Third Programme November 13, 1961.

Gloriana
Opera in 3 Acts.
Text by William Plomer.
First performance: London
(Covent Garden) June 8, 1953.

Below: *Peter Glossop in the title role of* Billy Budd.

The Turn of the Screw

Opera in Prologue and 2 Acts
Text by Myfanwy Piper, based on the novel by Henry James.
First performance: Venice, September 14, 1954.

A Midsummer Night's Dream

Opera in 3 Acts.
Text by Benjamin Britten and Peter Pears, based on Shakespeare's play.
First performance: Aldeburgh (re-opening of the Jubilee Hall after its rebuilding)
June 11, 1960.

Owen Wingrave

Opera for television in 2 Acts.
Text by Myfanwy Piper, based on a short story by Henry James.
First seen on BBC-2 TV on May 16, 1971.

Above: *The dancers in the English Opera Group's production of Death in Venice at Covent Garden.*

Death in Venice

Opera in 2 Acts.
Text by Myfanwy Piper, based on the short story by Thomas Mann.
First performance: Aldeburgh Festival, June 16, 1973. Performed at the Edinburgh Festival 1973, Venice, Brussels and Covent Garden.

Notes:
As with many of Britten's operas the action is tightly linked by Choral Dances, in this case where the boys on the beach take on the guise of young athletes in Greek games; they are very much a part of the visionary aspect of the opera rather than mere *divertimenti*.

FERRUCCIO (Benvenuto) BUSONI
(b. Empoli, Italy 1.4.1886; d. Berlin 27.7.1924)

An outstanding pianist and musical theorist, Busoni was, as a composer, a formidable intellectual whose creative flow has sometimes been felt to have been impeded by the sheer complexity of his mind. Yet his music is of a nature and quality that is extraordinarily impressive; his searching mystical and metaphysical temperament gives his best music an uncompromising aura. He began his concert career as pianist at the age of seven, and studied at Graz (with Wilhelm Meyer-Remy) and at Leipzig. He held teaching posts at Helsinki (where he met Sibelius and married Gerda Sjöstrand), Moscow and America, before settling in Berlin. He is best known for his piano music, especially the huge *Fantasia contrappuntistica* and for his transcriptions of Bach. He wrote four operas, of which the last, *Doktor Faustus*, was unfinished at his death and was completed by his pupil Phillip Jarnach. *Die Brautwahl*, to his own libretto based on a story by E. T. A. Hoffman, was produced in Hamburg in 1912, and the brief *Turandot*, with spoken dialogue and based on a play by Carlo Gozzi for which he had written incidental music (on which the opera is based), appeared in 1917.

Arlecchino
Comic Opera in 1 Act.
Text by Busoni.
First performance: Zürich May 11, 1917 (double bill with 'Turandot'). London (BBC) 1939; Venice 1940; Glyndebourne 1954.

Notes:
The work is highly satirical and anti-war. Busoni himself said: 'The title role gives my own confessions. The Abbé expresses human forbearance and tolerance. The tailor Matteo is the duped idealist, suspicious of nothing, Columbina—the woman. After *The Magic Flute* (which I value highly) it is the most moral libretto there is.' It also parodies Wagner.

Doktor Faust
Opera in 2 Prologues, 1 Interlude and 3 Scenes.
Text by Busoni (not after Goethe's drama but based upon older sources and puppet plays and Christopher Marlowe's 'Dr Faustus').
First performance: Dresden May 21, 1925. London (concert version) 1937; Florence 1942.

Die Brautwahl (1912)
Turandot (1917)

Left: *Ferruccio Busoni, pianist and composer, photographed during his last years in Zurich. Despite their intellectual leanings, his operas were described by E.J. Dent as being full of 'nobility and beauty'.*

ALFREDO CATALANI
(b. Lucca 19.6.1854; d. Milan 7.8.1893)

It sometimes happens that an artist suffers the double disadvantage of shortness of years and the contemporary presence of more ear-catching, though not necessarily superior, talents. This was the case with Catalani. He was of the generation of opera composers which included Puccini », Mascagni » and Leoncavallo »: but he was under 40 when he died and his talent was more fragile. He was probably more naturally gifted than Mascagni and Leoncavallo (though not than Puccini, of course); but he did not traffic in their kind of melodramatic *verismo* which pulls the crowd. Yet he was brilliantly endowed and composed a mass which was performed when he was 14. He studied with Bazin at the Paris Conservatoire and then at the Milan Conservatory. He composed a number of operas, of which the last, *La Wally*, is the best known. *Loreley*, which was in fact a new version of his first opera, *Elda* (1880) has also survived the pressure of time.

Loreley
Opera in 4 Acts.
Text by Zanardini.
First performance: Turin (Teatro Regio) February 16, 1890. London (Covent Garden) 1907; New York (Lexington Theatre) 1919.

Notes:
Like *La Wally*, this opera has strong associations with German Romanticism. Loreley, the legendary siren, is represented here a young orphan, jilted by her lover, Walter, Lord of Oberwessel. When Walter announces his intention of marrying Anna, Loreley casts her spell on him and Anna is jilted. Walter joins Loreley in a watery death and Anna dies of grief.

La Wally
Opera in 4 Acts.
Text by Luigi Illica after Wilhelmine von Hillern's Die Geyer-Wally.
First performance: Milan (La Scala) January 20, 1892. New York (Metropolitan) 1909 Manchester 1919.

La Falce (1875)	Ero e Leandro (1885)
L'Elda (1880)	Edmea (1886)
Dejanice (1883)	etc.

FRANCESCO CAVALLI
(b. Crema 14.2.1602; d. Venice 14.1.1676)

Cavalli, along with a number of others, among whom Pietro Antonio Cesti was prominent, kept Venetian opera's supremacy intact after the death of Monteverdi ». He took his name from his patron, a Venetian nobleman, his name at birth being Caletti-Bruni. He sang under Monteverdi at St Mark's and in 1640 became second organist at that church, rising to first organist in 1665 and *maestro di cappella* from 1668. Cavalli

Above: *Raymond Leppard and Jani Strasser at Glyndebourne during the* Ormindo *production.*

composed a good deal of church music, but virtually none of it has survived. His operas are a different matter: he wrote some 42 in all, of which 28 have survived in score. The most famous is *Giasone*, with *Ciro* a close second. However, neither is recorded: the two that have that distinction having been carefully (and brilliantly) edited for productions at Glyndebourne by Raymond Leppard. Cavalli's first opera, *Le Nozze di Teti e di Peleo*, was performed in 1639 at the Teatro San Cassiano, Venice, where most of his operas were produced and where he lived. In the middle of his life, Cavalli's reputation was diminished by a change in popular taste: Cesti's work made a more direct appeal to audiences desiring easier entertainment than Cavalli and his like normally provided. The consequent style depended largely on an increase in the number and quality of arias and ariettas at the expense of recitatives, and thus a diminution in dramatic tension and continuity.

L'Ormindo
Opera in 2 Acts.
Text by Giovanni Battista Faustini.
First performance: Venice (Teatro San Cassiano) 1644.

La Calisto
Opera in Prologue and 2 Acts.
Text by Giovanni Battista Faustini.
First performance: Venice (Teatro Sant' Apollinare) late 1651.

La nozze di Teti e di Peleo (1639)
Gli amori d'Apollo e di Dafne (1640)
Didone (1641)
La virtù de strali d'amore (1642)
Egisto (1643)
Doriclea (1645)
Giasone (1648)
Orimonte (1650)
Alessandro vincitor di·se stesso (1651)
Oristeo (1651)
Rosinda (1651)
Veremonda (1652)
Eritrea (1652)

Orione (1653)
Serse (1654)
Ciro (1654)
Statira (1655)
Erismena (1655)
Artemisia (1656)
Hipermestra (1658)
Elena (1659)
Ercole amante (1662)
Scipione Africano (1664)
Mutio Scevola (1665)
Pompeo Magno (1666)
etc.

IMANUEL CHABRIER

Ambert, Puy-de-Dòme 18.1.1841; d. Paris 13.9.1894)

hough he showed early musical gifts, which were recognised, Chabrier spent much of his life working in a Government Ministry. He took his degree in law and was for the rest of his life a musical amateur (in the best sense). But his natural gifts would not be subdued, and his compositions sparkle with Gallic exuberance and elegance. Best known for his orchestral pieces which are full of colour and vivacity, most notably the rhapsody *España*, he also wrote five operas (the last, *Briséis, ou les amants de Corinthe*, was unfinished at his death). The most famous is the brilliant comic opera *Le roi malgré lui*, although both *Gwendoline* and *Une Éducation manquée* contain excellent music, some of which is occasionally heard. Chabrier's operas have not been favoured on records, only some orchestral excerpts appearing with any regularity.

Une Éducation Manquée
Operetta in 1 Act.
Text by Eugène Leterrier and Albert Vanloo.
First performance: Paris (Théâtre des Arts) May 1, 1879. London 1961.

Gwendoline
Opera in 2 Acts.
Text by Catulle Mendès.
First performance: Brussels (Théâtre de la Monnaie) April 10, 1886.

Le Roi Malgré Lui
Opera in 3 Acts.
Text by Emile de Najac and Paul Burani, based on a comedy by Francois Ancelot.
First performance: Paris (Opéra-Comique) May 18, 1887. Karlsruhe 1890. Prague 1931.

L'Étoile (1877)   *Briséis (incomplete) (1899)*

GUSTAVE CHARPENTIER

(b. Dienze 25.6.1860; d. Paris 18.2.1956)

Studied at the Lille Conservatoire and then at the Paris Conservatoire in 1881. In 1885 he joined Massenet's » composition class and won the Prix de Rome in 1887 with *Didon*, a *scène lyrique*. From Rome came orchestral music — the successful *Impressions d'Italie*, and *La Vie du poète* (for soloists, chorus and orchestra)—and a fair amount of vocal music. Although he composed a great deal during a very long life, Charpentier is remembered by one work, the opera *Louise*, and for many years one aria kept his name alive, 'Depuis le jour'. He was an active worker and propagandist on behalf of the poor of Paris, especially the factory girls, and the founder of an academy for working girls, the Conservatoire Populaire de

Right: *Marcel Journet was Le Père in productions of Charpentier's Louise at La Scala in 1923 and Covent Garden in 1928.*

Mimi Pinson. He affected a Bohemian style of life and dress, fashionable at the time, and this was reflected in his music. *Julien*, a sequel to *Louise* which used material from the early *La Vie du poète*, was unsuccessful when it was produced at the Opéra-Comique in June, 1913.

Louise

Romance in 4 Acts.
Text by Charpentier.
First performance: Paris (Opéra-Comique) February 2, 1900. Brussels 1901; New York 1908; London (Covent Garden) 1909; New York (Metropolitan) 1921.

Notes:
Louise represented what appeared at the time as a new and daring realism in musical theatre; and it is sometimes held that this realistic approach keeps the opera alive. However, it is more true to say that the 'realism' is the dated element, and it is the vein of true and passionate lyricism that still attracts. It is also claimed, with justice, that the real 'heroine' of *Louise* is the city of Paris.

Julien

Opera in 4 Acts.
Text by Charpentier
First performance: Paris (Opéra-Comique) June 4, 1913. New York (Metropolitan) 1914.

LUIGI CHERUBINI
(b. Florence 14.9.1760; d. Paris 15.3.1842)

A most influential and serious-minded musician, Cherubini was the man Beethoven » considered (after himself) as the greatest living composer. Cherubini spent a large part of his life in Paris and is generally considered as a composer of the French school with Italian ancestry. He studied first with his father and then with Giuseppe Sarti in Venice. He spent the years 1785/6 in London in the service of George III, but two years later settled permanently in Paris, being appointed to the Royal Chapel in 1816, and becoming Director of the Paris Conservatoire in 1822. He produced some of his early works, including operas, during the period of the French Revolution. In 1805 he went to Vienna, where he met Beethoven. On his return to France, Cherubini was embittered and out of favour. He lived for ten years on the country estate of the Prince de Chimay where he composed church music, the form which occupied the latter part of his life. Still, he was a prolific composer in all forms, and wrote a great number of large scale works, including many operas. Only one, *Médée*, has retained anything like general popularity.

Demofonte (Démophoon)
Opera in 3 Acts.
Text by Jean François Marmontel.
First performance: Paris (Opéra) December 5, 1788.

Médée
Opera in 3 Acts.
Text by Francois Benoit Hoffmann.
First performance: Paris (Théâtre Feydeau) March 13, 1797. Berlin (in German) 1800; London (Her Majesty's) (in Italian) 1865.

Notes:
Most modern performances of *Médée* use the edition made by Franz Lachner in 1855, with interpolated recitatives (originally in German). This edition is used in the recordings. The Cetra record, though 'complete' in the larger sense, contains substantial cuts.

Anacreon
Opera in 3 Acts.
Text by R. Mendouze.
First performance: Paris (Opéra) October 4, 1803.

Quinto Fabio (1780)
Armida abbandonata (1782)
Adriano in Siria (1782)
Mesenzio (1782)
Lo sposo di tre (1783)
Idalide (1784)
Alessando nell' Indie (1784)
Demetrio (1785)
La finta principessa (1785)
Artaserse (1785)
Giulio Sabino (1786)
Didone abbandonata (1786)
Ifigenia in Aulide (1788)

Lodoiska (1791)
Elisa (1794)
L'Hôtellerie portugaise (1798)
La Punition (1799)
La Prisonnière (1799)
Les Deux Journées (1800)
Épicure (1800)
Faniska (1806)
Pimmalione (1809)
Le Crescendo (1810)
Les Abercérages (1813)
etc.

FRANCESCO CILEA
(b. Palmi, Calabria, 26.7.1866; d. Varazza 20.11.1950)

It was due to the good offices of Verdi's » friend, librarian at the Naples Conservatoire, Francesco Florimo, that the young Cilea seriously embarked upon a musical career. He entered the Naples Conservatoire in 1881 and produced his first opera, *Gina*, in 1881 while still a student. This led to a successful career as composer and pianist. His second opera, *La Tilda*, was commissioned by the publisher Sonzogno as a result of the success of *Gina* and was produced at the Teatro Pagliano, Florence, in 1892. Cilea was appointed professor at the Reale Instituto Musicale in Florence in 1896 and remained there for eight years. Cilea's operas have always maintained popularity in Italy; but only one, *Adriana Lecouvreur*, won him real fame abroad and has remained in general circulation. He was one of several musicians to base a composition on Alphonse Daudet's play *L'Arlésienne* (in Cilea's version, an opera in 4 Acts subsequently reduced to 3, it becomes *L'Arlesiana*).

L'Arlesiana
Opera in 4 Acts.
Text by Leopold Marenco, based on the drama by Alphonse Daudet.
First performance: Milan (Teatro Lirico) November 27, 1897.

Adriana Lecouvreur
Opera in 4 Acts.
Text by Arturi Colautti after Scribe.
First performance: Milan (Teatro Lirico) November 6, 1902. London (Covent Garden) 1904; New York (Metropolitan) 1907.

Gina (1889)	*Gloria (1907)*
La Tilda (1892)	

DOMENICO CIMAROSA
(b. Aversa, Naples, 17.12.1749; d. Venice 11.1.1801)

An enormously prolific composer (his output included at least 76 operas) and hugely popular in his own time, Cimarosa is now remembered chiefly for a charming oboe concerto arranged by Arthur Benjamin, and the delicious comic opera *Il matrimonio segreto (The secret marriage)*. He studied in Naples with Sacchini and Piccinni and immediately » succeeded with his operas. In 1787 he went to St Petersburg in the service of the court of Catherine the Great, but it did not work out. On his way back from Russia he stopped off in Vienna where the Emperor Leopold II invited him to compose an opera — *Il matrimonio segreto*. The Emperor was so delighted with its first performance that he had a meal prepared for the company — and demanded the entire performance over again. Cimarosa was appointed to succeed Salieri » as Kapellmeister to the court, but the Emperor's death the same year ended Cimarosa's tenure. He then returned to Naples and entered the King's service, but was imprisoned for his part in French revolutionary activities. On his release he headed for St Petersburg; but died at Venice on the way.

Il Fanatico per gli Antichi Romani

Opera in 2 Acts.
Text by Giovanni Palomba.
First performance: Naples (Teatro dei Fiorentini) Spring 1777.

I Due Baroni di Rocca Azura

Opera in 2 Acts.
Text by Giovanni Palomba.
First performance: Rome (Teatro Valle) February 1783.

Il Maestro di Capella

Intermezzo giocoso in 1 Act.
First performance: 1790.

Notes:
A brief comedy making fun of the trials of a pompous, conceited Kapellmeister and his difficulties with his colleagues. Although not an opera, complete recordings are available and we include it as an interesting example of Cimarosa's work.

Il Matrimonio Segreto

Comic opera in 2 Acts.
Text by Giovanni Bertati after the comedy by George Colman and David Garrick.
First performance: Vienna (Burg Theatre) February 7, 1792. Prague 1792; Leipzig 1792; London 1794; New York 1834.

Le stravaganze del conte (1772)
L'Italiana in Londra (1778)
Il pittore parigino (1781)
Il convito (1781)
La ballerina amante (1782)
L'Olimpiade (1784)
Artaserse (1784)
L'impresario in angustie (1786)
Cleopatra (1789)
La vergine del sole (1789)
I Traci amanti (1793)
Le astuzie femminili (1794)
Penelope (1794)
Gli Orazi ed i Curiazi (1796)
etc.

Left: *Cimarosa's* Il Matrimonio Segreto *so delighted Leopold II that he asked to hear the entire first performance again.*

41

Above: *Aaron Copland, born in 1900, is sometimes known as 'the Dean of American music', and is that country's best known composer.*

AARON COPLAND
(b. Brooklyn 14.11.1900)

Sometimes known as the 'Dean of American music', Copland studied first with Rubin Goldmark then went to Paris to study with Nadia Boulanger. In 1924 he won a Guggenheim scholarship which enabled him to spend a further two years in Europe; this influence, combined with that of Stravinsky », jazz and American folk music, produced a crisp and pointful musical style. Copland has written a good deal for the theatre (though more ballet than opera) and film music. His only true opera, *The Tender Land*, is a characteristic piece in his American rustic style. *The Second Hurricane* (1937), a school opera, was first performed at the Henry Street Music School, New York, by a cast of 150 children. It concerns the efforts of a small group of children to bring relief to flood victims, to a libretto by Edwin Denby. There is also a puppet show, *From Sorcery to Science*, written in 1939. As well as composing, Copland has done much writing and campaigning on behalf of American music.

The Tender Land
Folk opera in 2 Acts (later 3).
Text by Horace Everett.
First performance: New York, April 1, 1954.

Notes:
The Tender Land was commissioned by Richard Rodgers and Oscar Hammerstein to celebrate the 30th anniversary of the American League of Composers in 1954.

ALEXANDER DARGOMIZHSKY

(b. Tula 14.2.1813; d. St Petersburg 17.1.1869)

One of the lesser Russian nationalists, Dargomizhsky was a forerunner of 'The Mighty Five'. Tchaikovsky » named him a 'supreme example of the dilettante in music'; but although like several leading Russian composers he was mainly an amateur, he wrote a number of significant works and exerted an influence over the emergence of Russian national music later in the century. He wrote half a dozen operas, of which the best known is *Russalka* (or *The Water Sprite*) which is still performed in Russia. In *The Stone Guest*, orchestrated by Rimsky-Korsakov », he evolved a new kind of recitative and used Pushkin's text absolutely unchanged.

Russalka

Opera in 4 Acts.
Text by Alexander Dargomizhsky after Pushkin.
First performance: St Petersburg May 16, 1856. New York 1922; London (Covent Garden) 1931.

Notes:
Certain arias in this opera have always been great favourites with the world's leading singers. Chaliapin made a formidable impression as the Mad Miller in London in 1931.

Esmeralda (1847)   The Stone Guest (1872)
The Triumph of Bacchus (1867)

Below: *Chaliapin as the Mad Miller in Dargomizhky's* Russalka, *a part he played in London in 1931.*

CLAUDE DEBUSSY
(b. Saint-Germain-en-Laye 22.8.1862; d. Paris 25.3.1918)

After taking lessons from one of Chopin's pupils, Mme Mauté de Fleurville, Debussy entered the Paris Conservatoire in 1873 where he studied with Lavignac, Marmontel and Durand. For two summers he was private musician to Nadezhda von Meck, the former patroness of Tchaikovsky ». In 1884 he won the Grand Prix de Rome with the cantata, or 'Scene Lyrique', *L'Enfant prodigue*. He began to find his artistic feet with the Rossetti setting (in French translation) *La Damoiselle élue* and became completely established with the orchestral *Prélude à l'après-midi d'un faune*. He was twice married, and in addition to his compositions he was a noted critic and musical journalist, being appointed music critic of *La Revue blanche* in 1901. For the last decade of his life Debussy suffered from cancer, which resulted in his death at 55 in 1918. He completed only one full opera, *Pélleas et Mélisande*, one of the supreme and most influential masterpieces of modern lyric theatre. But this is not Debussy's only dramatic work. There is the music he wrote for Gabriele d'Annunzio's *Le Martyre de saint Sébastien*; and *L'Enfant prodigue* has been presented as a one-act opera, though without marked success. Debussy continued to plan further operas until the end of his life, but none came to fruition. These include a version of the Tristan legend and one on Orpheus; a Shakespeare piece, *Comme il vous plaira* (As You Like It); and two based on stories by Edgar Allan Poe. Much of Debussy's non-stage music (the *Images*, *Nocturnes* and *La Mer* for orchestra; the *Préludes*, *Images*, *Estampes*, *Children's Corner* for piano in particular) is well known and widely popular.

Pélleas et Mélisande
Opera in 5 Acts.
Text by Maurice Maeterlinck from his play.
First performance: Paris (Opéra-Comique) April 30, 1902. Brussels 1907; New York (Metropolitan) 1908; London (Covent Garden) 1909.

LÉO DELIBES
(b. Saint-Germain-du-Val 21.2.1836; d. Paris 16.1.1891)

After studying at the Paris Conservatoire under Adolphe Adam » Delibes held a number of appointments in the theatre and as church organist, but in 1881 returned to the Conservatoire as professor. Best known today as the composer of the two popular and expert ballets, *Coppélia* and *Sylvia*, Delibes wrote a series of lively operettas and a number of serious operas, one of which, *Lakmé*, with its famous 'Bell Song', used to be a favourite with coloratura sopranos and still holds its own in France. Another Delibes opera, *Le Roi l'a dit* after Victor Hugo, is one of these works that seems to hover on the brink of revival without actually achieving it — at least outside France. The 5 Act *Kassya* was completed by Massenet » after Delibes's death and given at the Opéra-Comique in March, 1893.

Above: *Some famous Lakimés— Lily Pons (l), Amelita Galli-Curci (r) and Luisa Tetrazzini (c).*

Lakmé

Opera in 3 Acts.
Text by Edmond Gondinet and Philippe Gille after 'Le Mariage de Loti'.
First performance: Paris (Opéra-Comique) April 14, 1883. Frankfurt (in German) 1833; London (Gaiety) 1885; New York (in English) 1886.

Notes:
This is a piece of much charm, but somewhat dated by its general idiom and its 'orientalisms', of a kind much favoured in the late 19th century. The original version was in the opéra-comique tradition with spoken dialogue. Subsequently the score was revised and the music made continuous; this is the version nowadays heard, and used in recordings. The theme of the impact of Western military personnel on the people of the East anticipates, as do certain aspects of the music, Puccini's » *Madama Butterfly.*

Le Roi l'a dit (1873)   *Kassya (1893)*
Jean de Nivelle (1880)   *etc.*

45

Above: *One of the last pictures of Delius, taken at his French home.*

FREDERICK DELIUS

(b. Bradford 29.1.1862; d. Grez-sur-Loing 10.6.1934)

Delius was born into a prosperous wool-trading family of German descent. It was also a musical family, though Delius was originally expected to follow a business career. When it was clear he was determined to become a musician, he was sent off to manage an orange grove in Florida, where he came under the important influence of Thomas Ward, organist at Jacksonville. Subsequently he studied at Leipzig. In 1887 he went to Norway and on his return to Leipzig met Grieg, whose advocacy was instrumental in persuading Delius's father that his son should devote his life to music. While at Leipzig Delius was deeply impressed by a great deal of music by Beethoven », Brahms, Wagner » and Tchaikovsky »—in spite of the legend that Delius despised all music but his own and that he had no time for 'academic' composers. From 1890 Delius lived in France, first in Paris and from 1897 at Grez-sur-Loing in the Seine-et-Marne district, beside the river which played so important a part in his creative work. In that year he married the painter Jelka Rosen. Delius composed six operas. Only two, *A Village Romeo and Juliet* and *Koanga*, have achieved any real popularity, though his last opera, *Fennimore and Gerda*, has been recorded and the first, *Irmelin*, was produced at Oxford under Sir Thomas Beecham, Delius's foremost interpreter and the man who did more than anyone to propagate the gospel of his art. It is worth noting that, in respect of his operas as of all his music, the long-held idea that Delius was primarily a harmonic composer somewhat deficient in melody, is way off the mark. The truth is that his melody and harmony are closely interwoven, totally interdependent, the rich harmonies a continual seedbed for long weaving strands of melody, the melody provoking richness of harmony. Only in this interaction of melody and harmony does the music of Delius ultimately fulfil itself. During the last years of his life Delius was blind and paralysed. But his mind remained active to the end and he was able to continue composing through the devoted services of Eric Fenby, who acted as his amanuensis from 1928 until Delius's death in 1934.

Irmelin

Opera in 3 Acts. (Written 1890-92.)
Text by Delius.
First performance: Oxford (New Theatre) May 4, 1953.

Koanga

Opera in Prologue, 3 Acts and Epilogue.
Text by C. F. Keary after George Washington Cable's 'The Grandissime'.
First performance: Elberfeld (Municipal Theatre) March 30, 1904. London (Covent Garden) 1935.

A Village Romeo and Juliet

Lyric Drama in Six Scenes.
Text by Jelka Delius after Gottfried Keller's 'Romeo und Julia auf dem Dorfe'.
First performance: Berlin (Komische Oper) February 21, 1907. London (Covent Garden) 1910.

Fennimore and Gerda

Music drama in 11 Pictures.
Text by Delius after Jens Peter Jacobsen's novel 'Niels Lyhne'.
First performance: Frankfurt, October 21, 1919.

Notes:
This opera is something of an oddity, in that the Gerda of the title does not appear until the end and plays no part in the dramatic action. The 11 'pictures' are linked by orchestral interludes which contain some of Delius's best music.

GAETANO DONIZETTI

(b. Bergamo 29.11.1797; d. Bergamo 8.4.1848)

This talented and industrious man was once thought to have been of Scottish descent (due partly to his predilection for Scots subjects for his operas); but this theory was disproved some time ago. Donizetti studied first at the Instituto Musicale of his native Bergamo and then at the Liceo Filharmonico in Bologna, under Mattei. He began writing operas early in his career, and after three unperformed works began his career proper with *Enrico di Borgogna* which was produced in Venice at the Teatro San Luca on November 14, 1818. Thereafter he composed operas prolifically, producing over 70 before he died, paralysed and the victim of melancholia, in the town where he was born. Donizetti, like his contemporaries Bellini » and Rossini », wrote for the great race of *bel canto* singers of that era, such as Rubini, Pasta and Grisi, and his musical style reflects those circumstances even more than Bellini's. It is sometimes facile, often superficial; yet he had a genuine dramatic gift and was a thoroughly trained musician who could handle any task to which he set his hand. Because of the decline of the type of singers and singing for which his work was designed, his operas fell into neglect for a considerable period. There were always exceptions, like *Lucia di Lammermoor* and the delectable comedies *Don Pasquale* and *L'elisir d'amore*; and the modern revival, led by the late Maria Callas, of true *bel canto* has readjusted the perspectives. But the large bulk of his operatic productions has sunk into history and will probably not surface again except in excerpt form on various recordings.

Emilia di Liverpool

Opera in 2 Acts.
Text by unknown person, revised Giuseppe Checcherini, based on a melodrama by Scatizzi.
First performance: Naples (Teatro Nuovo) July 28, 1824. Revised version Naples (Teatro Nuovo) Lent 1828.

Left: *Gaetano Donizetti, composer of over 70 operas.*

Right: *A performance of Donizetti's best comic opera, L'Elisir d'Amore. He wrote it in 1832 at the age of 34 just after establishing himself with Anna Bolena. In response to an urgent demand from the management of the Canobbiana he managed to complete the work in 14 days. When he was asked to whom the published score was to be dedicated he said: 'To the fair sex of Milan—who know how to bestow it'.*

Anna Bolena

Opera in 2 Acts.
Text by Felice Romani.
First performance: Milan (Teatro Carcano) 26.12.1830. London 1831; New York 1843.

Notes:
In most modern productions the structure is altered to move Act 1, Scene 3 into Act 2. *Anna Bolena* was one of the leading vehicles for the late Maria Callas, who revived the art of *bel canto* in the 1950s. It was also the opera in which she made her triumphant return to the Italian stage after the scandal during a performance of Bellini's » *Norma* in 1957, when, ill and unable to continue, she withdrew after the first Act and was accused of insulting the President.

Ugo, Conte di Parigi

Opera in 2 Acts.
Text by Felice Romani.
First performance: Milan (La Scala) March 13, 1832.

L'Elisir d'Amore

Opera in 2 Acts.
Text by Felice Romani after Eugène Scribe's 'Le Philtre'.
First performance: Milan (Teatro della Canobbiana) May 12, 1832. London 1836; New York 1838.

Lucrezia Borgia

Opera in Prologue and 2 Acts.
Text by Felice Romani after Victor Hugo.
First performance: Milan (La Scala) December 26, 1833. London 1839; New York 1844.

Rosamonda d'Inghilterra

Opera in 2 Acts.
Text by Felice Romani.
First performance: Florence (Teatro Pergola) February 27, 1834.

Notes:
Later revised as *Eleonora di Gujenna*. The libretto was not written for Donizetti, having been set by Carlo Coccia in 1829.

Maria Stuarda

Opera in 3 Acts.
Text by Giuseppe Bardari.
First performance: Naples (Teatro San Carlo) October 19, 1834 (as 'Buondelmonte'). Milan (La Scala) December 30, 1835 (as 'Maria Stuarda').

Notes:
Because of censorship difficulties, *Maria Stuarda* was originally presented as *Buondelmonte* with a text radically altered by Pietro Salatino and the action removed from Tudor England to Renaissance Italy. The story, after Schiller, is of course apocryphal; the meeting between Mary and Elizabeth never took place.

Below: *Joan Sutherland, portrayer of so many Donizetti heroines, in the Covent Garden Maria Stuarda.*

Gemma di Vergy

Opera in 2 Acts.
Text by Emanuele Bidera after Alexandre Dumas's 'Charles VII chez ses grands vassaux'.
First performance: Milan (La Scala) December 26, 1834.

Above: Lucia di Lammermoor, *with its famous sextet, is one of Donizetti's best-known works. Here the American soprano Beverly Sills take the leading role.*

Lucia di Lammermoor

Opera in 3 Acts.
Text by Salvatore Cammarano after Walter Scott's 'The Bride of Lammermoor'
First performance: Naples (Teatro San Carlo) September 26, 1835. Vienna 1835; London (Her Majesty's) 1838; New Orleans (in French) 1841.

Il Campanello di Notte

Opera in 1 Act.
Text by Donizetti.
First performance: Naples (Teatro Nuovo) June 1, 1836.

Notes:
Based on a vaudeville by Brunswick, Trion and Lhérie, *La Sonnette de nuit*, it concerns an apothecary whose wedding night is constantly disturbed by his wife's former lover ringing on the night bell.

L'Assedio di Calais

Opera in 3 Acts.
Text by Salvatore Cammarano, after du Belloy's 'Le siège de Calais'.
First performance: Naples (Teatro San Carlo) November 19, 1836.

Roberto Devereux, Conte d'Essex

Opera in 3 Acts.
Text by Salvatore Cammarano after François Ancelot's 'Elisabeth d'Angleterre'
(with plagiarisms from a libretto by Felice Romani).
First performance: Naples (Teatro San Carlo) October 29, 1837.

La Fille du Régiment

Opera in 2 Acts.
Text by Jules Henri Vernoy de Saint-Georges and Jean François Alfred Bayard.
First performance: Paris (Opéra-Comique) February 11, 1840. Milan (in Italian)
1840; New Orleans (in French) 1843; London (Her Majesty's) (in Italian) 1847;
New York (Metropolitan) 1902.

Poliuto

Opera in 3 Acts.
Text by Salvatore Cammarano. Expanded into 4 Acts (in French), text by Eugène
Scribe, as Les Martyrs. Based on Corneille's 'Polyeucte'.
First performance: (as Les Martyrs) Paris (Opéra) April 10, 1840; (as Poliuto)
Naples (Teatro San Carlo) November 30, 1848.

La Favorite

Opera in 4 Acts
Text by Alphonse Royer and Gustave Vaëz after Baculard-Darnaud's 'Le Comte
de Comminges' (plus Eugène Scribe).
First performance: Paris (Opéra) December 2, 1840. New Orleans 1843; Milan
(La Scala, in Italian) 1843; London (Drury Lane, in English) 1843.

Linda di Chamounix

Opera in 3 Acts.
Text by Gaetano Rossi.
First performance; Vienna (Kärthnerthortheater) May 19, 1842. London 1843;
New York (Palmo's Opera House) 1847.

Below: La Fille du Régiment *opened the way to the new French operetta.*
Joan Sutherland has made the role of Marie very much her own.

Don Pasquale

Opera in 3 Acts.
Text by Donizetti and Giovanni Ruffini after Angelo Anelli's 'Ser Marc' Antonio'.
First performance: Paris (Théâtre-Italien) January 3, 1843. Milan (La Scala) 1843; London (Her Majesty's Theatre) 1843; New York (in English) 1846.

Maria di Rohan (Il Conte di Chalais)

Opera in 3 Acts.
Text by Salvatore Cammarano, based on Lockroy's 'Un duel sous le cardinal de Richelieu'.
First performance: Vienna (Kärthnerthortheater) June 5, 1843.

Don Sébastian de Portugal

Opera in 5 Acts.
Text by Eugène Scribe, based on Barbosa Machado's 'Memoirs'.
First performance: Paris (Opéra) November 13, 1843.

Il Duca d'Alba

Opera in 4 Acts.
Text by Eugène Scribe and Charles Duveyrier.
First performance: Rome (Teatro Apollo) (in Italian) March 22, 1882.

Notes:
Donizetti left the opera incomplete, having worked on it in 1839. It was revised after his death: the libretto was translated into Italian by Angelo Zanardini and the score was edited by Matteo Salvi.

Enrico di Borgogna (1818)
Una follia (1818)
Piccioli virtuosi ambulanti (1819)
Pietro il Grande (1819)
Le nozze in villa (1821)
Zoraide di Granata (1822)
La zingara (1822)
La lettera anonima (1822)
Chiara e Serafina (1822)
Alfredo il Grande (1823)
Il fortunato inganno (1823)
L'aio nell' imbarazzo (1824)
Alahor in Granata (1826)
Il castello degli invalidi (1826)
Elvida (1826)
Olivo e Pasquale (1827)
Gli esiliati in Siberia (1827)
Il borgomastro di Saardam (1827)
Le convenienze ed inconvenienze teatrali (1827)
L'esule di Roma (1828)
La regina di Golconda (1828)
Gianni di Calais (1828)
Il giovedì grasso (1828)

Il paria (1829)
Il castello di Kenilworth (1829)
I pazzi per progetto (1830)
Il diluvio universale (1830)
Imelda de' Lambertazzi (1830)
Francesca di Foix (1831)
La romanziera e l'uomo nero (1831)
Fausta (1832)
Sancia di Castiglia (1832)
Il furioso all'isola di San Domingo (1833)
Parisina (1833)
Torquato Tasso (1833)
Marino Faliero (1835)
Belisario (1836)
Betly (1836)
Pia de' Tolomei (1837)
Maria di Rudenz (1838)
Gianni di Parigi (1839)
Adelia (1841)
Maria Padilla (1841)
Catarina Cornaro (1844)
Rita (1860)
etc.

ANTONÍN DVOŘÁK
(b. Nelahozeves 8.9.1841; d. Prague 1.5.1904)

The son of a butcher and innkeeper, Dvořák absorbed nation. folk and church music as a youth. When his musical gift revealed themselves fully, he was sent to the organ school in Prague and subsequently joined the orchestra of the Czech National Theatre under the direction of Smetana ». His compositions soon began to establish his reputation at home and abroad. He composed fruitfully and at length in all forms, and wrote 10 operas, of which *Rusalka* has maintained an international foothold, and the diverting *The Devil and Kate* reveals a lively vitality. His serious, tragically inclined operas are not among his most successful compositions. Dvořák spent time in both England and America. His most famous symphony (No. 9) and some chamber music emanated from his American visits. He undertook his first visit to England in 1884 where he made a strong impression with his *Stabat Mater*, and became an Honorary Doctor of Music at Cambridge in 1891. He married in 1873 and in 1884 bought himself a country property which was his home for the rest of his life, alternating with travels abroad and periods in Prague. He was friends with many great international figures in music, including Brahms, Tchaikovsky » and Sibelius. As a man he appears to have been as amiable and well disposed as his music. His son-in-law was the celebrated Czech composer Josef Suk (1874-1935).

The Devil and Kate (Čert a Káča)
Opera in 3 Acts.
Text by Adolf Wenig.
First performance: Prague (National Theatre) November 23, 1899. Oxford 1932.

Rusalka
Opera in 3 Acts.
Text by Josef Kvapil.
First performance: Prague (National Theatre), March 31, 1901. Vienna 1910; Stuttgart 1929; London (John Lewis Musical Society) 1950; Sadler's Wells 1959.

Left: *Antonín Dvořák.*

King and Collier (1874)
Vanda (1876)
The Peasant a Rogue (1878)
The Pigheaded Peasants (1881)
Dimitrij (1882)
The Jacobin (1889)
Armida (1904)
Alfred (1938)
etc.

FERENC ERKEL
(Gyula 7.11.1810; d. Budapest 15.6.1893)

The founder of Hungarian national opera, Erkel came from a family long noted as musicians. He showed early promise and at the age of ten was able to deputise for his father at the organ of the local church. He studied music from an early age, especially at Pozsony, which, being near Vienna, provided opportunities for musical experience. Erkel became music master to the family of Count Csáky at Kolozsvár in 1827 and remained in that position until 1834, when he entered the service of the Countess Stainlen-Saalfeld. In 1836 he became assistant conductor at the Municipal Theatre in Pest and then joined the newly-established National Theatre as musical director. He was already preoccupied with a Hungarian national opera and his first work in this direction was *Bátori Mária*, produced in August 1840. His second, *Hunyadi László*, became one of his and his country's most famous and successful operas. He was prominent in the formation of the Philharmonic Society in 1853 and became its President Conductor. He was also a considerable writer on and editor of Hungarian national music. Erkel was not the first to write Hungarian opera, but he was the virtual creator of the true national style. His operas, like those of composers in several other countries, were an offshoot of national liberation movements and inner national aspirations.

Hunyadi László
Opera in 4 Acts.
Text by Béni Egressy based on Lörinc Tóth.
First performance: Pest (National Theatre) January 27, 1844.

Notes:
Like most of Erkel's music, this opera strikes a strong patriotic note. One chorus was taken as a national affirmation, in much the same manner as several of Verdi's were in Italy at the time of the struggles for national independence.

Bánk Bán
Opera in 3 Acts.
Text by Béni Egressy based on József Katona.
First performance: Pest (National Theatre) March 9, 1861.

Notes:
This is another strongly nationalistic work, its subject the liberation of Hungary from oppressive foreign rule. *Bánk Bán* was written between 1844 and 1852, but it was not produced until 1861 because of the political situation and the setback to Hungarian national aspiration in 1849, when an uprising proved abortive.

Bátori Mária (1840)	*Brankovics György (1874)*
Erzsébet (1857)	*Névtelen hösök (1880)*
Sarolta (1862)	*Istvan király (1885)*
Dózsa György (1867)	

MANUEL DE FALLA

(b. Cadiz 23.11.1876; d. Alta Gracia, Argentina, 14.11.1946)

Spain's premier modern composer studied the piano from the age of eight, and then with the great man of the Spanish music renaissance, Felipe Pedrell, who gave Falla the most powerful impetus towards his ultimate goal—the creation of a genuinely international style based on the various idioms of Spanish music. In 1907 Falla went to Paris, where he was encouraged by the leading French composers, including Debussy », Ravel » and Dukas, as well as his compatriot Isaac Albéniz. Falla returned to Spain in 1914 and did not leave again until he went to Argentina in 1939, where he stayed until his death. He was a withdrawn, ascetic, celibate, deeply religious, totally dedicated man and artist, who lived to become the embodiment of the historic spirit of Spain. He wrote only a little music; but four of his most important works were for the theatre—two ballets, one opera and a puppet opera. The opera, *La vida breve*, the first of his works he wished to acknowledge, won first prize in a competition organized by the Real Academia de Belles Artes in 1904, but despite the terms which stated that the winning work should be produced at the Teatro Real in Madrid, was given first at Nice in a French translation and did not reach Madrid until 1914. The puppet opera *El retablo de Maese Pedro* was commissioned by the Princesse de Polignac in 1923, for performance in her private theatre.

Below: *Conductor Garcia Navarro and singer Teresa Berganza, who collaborated in a recording of Falla's* La Vida Breve.

Above: *Manuel de Falla, whose music is full of the true spirit of Spain.*

La Vida Breve
Opera in 2 Acts (originally 1 Act).
Text by Carlos Fernández Shaw.
First performance: Nice (Casino Municipal) April 4, 1913. Paris (Opéra-Comique) 1914 (both in French); Madrid (Teatro de la Zarzuela) 1914.

Notes:
Two misconceptions about *La vida breve* persist—that it is a kind of offshoot of the *zarzuela* style; and that Salud is a gypsy. The opera has nothing to do with *zarzuela*, despite the fact that its librettist was a leading writer in the *zarzuela* field. Salud is not a gypsy but a typification of the southern Spanish woman. Falla himself was insistent on this point.

El Retablo de Maese Pedro
Puppet opera in 6 scenes.
Text by Falla after an episode in 'Don Quixote' (Cervantes).
First performance: Seville (Teatro San Fernando) March 23, 1923. Paris (house of Princesse Edmond de Polignac) 1923; Clifton, Bristol, England (Victoria Rooms) 1924; New York 1925.

FRIEDRICH VON FLOTOW

(b. Teutendorf 26.4.1812; d. Darmstadt 24.1.1883)

Of noble birth, Flotow was originally intended for a diploma. career. But he went to Paris in 1827 to study under Reicha an. began to compose after the revolution of 1830, presenting his stage works at private aristocratic houses. He achieved public recognition in 1839 with *Le Naufrage de la Méduse* in collaboration with Albert Grisar and Pilati. (He later rewrote this as *Die Matrosen* in 1845.) A serious opera, *Alessandro Stradella*, which he recast from some incidental music, showed that his talent was somewhat slighter than his ambition —but his lighter operas contain much charming and diverting music. His gift was clearly for the theatre; he wrote some 30 operas and operettas in various languages, plus a number of ballets and some incidental music. He also wrote an amount of instrumental music and songs. His most famous work, *Martha*, had a long run of international popularity. Between 1856 and 1863 Flotow was intendant at the theatre at Schwerin, and then returned to Paris before settling near Vienna.

Alessandro Stradella

Opera in 3 Acts.
Text by 'W. Friedrich' (Friedrich Wilhelm Riese).
First performance: Hamburg, December 30, 1844. London (Drury Lane) 1846, (Covent Garden) 1864.

Below: *Gigli as Lionel in the 1930 Covent Garden* Martha.

Martha

Opera in 4 Acts.
Text by W. Friedrich after 'Lady Henriette, ou La Servante de Greenwich' by Vernoy St Georges.
First performance: Vienna (Kärtnertor Theatre) November 25, 1847. London (Drury Lane) 1849; London (Covent Garden) (in English) 1858; Paris (Théâtre-Lyrique) 1865; New York (Metropolitan) 1884.

Notes:
The famous aria 'Ach, so fromm' or 'M'appari' was not in the original score but was interpolated for the production at the Paris Théâtre-Lyrique on December 16, 1865. The number was 'borrowed' from Flotow's opera in 2 Acts, *L'Ame en Peine* (1846). *Martha* is nowadays more a matter of extracts than a complete opera. Its rustic charms have faded somewhat, but its famous numbers remain popular; most notably 'M'appari' (since Caruso made a great hit with it) and 'The Last Rose of Summer' ('Die letzte Rose'), an old Irish tune with words by Thomas Moore which Flotow cunningly incorporated into his score. It is still a work of considerable charm and will no doubt earn its revival in due course.

Pierre et Catherine (1835)
Rob Roy (1836)
Sérafine (1836)
Alice (1837)
Le Comte de Saint-Mégrin (1838)
Le Naufrage de la Méduse (1839)
La Duchesse de Guise (1840)
L'Esclave de Camoëns (1843)
Die Matrosen (1845)
L'Âme en peine (Léoline) (1846)
Sophia Catharina (1850)
Indra (1852)

Rübezahl (1853)
Albin (1856)
Pianella (1857)
La Veuve Grapin (1859)
Naida (1865)
Zilda (1866)
Am Runenstein (1868)
L'Ombre (1870)
Il fiore di Harlem (1876)
Alma, l'incantatrice (1878)
etc.

JOHN GAY
(b. Barnstaple 16.9.1685; d. London 4.12.1732)

Gay is usually credited with the creation of one of the first and most successful ballad operas in England, *The Beggar's Opera*. In reality, his musical contribution was simply to select various popular airs to which he added the lyrics and wrote the interspersed dialogue. The actual music was already familiar, and was arranged by Johann Christoph Pepusch (1667-1752), a German composer who settled in London around 1700. It was Gay, however, who invented the story to go with it—a tale of bawdy realism, full of rogues, beggars, highwaymen and receivers. The public of the time flocked to see it and made *The Beggar's Opera* one of the most successful entertainments of the day. It had a tremendous influence, not only on further ballad-operas, including Gay's own less successful *Polly*, but on

British opera as a whole. It freed opera from the dictates of the Italian and German schools and gave it its own national style. After being played countless times and becoming something of a legend, *The Beggar's Opera* was somewhat neglected until revived nearly 200 years later by Nigel Playfair, with the music skilfully revised by Frederic Austin, at the Lyric, Hammersmith in 1920. The production ran for 1,463 performances. Later revivals have always found an affectionate audience for this sturdy masterpiece, which also inspired a new copy in Kurt Weill's » *Die Dreigroschenoper*.

The Beggar's Opera
Ballad Opera in 3 Acts.
Text by John Gay.
Music collected and arranged by Pepusch.
First performance: London (Lincoln's Inn Fields) January 29, 1728. London (Covent Garden) 1732; New York 1750; Revived London (Covent Garden) (2 Acts) 1813 and 1878 (with Sims Reeves); New version (arranged Frederick Austin) London (Lyric, Hammersmith) 1920 London (Criterion) 1935 New version arranged Benjamin Britten, Cambridge 1948; Vienna 1949; Hamburg 1950.

GEORGE GERSHWIN
(b. New York 26.9.1898; d. Hollywood 11.7.1937)

Throughout his short working life Gershwin was always torn between his natural ability to write first-rate music in a popular idiom, which made him very successful, and an ambitious streak which constantly led him to desire a reputation in the more 'respectable' fields of composition. He was also an excellent pianist and could have made a living as a performing musician. He was greatly influenced in his early days, when he worked in Tin Pan Alley, by the music of such composers as

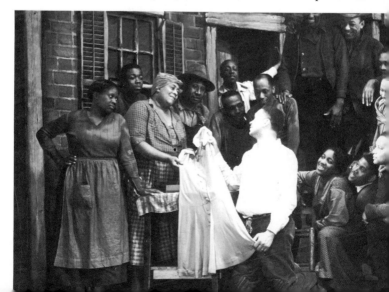

Jerome Kern and Irving Berlin. He soon built a reputation as a writer for the musical theatre; his first full-length show was *La La Lucille* in 1919 which led to such shows as *Lady Be Good* (1924) and *Funny Face* (1927), which have survived in the unforgettable hit-songs that he wrote for them. Some of his best songs were written, at the end of his career, for Hollywood films. He could easily have rested on his reputation as one of the best popular songwriters of the century; but he was persuaded by Paul Whiteman that he could and should write a larger scale work for his band to perform, and the undoubted success of *Rhapsody in Blue* in 1924 (although there were critical reservations about it) led him to write other works like *An American in Paris*, and a Piano Concerto, and to the confident belief that he could write a serious folk opera and the eventual production of *Porgy and Bess*. The acceptance of this work came gradually and Gershwin never knew its full acclaim, which came with revival performances after his sudden and tragic death of a brain tumour at the age of 38.

Porgy and Bess
Opera in 3 Acts.
Text by DuBose Heyward and Ira Gershwin, based on the play 'Porgy' by Dorothy and DuBose Heyward.
First performance: Boston (Colonial Theater) September 30, 1935. New York (Alvin Theater) October 10, 1935; Zürich 1945; London 1953.

Notes:
Gershwin first read DuBose Heyward's 'Porgy' in 1926; he immediately knew that it was the ideal subject for an opera and wrote to the author, who agreed that he should set it. But it was not until 1932 that they were able to go ahead. In the meantime the Theatre Guild had asked for permission to have it made into

Below: *The original New York production of* Porgy and Bess.

a musical by Jerome Kern and Oscar Hammerstein II to star Al Jolson. Heyward kept faith with Gershwin and the idea of an opera, and they set to work. It took the composer 11 months to write the piano score and nine months to orchestrate. It was enthusiastically received by the audiences at the opening performances in Boston and New York but received mixed notices, only ran for 124 performances and made a heavy loss. The real acclaim was to come with the revivals in the 1950s, when its fine songs were already accepted as classics.

UMBERTO GIORDANO
(b. Foggia 27.8.1867; d. Milan 12.11.1948)

The son of an artisan, he was at first intended to follow in the trade, until his musical gift was recognised. He studied at Naples Conservatoire, and while still a student composed an opera, *Marina*, which attracted the attention of the publisher Sonzogno who commissioned a work from him—a piece of somewhat bloodthirsty melodrama, *Mala vita*, which was successful. From then on Giordano produced a stream of effective but often unsophisticated operas. Of these, only *Andrea Chénier* has remained popular, though one or two others are occasionally heard. He married a wealthy lady and lived comfortably; but he never repeated his early successes or really fulfilled his promise.

Andrea Chénier
Opera in 4 Acts.
Text by Luigi Illica.
First performance: Milan (La Scala) March 28, 1896. New York (Academy of Music) 1896; London (in English) 1903.

Fedora
Opera in 3 Acts.
Text by Arturo Colautti after Sardou.
First performance: Milan (Teatro Lirico) November 17, 1898. New York (Metropolitan) 1906.

Mala vita (1892)
Regina Diaz (1894)
Siberia (1903)
Marcella (1907)
Mese Mariano (1910)
Madame Sans-Gêne (1915)
La cena delle beffe' (1924)
Il re (1929)
etc.

Right: *Renata Tebaldi, a famous Madeleine, who played the role in the Giordono commemoration performance of Andrea Chénier in 1949 and later recorded the opera.*

MIKHAIL IVANOVICH GLINKA
(b. Novospasskoye, Smolensk 1.6.1804; d. Berlin 15.2.1857)

Glinka came from a wealthy, if not musical, family. His father intended him for government service, which he entered briefly in 1824. But the young Glinka was determined to devote his life to music. He travelled and studied abroad in his youth, but returned to Russia on the death of his father in 1834, married and settled in St Petersburg. Although he remained essentially an amateur, he made his mark and it was an important one: he is often considered the founder of Russian national music. There is some truth in this; certainly later Russians (notably Tchaikovsky ») had great admiration for and were influenced by Glinka. Of his two operas, the first, *A Life for the Tsar* was the most influential—an epoch-making work—even though it contains much pseudo-Italianism and is by no means entirely original, except in the superb choruses. His second opera *Ruslan and Ludmila* catches the true Russian national note.

A Life for the Tsar (Ivan Susanin)
Opera in 4 Acts and Epilogue.
Text by Georgy Fedorovich Rosen.
First performance: St Petersburg (Bolshoi Theatre) December 9, 1836.

Notes:
The original title was *Ivan Susanin*, but when the Emperor accepted the dedication it was changed to *A Life for the Tsar*. After the 1917 revolution the original title was restored and is now used exclusively in the Soviet Union.

Ruslan and Ludmila
Opera in 5 Acts.
Text by Glinka, V. F. Shirkov, N. V. Kukolnik and others, after Pushkin.
First performance: St Petersburg (Bolshoi Theatre) December 9, 1842.

Below: *The final scene of* Ivan Susanin *at the Bolshoi Theatre, with the singers riding real horses on stage.*

CHRISTOPH WILLIBALD GLUCK

(b. Erasbach 2.7.1714; d. Vienna 15.11.1787)

After encountering the familiar parental opposition to a musical career, Gluck studied at Prague University and entered the service of Prince Melzi and studied with Sammartini in Milan. He visited London in 1745 where he met Handel ». During all this time Gluck was producing operas in the conventional Italian style, and it was not until he settled in Vienna in 1752 that he began his great work of opera reform. Previously, operas had been tailored to the traditional conceits of the period, when the drama was subservient to the vocal pyrotechnics of a tribe of virtuoso singers who thought that opera's sole purpose was to display their talents. Gluck's aim was to effect an equal marriage of music and drama; the expurgation of extraneous matter, and a more flexible and expressive style in which the music moved the drama on and added a further dimension to it. Yet for all the success of his reforming zeal, Gluck was no pedant; he could, when occasion required, return to the older tradition and make the best of it. It was this lack of rigidity that enabled him to carry out his reforms—even though his actual creative genius was not of the highest order. Gluck composed a great number of operas, but only a few have maintained their popularity. Of these, the most famous by far is *Orfeo*, which exists in both French and Italian versions.

Orfeo ed Euridice (Orphée)

Opera in 3 Acts.
Text by Raniero da Calzabigi.
First performance: Vienna (Burg Theatre) October 5, 1762. Frankfurt o/M 1764; Parma 1769; London (with additions) 1770; New York (Winter Garden Theatre) (in English) 1863.

Notes:
The part of Orfeo was originally written for male alto. When the new version was produced for Paris (*Orphée*, trans. Pierre Louis Moline; Paris [Opéra] August 2, 1774) Gluck rewrote it for tenor. It was Berlioz » who restored the original voicing, allotting the part to contralto, the version usually heard today.

La Rencontre Imprévue

Opera.
Text by L. H. Dancourt.
First performance: Vienna (Burg Theatre) January 7, 1764.

Alceste

Opera in 3 Acts.
Text by Raniero da Calzabigi.
First performance: Vienna (Burg Theatre) December 26, 1767. Paris (Opéra) (French) 1776.

Paride ed Elena

Opera in 4 Acts.
Text by Raniero da Calzabigi.
First performance: Vienna (Burg Theatre) November 3, 1770.

Above: *Kathleen Ferrier in her most famous role as* Orfeo.

Iphigénie en Aulide
Opera in 3 Acts.
Text by François Louis and Lebland du Roullet after Racine and Euripides.
First performance: Paris (Opéra) April 19, 1774.

Armide
Opera in 5 Acts.
Text by Philippe Quinault after Tasso.
First performance: Paris (Opéra) September 23, 1777.

Iphigénie en Tauride
Opera in 4 Acts.
Text by Nicolas-Francois Giullard after Euripides.
First performance: Paris (Opéra) May 18, 1779. Vienna (in German) 1781;
London (in Italian) 1796; New York (Metropolitan) (in German) 1916.

Artaserse (1711)
Demetrio (1742)
Demofoonte (1742)
Il Tigrane (1743)
La Sofonisba (1744)
Impermestra (1744)
Poro (1744)
Ippolito (1745)
La caduta de'giganti (1746)
Artamene (1746)
Le nozze d'Ercole e d'Ebe (1747)
Semiramide riconosciuta (1748)
La contesa dei numi (1749)
Ezio (1750)
Issipile (1752)
La clemenza di Tito (1752)
Le cinesi (1754)
La danza (1755)
La vestale (1755)
Les Amours champestres (1755)

Antigono (1756)
Il re pastore (1756)
Le Chinois poli en France (1756)
Le Déguisement pastoral (1756)
L'Isle de Merlin (1758)
La Fausse Esclave (1758)
La Cythère assiégée (1759 and 1775)
L'Arbre enchanté (1759)
Tetide (1760)
L'Ivrogne corrigé (1760)
Le Cadi dupé (1761)
Il trionfo di Clelia (1763)
Il Telemacco (1765)
Il Parnaso confuso (1765)
Il prologo (1767)
Le feste d'Apollo (1769)
Armide (1777)
Écho et Narcisse (1779)
etc.

65

CHARLES GOUNOD

(b. Paris 18.6.1818; d. Saint-Cloud 18.10.1893)

Gounod received his first musical education from his concert pianist mother. Later he entered the Paris Conservatoire, where he studied under Halévy , Paer and Lesueur before winning the Prix de Rome in 1839. While in Rome he was greatly influenced by Italian music (especially Palestrina), and by Italian life and art in general. Travels in Germany and Austria introduced him to German music and musicians. The theatre occupied Gounod's energies for the major part of his life. He composed 13 operas between 1850 and 1880 (including the unfinished *Maître Pierre*) and a considerable amount of incidental music. At one time Gounod appeared to be on the point of taking holy orders, and all his life he composed widely for the church; he also composed much orchestral and instrumental music and songs. As an opera composer Gounod is remembered principally by *Faust*, one of the most successful operas ever written, though its popularity has declined somewhat in our own time. His *Roméo et Juliette*, a not altogether convincing adaptation of Shakespeare (as *Faust*, for all its musical brilliance, is not a very profound adaptation of Goethe) contains a good deal of fine music but has not held its place in the repertory. Perhaps Gounod's most attractive operatic

production is *Mireille,* with its warm lyricism and Provençal setting. It well deserves a revival.

Sapho
Opera in 3 Acts.
Text by Emile Augier.
First performance: Paris (Opéra) April 16, 1851. Paris 1884 (revised in 4 Acts).

Faust
Opera in 5 Acts.
Text by Jules Barbier and Michel Carré after Goethe.
First performance: Paris (Théâtre-Lyrique) March 19, 1859. Paris (Opéra) 1869 (new version with recitative and ballet); Liège 1860; London (Her Majesty's Theatre) (in Italian) 1863; New York (in Italian) 1863.

Mireille
Opera in 5 Acts.
Text by Michel Carré after Frédéric Mistral's 'Mirèo' (poem).
First performance: Paris (Théâtre-Lyrique) March 19, 1864. Paris 1864 (revised in 3 Acts); London (Her Majesty's Theatre) (in Italian) 1864; Chicago (in English) 1880.

Below: *Gounod's* Faust *at the Royal Opera House, Covent Garden.*

Notes:
In other versions, Mireille dies in Vincent's arms, seeing, like the doomed Marguerite of *Faust*, a vision of heaven.

Roméo et Juliette
Opera in 5 Acts.
Text by Barbier and Carré.
First performance: Paris (Théâtre-Lyrique) April 27, 1867. Paris (Opéra) 1888 (with ballet).

Le Tribut de Zamora
Opera in 5 Acts.
Text by Adolphe Philippe d'Ennery and Jules Brésil.
First performance: Paris (Opéra) April 1, 1881.

La Nonne sanglante (1854)	*La Reine de Saba (1862)*
Le Médecin malgré lui (1857)	*Cinq-Mars (1877)*
Philémon et Bacchus (1859)	*Polyeucte (1878)*
La Colombe (1859)	*etc.*

ENRIQUE GRANADOS
(b. Lérida 27.7.1867; d. at sea 24.3.1916)

Granados was one of several Spanish composers to study with Felipe Pedrell and to be encouraged in his ambitions towards the renaissance of Spanish music. Also, like others of his time, he went to Paris, although for only two years; ill health prevented him from making the most of it. On his return to Spain, he revealed his great talents as a concert pianist. As a composer Granados's work centred on the piano, for which he wrote many pieces, often little more than well turned genre pieces in the 19th Century Romantic style. Yet with the two books of *Goyescas*, based upon the paintings, drawings and tapestries of Francesco Goya, he found an original and genuinely Spanish idiom. These piano pieces have more than a direct bearing on the one opera out his seven to have gained international acceptance, also called *Goyescas*. The opera is unusual, because it was built out of the piano pieces, a reversal of the more familiar practice. Its launching was tragic, as Granados was drowned when the ship on which he was returning to Spain from New York after the première was torpedoed in the English Channel by a U-boat.

Goyescas
Opera in 3 Tableaux.
Text by Fernando Periquet after Goya and based on Granados's piano 'Goyescas'.
First performance: New York (Metropolitan) January 28, 1916.

Maria del Carmen (1898)	*Gaziel (1906)*
Picarol (1901)	*Liliana (1911)*
Follet (1903)	*etc.*

ANDRÉ ERNEST GRÉTRY
(b. Liège 11.2.1741; d. Montmorency 24.9.1813)

Above: *André Gretry was an important composer of over 70 operas.*

An enormously prolific and in his day important composer of operas, today virtually none of Grétry's operatic music survives or is widely performed. He wrote over 70 operas and operettas and these contain much delightful, intelligent music, even if technically they tend to be somewhat plain and simplistic. We are indebted to Sir Thomas Beecham for preserving some totally charming ballet and orchestral excerpts. Grétry was a French composer of Walloon descent who played a major part in the French musical life of the late 18th and early 19th Centuries. He was an inspector of the Paris Conservatoire when it was founded in 1795, and was one of the founder members of the Institut de France, the same year. In France his operas still retain some popularity.

Zémire et Azor
Opera in 4 Acts.
Text by Jean François Marmontel.
First performance: Fontainebleau, November 9, 1771. Paris (Comédie-Italienne) December 16, 1771.

Le Magnifique
Opera in 3 Acts.
Text by Jean-Michel Sedaine, after La Fontaine.
First performance: Paris (Comédie-Italienne) March 4, 1773.

Le Jugement de Midas
Opera in 3 Acts.
Text by Thomas d'Hele.
First performance: Paris (privately) March 28, 1778. Paris (Comédie-Italienne) June 27, 1778.

Le Tableau parlant (1769)
Les Fausses Apparences, or
* L'Amant jaloux (1778)*

Richard Coeur de Lion (1784)
etc.

GEORGE FRIDERIC HANDEL

(b. Halle 23.2.1685; d. London 14.4.1759)

Above: *Handel turned to oratorio later in life, after a career spent battling against operatic conventions.*

The operatic world of Handel's time was dominated by a race of fashionable, frequently gifted, but mostly conceited singers, for whom Handel wrote. He was obliged to use the contemporary forms and conventions in his operas and rarely rebelled, as Gluck » did; although there is the story of him holding an obstreperous *prima donna* out of the window and threatening to drop her into the street if she did not mend her ways (there is an even better story that it was, in fact, two *prima donne*, one in each hand, who had persisted in quarrelling in his presence. But for the most part Handel abided by the rules of the day and composed accordingly. Of course, being a man of genius, he frequently turned it to his own advantage; his operas are full of superb arias and deep expression; and as he grew older he subtly tightened and economised the structure and form of his operas so that the worst excesses were at least tamed. But whatever else may be argued, Handel's operas are an essential part of his genius, without which no proper understanding of him is possible. Handel's early career was as a musician in the Hamburg opera house, where his first stage work, *Almira*, was produced. He then moved to Italy for five years, where he associated with, Alessandro Scarlatti », founder of the Neapolitan school of opera, then settled permanently in London and became a naturalised Englishman. We need not go into the details of his career as an opera impresario and composer, except perhaps to note that his turning from opera to oratorio for the last 20 years of his life was commercially rather than artistically motivated. He finally found the embattled London operatic scene too perilous and unrewarding and decided to give the English what they wanted—large and splendid oratorios on biblical subjects.

Rodrigo
Opera in 3 Acts.
Text by: Unknown.
First performance: Florence, c. 1707.

Agrippina
Opera in 3 Acts.
Text by Vincenzo Grimani.
First performance: Venice (Teatro San Giovanni Crisostimo) December 26, 1709.

Rinaldo
Opera in 3 Acts.
Text by Giacomo Rossi (Italian) and Aaron Hill (English) after Tasso.
First performance: London (Queen's Theatre) February 24, 1711. Dublin 1711; Naples 1718.

Notes:
The plot is confusing but the action highly spectacular, as befitted Handel's first operatic success in London. Argante's first aria, accompanied by trumpets, was taken from Handel's *Aci, Galatea e Polifemo* (not *Acis and Galatea*). *Rinaldo*, written in haste, contains many borrowings.

Il Pastor Fido
Opera in 3 Acts.
Text by Giacomo Rossi after Battista Guarini.
First performance: London (Queen's Theatre) November 22, 1712.

Teseo
Opera in 3 Acts.
Text by Nicola Francesco Haym.
First performance: London (Queen's Theatre) January 10, 1713.

Radamisto

Opera in 3 Acts.
Text by Nicola Francesco Haym, from 'L'amor tiranico'.
First performance: London (King's Theatre) April 27, 1720.

Ottone

Opera in 3 Acts.
Text by Nicola Francesco Haym.
First performance: London (King's Theatre) January 12, 1723.

Giulio Cesare in Egitto

Opera in 3 Acts.
Text by Nicola Francesco Haym.
First performance: London (King's Theatre) February 20, 1724.

Above: *Huguette Tourangeau sings the role of Sextus, son of Pompey's widow Cornelia, in Handel's opera* Giulio Cesare in Egitto.

Tamerlano

Opera in 3 Acts.
Text by Agostino Piovene/Nicola Francesco Haym.
First performance: London (King's Theatre) October 31, 1724.

Rodelinda

Opera in 3 Acts.
Text by Antonio Savi/Nicola Francesco Haym.
First performance: London (King's Theatre) February 13, 1725.

Scipione

Opera in 3 Acts.
Text by Paolo Antonio Rolli after Zeno's 'Scipione nelle Spagne'.
First performance: London (King's Theatre) March 12, 1726.

Alessandro

Opera in 3 Acts.
Text by Paolo Antonio Rolli after Mauro's 'La superbia d'Alessandro'.
First performance: London (King's Theatre) May 5, 1726.

Admeto

Opera in 3 Acts.
Text by Nicola Francesco Haym or Paolo Antonio Rolli after 'L'Antigona delusa da Alceste'.
First performance: London (King's Theatre) January 31, 1727.

Lotario

Opera in 3 Acts.
Text from Salvi's 'Adelaide'.
First performance: London (King's Theatre) December 2, 1729.

Partenope

Opera in 3 Acts.
Text by Silvio Stampiglia.
First performance: London (King's Theatre) February 24, 1730.

Poro

Opera in 3 Acts.
Text by Samuel Humphreys from Metastasio's 'Alessandro nell' Indie'.
First performance: London (King's Theatre) February 2, 1731.

Ezio

Opera in 3 Acts.
Text by Samuel Humphreys from Metastasio's original.
First performance: London (King's Theatre) January 15, 1732.

Sosarme

Opera in 3 Acts.
Text by Matteo Noris from his play 'Alfonso primo'; English version by Samuel Humphreys.
First performance: London (King's Theatre) February 15, 1732.

Notes:
Dramatically this is one of Handel's weakest operas, but musically it is one of the finest. The plot is muddled (which is not unusual) and lacking in true drama (which is less usual), and is hardly worth detailing; what matters is the string of superb arias and concerted numbers Handel poured into it, especially in Act 2, where one marvellous number succeeds another.

Orlando
Opera in 3 Acts.
Text by Grazio Bracciolo after Ariosto's 'Orlando furioso'.
First performance: London (King's Theatre) January 27, 1733.

Arianna
Opera in 3 Acts.
Text by Pietro Pariati's 'Arianna e Teseo'.
First performance: London (King's Theatre) January 26, 1734.

Ariodante
Opera in 3 Acts.
Text by Antonio Salvi after Ariosto's 'Orlando furioso'.
First performance: London (Covent Garden) January 8, 1735.

Alcina
Opera in 3 Acts.
Text by Antonio Marchi after Ariosto's 'Orlando furioso'.
First performance: London (Covent Garden) April 16, 1735.

Atalanta
Opera in 3 Acts.
Text by Belisario Valeriani's 'La caccia in Etolia'.
First performance: London (Covent Garden) May 12, 1736.

Arminio
Opera in 3 Acts.
Text by Antonio Salvi.
First performance: London (Covent Garden) January 12, 1737.

Berenice
Opera in 3 Acts.
Text by Antonio Salvi.
First performance: London (Covent Garden) May 18, 1737.

Faramondo
Opera in 3 Acts.
Text by Apostolo Zeno.
First performance: London (King's Theatre) January 3, 1738.

Serse (Xerxes)
Opera in 3 Acts.
Text by Niccolò Minato.
First performance: London (King's Theatre) May 15, 1738.

Notes:
This, one of Handel's last operas before he turned to oratorio, shows his formal skill and powers of characterisation at their best. In its mixture of the serious and the comic, as well as in its

74

range of expression, it anticipates Mozart. The opera opens with the famous Larghetto aria 'Ombra mai fù, which time has somehow transmogrified into 'Handel's Largo', with religioso connotations. The aria, far from being religious, is sung by Serse, a character so eccentric that he has fallen in love with a plane tree and thanks it in song for offering shade on a hot day. For the rest, *Serse* contains the familiar ingredients of the opera seria—love, war, intrigue and a fair degree of posturing. But the music is superb.

Above: Joan Sutherland in Handel's Alcina at Dallas.

Deidamia
Opera in 3 Acts.
Text by Paolo A. Rolli.
First performance: London (Lincoln's Inn Fields Theatre) January 10, 1741.

Almira (1705)
Nero (1705)
Florindo Daphne (1708)
Amadigi di Gaula (1715)
Floridante (1721)
Flavio (1723)

Riccardo Primo (1727)
Siroe (1728)
Tolomeo (1728)
Giustino (1737)
Imeneo (1740)
etc.

JOSEPH HAYDN

(b. Rohrau, 31.3.1732; d. Vienna 31.5.1809)

Until a few years ago many music lovers would have been surprised to learn that Haydn wrote more than 20 operas—and some would have been surprised to hear that he had written any at all. However, opera was an important part of his musical duties at Esterház, the great palace of the Esterházy family; it was widely said at the time that if one wanted to hear good opera, one went to Esterház. He had first entered their service in 1761, when his previous employer, Count Morzin, had disbanded his orchestra. The following year Prince Paul Anton Esterházy died and was succeeded by his brother, Prince Nicolaus, under whom Haydn lived and worked happily until Nicolaus's own death in 1790. Thereafter there was no Esterházy musical establishment; but Haydn continued in the family employ for the remainder of his life, his freedom to travel and accept outside engagements greatly increased. Haydn was the son of a wheelwright and suffered a good deal of poverty in his youth. As a small boy he was a chorister at St Stephen's Cathedral in Vienna, but afterwards eked out a living by freelance performing and teaching. He married in 1760; like Mozart », he courted one of two sisters but had to marry the other (in his case when his first choice entered a convent); but unlike Mozart he found no happiness in his choice. Thus he

Below: *Joseph Haydn, composer of more than 20 operas.*

became something of a judicious philanderer. In composition he was largely self-taught; and his engagement at Esterház encouraged him to develop his talent and his originality to the full. In addition to his operas proper, Haydn wrote a number of puppet operas, a form which interested him considerably.

Acide e Galatea
Festa teatrale— opera seria.
Text by Giannambrogio Migliavacca.
First performance: Esterház, January 11, 1763.

L'Infedeltà Delusa
Burletta.
Text by: Unknown.
First performance: Esterház, July 26, 1773.

Notes:
Vespina's disguises perhaps anticipate, on a lesser scale, Mozart's Despina in Così fan tutte. L'Infedeltà delusa was produced for the visit of the Empress Maria Theresa to Esterház during September 1773.

Il Mondo della Luna
Dramma giocoso in 3 Acts.
Text by Carlo Goldoni
First performance: Esterház, August 3, 1777.

La Vera Costanza
Drama giocosa in 3 Acts.
Text by Francesco Puttini.
First performance: Esterház, April 2, 1779.

L'Isola Disabitata
Anzione teatrale in 2 Parts.
Text by Pietro Matastasio.
First performance: Esterház, December 6, 1779.

La Fedelta Premiata
Dramma giocoso in 3 Acts.
Text from Giovanni Battista Lorenzi's 'L'infedelità fedele'.
First performance: Esterház, February 25, 1781.

Orlando Paladino
Dramma eroicomico in 3 Acts.
Text by Nunziato Porta after Ariosto.
First performance: Esterház, December 6, 1782.

Der krumme Teufel (1752)
La Marchesa Nespoli (1762)
La vedova (1762)
Il dottore (1762)
Il Sganarello (1762)
La cantarina (1767)

Lo speziale (1768)
Le pescatrici (1770)
Il incontro improviso (1775)
Armida (1784)
etc.

HANS WERNER HENZE
(b. Gütersloh 1.7.1926)

Henze probably ranks with Benjamin Britten » as the most important opera composer of the post-World War II period. Many have written one or two operas: Henze and Britten have kept the stream flowing. Henze studied with Wolfgang Fortner at Heidelberg and then with René Leibowitz in Paris. He adopted a deliberately 'progressive' stand, influenced by Schoenberg » but not adhering to Schoenberg's strict principles. He worked much in ballet during the 1950s, gaining considerable theatre experience which he has put to good use in his operas. He composed six operas of admirable quality before 1970, when he announced that he considered opera 'finished' as a medium, though he admitted that there would still be music and drama. His strong Marxist sympathies have a good deal to do with his attitude and appear to have influenced his music and position in recent years, sometimes in a way that unquestionably tends to undermine his best creative abilities by leading him to put emphases in the wrong places. But he remains a potent force in contemporary music and, whatever the form his future musical dramas may take, the operas he has written are a major contribution. They have been often produced, especially in Europe, but regrettably little recorded.

Elegie fur Junge Liebende (Elegy for Young Lovers)
Opera in 3 Acts.
Text by W. H. Auden and Chester Kallman (in English).
First performance: Schwetzingen Festival (Munich Opera) (in German), May 20, 1961. Glyndebourne (in English) July 19, 1963.

Notes:
The story concerns a group of people in an Austrian Alpine hotel: the poet Gregor Mittenhofer, his young mistress Elisabeth, his patroness and secretary Carolina, Dr Reischmann and his son Toni, and the widow Mack whose husband disappeared 40 years before when in the mountains on their honeymoon. The plot builds to the birth of a poem by Mittenhofer, which he eventually reads in public, after Elisabeth and Toni have died together in the mountains. This brief outline gives only the bare bones: the variety of meanings and the psychological insights into each character provide the highly distinctive and memorable 'flesh'.

Das Wundertheater (1949)
Ein Landarzt (1951)
Boulevard Solitude (1952)
Das Ende einer Welt (1953)
König Hirsch (1956)
Der Prinz von Homburg (1960)
The Bassarids (1966)
etc.

Left: *Hans Werner Henze.*

PAUL HINDEMITH
(b. Hanau 16.11.1895; d. Frankfurt 28.12.1963)

One of the most important and influential German composers of the 20th century, Hindemith studied in Frankfurt where he became leader of the orchestra in 1915 and founded a string quartet with the Turkish violinist Licco Amar. As well as making headway with his own works, he taught composition at the Berlin Hochschule until 1938, when he and hs works were condemned as 'degenerate' under Nazism. During the later 1930s Hindemith was active in the administration of music in Turkey, and in 1939 emigrated to the US. After World War II he returned to Europe, where he continued to compose and played a leading part in the revival of German music after the Nazi aberration. Hindemith was the inventor of what became known as *Gebrauchsmusik*, or 'utility music', of which he wrote a number of examples. By no means all his music falls into this category or was meant to; but it did have a considerable impact on the post-1918 musical world. Hindemith composed a number of operas, of which the experimental *Cardillac* became best known on the stage. Both *Mathis der Maler* and *Die Harmonie der Welt*, although occasionally staged, have become best known through the symphonic music Hindemith extracted from them.

Cardillac
Opera in 3 Acts (originally 4).
Text by Hindemith from Ferdinand Lion after E. T. A. Hoffmann.
First performance: Dresden, November 9, 1926. Zurich (revised version) 1952.

Mathis der Maler
Opera in 7 Scenes.
Text by Hindemith, based on the altar-piece of the 16th-century painter Matthias Grünewald.
First performance: Zurich, May 28, 1938. Stuttgart 1946.

Die Harmonie der Welt
Opera in 5 Acts.
Text by Hindemith, based on the life and theories of the 17th-century German astronomer Johann Kepler.
First performance: Munich, August 11, 1957.

Mörder, Hoffnung der Frauen (1921)
Das Nuschi-Nuschi (1921)
Sancta Susanna (1922)
Hin und Zurück (1927)
Neues vom Tage (1929)
Der lange Weinachtsmahl (1961)
etc.

Left: *Paul Hindemith, once the leader of the orchestra at the Frankfurt Opera.*

79

GUSTAV HOLST

(b. Cheltenham 21.9.1874; d. London 25.5.1934)

A leading English composer of the so-called 'renaissance', Holst (of Swedish descent) was a potent and enigmatic figure. He studied under Stanford at the Royal Academy, where he was a close friend of Ralph Vaughan Williams », and subsequently became a trombonist with the Carl Rosa Opera Company. In 1903 he became music master at Edward Alleyn School and in 1907 musical director at Morley College, but it was his appointment in 1905 as music master at St Paul's School for Girls in Westminster that set a seal on his subsequent life. Holst was a great teacher, a man of sympathy and perception and a musician who combined a severely practical approach to the making of music with a far-ranging imagination in the composition of it. Later in life, painful neuritis resulting from an accident made the act of writing an arduous task; this has sometimes been seen as the primary reason for the increasing economy and austerity of his music, as well as for the frequent use of ostinatos; this seems a specious argument—both the economy and the ostinatos stemmed from some deeper necessity of his creative being, even if the effects of his physical infirmity may have accorded with the natural bent of his talent. Holst wrote nine operas and operettas, three of which remained unpublished. Throughout his life Holst had an abiding interest in Sanskrit: two adjacent operas in his catalogue are derived from that source, and those, separated by only two years, are

remarkable for their stylistic contrast. The first, *Sita* (1906) is large and extravagant ('good old Wagnerian bawling', Holst himself said of it). *Sávitri* (1908) is so different that it is only recognisable as being by the same hand by exercising imaginative insight into the creative processes of both operas. Of Holst's other operas, the ballet music from *The Perfect Fool* has become especially popular.

Sávitri
Chamber Opera in 1 Act.
Text by Holst from the Mahabharata.
First performance: London (Wellington Hall) December 5, 1916.

The Perfect Fool
Opera in 1 Act.
Text by Holst.
First performance: London (Covent Garden) May 14, 1923.

The Tale of the Wandering Scholar
Opera in 1 Act (Op. 50)
Text by Clifford Bax.
First performance: Liverpool (private) 1934.

Lansdown Castle (1893)
At the Boar's Head (1924)
etc.

Below: *A rare performance of Holst's* Savitri *at the Snape, Aldeburgh, in June 1974.*

ENGELBERT HUMPERDINCK

(b. Siegburg 1.11.1854; d. Neustrelitz 27.11.1921)

Many of those who think the music dramas of Wagner » heavy, obtuse and overbearing may be surprised that the most successful (and enduringly popular) opera of Engelbert Humperdinck, one of Wagner's most devoted followers and his assistant in the production of *Parsifal* at Bayreuth, should be the entrancing fairy tale *Hänsel und Gretel*. In fact, *Hänsel und Gretel* goes back beyond the woodland scenes in Wagner's *Siegfried* to the roots of German Romantic opera in Weber », to the magic elements in *Der Freischütz* and *Oberon*. Humperdinck studied first in Cologne and then in Munich and met Wagner in 1879. Travels through Europe brought him to Barcelona, where he was professor at the Conservatoire in 1885-87. He subsequently taught at the Hoch Conservatoire in Frankfurt between 1890 and 1896, during which period he also worked as music critic for the influential *Frankfurter Zeitung*. In 1896 he was granted a professorship at the instigation of Kaiser Wilhelm II (who hated Wagner), and in 1900 became head of the Meisterschule for composition in Berlin. Humperdinck wrote seven operas, but only the first, *Hänsel und Gretel* for which his sister wrote the text, has significantly outlived him.

Hänsel und Gretel

Fairy tale opera in 3 Acts.
Text by Adelheid Wette after the Brothers Grimm.
First performance: Weimar (Court Theatre) December 23, 1893. Basle 1894; London (Daly's Theatre) (in English) 1894; New York (in English) 1895.

Below: *The 1976 BBC-2 TV version of Humperdinck's* Hänsel und Gretel.

Die sieben Geislein (1895)
Dornröschen (1902)
Die Heirat wider Willen (1905)
Königskinder (1910)
Die Marketenderin (1914)
Gaudeamus (1919)

LEOŠ JANÁČEK

(b. Hukvaldy, Moravia, 3.7.1854; d. Moravia-Ostrava 12.8.1928)

Above: *A scene from the English National Opera production of Janáček's* The Adventures of Mr Brouček *at the London Coliseum.*

Usually accounted one of the three great Czech composers (the others were Dvořák » and Smetana »), Janáček was lastingly influenced by the folk music and dialect of northern Moravia. His family was poor (his father was a local schoolteacher) but were keen musical amateurs and he learnt his first music at home. He began his serious musical studies at the Augustine monastery in Brno and then went to the Organ School in Prague. He quarrelled with his teacher, returned to Brno, after briefly visiting Vienna and Leipzig, and became conductor of the Brno Philharmonic Society. Around this time he began to compose. All his life he held teaching posts and was greatly revered by his pupils.

Janáček's musical style was formed out of the elements of national folk song and its associated rhythms, the inflexions of Moravian speech, and the sounds of nature, which he heard with the keenest of ears and reproduced in his music with an absolute accuracy which sometimes amounted to deliberate onomatopoeia. Janáček wrote 11 operas. For a long time only one or two, notably *Jenůfa*, were popular outside his homeland; but in recent years others have been recognised as masterpieces and performed throughout the world. He was a true original, in some respects the Moravian counterpart of Bartók » in Hungary and Manuel de Falla » in Spain, but basically unique: he has been seen as one of the seminal figures of modern music, outside the Schoenberg » orbit.

Jenůfa (Její Pastorkyňa)
Opera in 3 Acts.
Text by Janáček after Gabriela Preissová's drama of Moravian rural life.
First performance: Brno, January 21, 1904. Vienna (State Opera) (in German)
1918; New York (Metropolitan) (in German) 1924.

Mr Brouček's Excursion to the Moon (Výlet Pana Broučka na Mešic)
Opera in 1 Act.
Text by Viktor Dyk and others after Svatopluk Čech.
First performance: Prague (National Theatre) April 23, 1920.

Mr Brouček's Excursion into the 15th Century (Výlet Pana Broučka do XV Stol)
Opera in 1 Act.
Text by Frantisek Procházka after Svatopluk Čech.
First performance: Prague (National Theatre) April 23, 1920.

These two one-Act operas, though composed some years apart
(the first was begun in 1908, but not completed until seven
years later; the second dates from 1917) are linked together as
one opera to provide a single evening's entertainment, known as
The Excursions of Mr Brouček.

Notes:

In both works, Janáček shows a sardonic wit and a vein of sharp-edged parody as he pillories, albeit with good humour, the foibles of mankind, including excessive patriotism and the pomposities of pretentious 'artists'.

Kátya Kabanová

Opera in 3 Acts.
Text by Janáček after Vincenc Cervinka's translation of Ostrovsky's 'The Storm'.
First performance: Brno, November 23, 1921. Cologne (in German) 1922;
London (Sadler's Wells) 1951.

The Cunning Little Vixen (Príhody Lišky Byštrousky)

Opera in 3 Acts.
Text by Rudolf Tesnohlidek.
First performance: Brno, November 23, 1924.

The Makropulos Affair (Vec Makropulos)

Text by Janáček after Karel Capek.
First performance: Brno, December 18, 1926. Prague 1928; Frankfurt 1929;
London (Sadler's Wells) 1964; Edinburgh 1970; New York (City Opera) 1970.

From the House of the Dead (Z Mrtvého Domu)

Opera in 3 Acts.
Text by Janáček after Dostoyevsky (unfinished).
First performance: Brno, April 12, 1930. Berlin (Kroll Opera) 1931; Wiesbaden
1954; Edinburgh 1964.

Notes:

The text, based fairly freely on Dostoyevsky's autobiographical novel *The House of the Dead*, is set to music of extraordinary originality and effectiveness; a kind of sophisticated simplicity. The all-male cast (though in the recording the part of the boy Alyeya is taken by a soprano) gives the opera a particular textural stamp —it has been seen as in some ways a forerunner of Britten's *Billy Budd*—and has not endeared it to wider audiences. Rather than deploying a conventional 'plot', it is a series of episodes in the life of the central figure, with subsidiary characters presented with penetrating insight. In some ways it anticipates the writings of Solzhenitzyn: only the political system has (nominally) altered.

Left: Jenůfa *was the only one of Janáček's operas to be known outside his homeland until the revival of interest in his work during recent years.*

Pocátek románu (The Beginning of a Romance) (1894)
Její pastorkyna (Her Foster-Daughter) (1904)
Sárka (1925)
Osud (Fate) (1934)
etc.

DIMITRI KABALEVSKY
(b. St Petersburg (Leningrad) 30.12.1904)

Above: *In the front row, three well-known Russian composers—Kabalevsky, Glière and Prokofiev.*

Best known outside Russia for his suite *The Comedians* and for a number of symphonies and concertos, Kabalevsky appears to have fitted easily into official Soviet artistic requirements, composing fluently in a straightforward, melodious, non-experimental—and sometimes banal—style, especially (and inevitably) in his 'official' choral/orchestral productions. He showed early aptitude for the piano and entered the Scriabin School of Music in Moscow in 1918; then he studied piano with Catoire and composition with Miaskovsky at the Moscow Conservatoire, where he later became professor of composition. Kabalevsky was a genuinely and, at his best, distinctively gifted musician who played a leading part in Soviet musical life. Like most leading Russian composers, he was deeply influenced by folk material. He composed five operas, of which *Colas Breugnon* is most familiar, notably from its rumbustious overture.

Colas Breugnon (The Craftsman of Clamecy)
Opera in 3 Acts.
Text by V. Bragin after Romain Rolland's novel 'Colas Breugnon'.
First performance: Leningrad, 1938. Revised 1968.

Notes:
The opera is now more generally known under the name of its eponymous hero, replacing the original title *The Craftsman of Clamecy* (or, sometimes, *The Master of Clamecy*).

Before Moscow (1942)   *Armoured Train 14-69 (1956)*
The Family of Tarras (1944)   *etc.*
Nikita Vershinin (1954)

86

ZOLTÁN KODÁLY

(b. Kecskemét 16.12.1882; d. Budapest 6.3.1967)

Kodály was, with Béla Bartók », the leading Hungarian composer of the first half of the 20th century. Like Bartók, with whom he collaborated in collecting and editing Hungarian folk song, he was a dedicated folk music enthusiast. Kodály had no serious musical education until he entered the Budapest Conservatoire in 1900 (simultaneously studying science at the University of Budapest). In 1906, after writing his thesis on folk song, he became a professor at the Conservatoire and in 1919 was appointed deputy director. He was active in the Institute for the Study of Continental Music through the 1920s and 1930s, and in 1945 became president of the new Hungarian Arts Council. He became Honorary Doctor of Music at Oxford University in 1960, and was awarded the Gold Medal of the Royal Philharmonic Society in 1967, the year of his death.

Kodály wrote a great deal of music in various forms, especially choral works. He was also a notable musicologist with much published work to his credit. Kodály wrote no real opera, though two of his works for the theatre may be admitted. In both, Kodály, noting the failure of Bartók's *Bluebeard's Castle* with theatre audiences, set himself to accustom those audiences to the sound and texture of Hungarian folk song. *Háry János*, basically a play with music but also described as a comic opera, and *The Spinning Room*, a sequence of choruses, songs, ballads and dances in seven scenes and one Act, were both originally designed to bring folk material to the theatre as a preparation for 'work of a higher order'. Perhaps the exact category of each is not very important; both are delightful exercises. There is a third work which approaches operatic classification: *Czinka Panna*, with text by Béla Balázs. This was a purely occasional piece written for the celebration of the 1848 Centenary and has not been heard outside Hungary.

Below: *Adrienne Csengery, György Melis and Gabriella Számado in a scene from* Háry János.

Háry János
Comic Opera in 3 Acts.
Text by Béla Paulini and Zsolt Harsányi, after János Garay's poem.
First performance: Budapest, October 16, 1926.

Notes:
Háry János (or János Háry as he would be called in Hungary)
was an historical figure; the poet János Garay knew him in his
old age—but the tales themselves go back to Magyar folklore.
The stories are told by an old peasant soldier, veteran of the
Napoleonic Wars. In accordance with the old tradition that a
speaker who begins with a sneeze is telling the truth, the work
commences thus.

The Spinning Room (Székelyfonó)
L yric scenes with folk songs from Transylvania.
First performance: Budapest (Royal Hungarian Opera) April 24, 1932.

Notes:
Even less a true opera than *Háry János*. The slight dramatic
continuity is itself derived from folklore. The work has been
called a 'dramatic rhapsody' or 'operatic folk ballad', but it
really has no classification. However, it contains some excellent
music, mostly choral, and effectively displays Kodály's
'Hungarian counterpoint', as he liked to call it, a notable feature
being the playing of two folk tunes simultaneously (a parallel
with Charles Ives); also part-writing in imitation.

ERICH WOLFGANG KORNGOLD
(b. Brno 29.5.1897; d. Hollywood 29.11.1957)

Korngold is best known for his film scores, including many for
Errol Flynn epics, of which a useful compilation has been made
by RCA (SER5664). But in his youth he was seen as a virtual
prodigy in Vienna, where several of his 'serious' works made a
great impression. He composed orchestral music, including a
symphony recorded by the late Rudolf Kempe, and a violin
concerto recorded by Heifetz (it was originally written for
Hubermann). But his primary fame came from his operas, two
of which, *Der Ring des Polycrates* and *Vera Violanta* were
premiered by Bruno Walter in Munich; but the most successful,
Die tote Stadt, was the only one to have been recorded.
Korngold's operatic style is derived from a German form of
verismo with elements of expressionism—effective, if at times
somewhat diffusely focused.

Der Ring des Polykrates
Opera in 1 Act.
Text based on a comedy by Heinrich Teweles.
First performance: Munich, March 28, 1916.

Die tote Stadt

Opera in 3 Acts.
Text by Erich and Julius (father) Korngold (as 'Paul Schott') after Georges Rodenbach's play 'Bruges-la-morte'.
First performance: Hamburg and Cologne (simultaneous production) December 4, 1920. New York (Metropolitan) 1921; Prague 1922.

Die Kathrin

Opera in 2 Acts.
Text by Korngold.
First performance: Stockholm, October 1939.

Violanta (1916)
Das Wunder de Heliane (1927)
etc.

Below: Korngold's Die tote Stadt *revived in Munich and New York.*

ÉDOUARD LALO

(b. Lille 27.1.1823; d. Paris 22.4.1892)

Of Spanish descent, Lalo studied violin and cello at the Lille Conservatory and then in Paris. He studied composition privately and played the viola in the Armingaud-Jacquard Quartet. He started to compose seriously around 1865, the year he married the singer Mlle Bernier de Maligny, who frequently performed his songs. He is now best remembered for his *Symphonie espagnole*, written in 1873, and his Cello Concerto of 1883, but he became quite a prolific composer of all forms of music. Of his three attempts at opera, the first, *Fiesque* (1866), was never produced; and the third, *La Jacquerie*, was left unfinished and given a posthumous production in 1895. The second, *Le Roi d'Ys* (1888), became well known and is still performed in France. Its *Aubade* was made famous by Melba, and the Overture is a popular concert item.

Above: *A production of* Le Roi d'Ys *at the Paris Opéra.*

Le Roi d'Ys

Opera in 3 Acts.
Text by Edouard Blau.
First performance: Paris (Opéra-Comique) May 7, 1888. New Orleans 1890;
London (Covent Garden) 1901.

RUGGIERO LEONCAVALLO
(b. Naples 8.3.1858; d. Florence 9.8.1919)

Some opera composers write their own libretti, and some are quite good at it; Leoncavallo was one of these. He was well trained for the task. After studying music at the Naples Conservatoire, he went to Bologna to attend the literary classes held there by the Italian poet and writer Giosué Carducci. He then embarked, with varying success, on a career of opera composing, being one of those who made a huge impact with an early work and spent the rest of his life trying to repeat it. Not that *I Pagliacci* is necessarily his best opera, though it is no doubt his most theatrically effective. He also wrote a *La Bohème* which had a modest success—but Puccini's » version was produced at precisely the same time. Of Leoncavallo's other operas little is now heard outside Italy, where Italian opera houses do him occasional honour by production. His ambitious trilogy dealing with the Italian Renaissance under the overall title 'Crepusculum' never came to final fruition, though the first piece, *I Medici*, was produced (but failed to impress). Production was achieved with *Zazà* and with *Der Roland*, an opera commissioned by Kaiser Wilhelm II, based on Willibald Alexis's romance *Der Roland von Berlin*. Leoncavallo's later works, some pretty slight, never repeated the success of *I Pagliacci*.

I Pagliacci

Opera in Prologue and 2 Acts.
Text by Leoncavallo.
First performance: Milan (Teatro del Verme) May 21, 1892. Vienna 1892;
London (Covent Garden) 1893; New York (Metropolitan) 1893.

Notes:
I Pagliacci, robust and somewhat coarse like its creator, was an example of unabashed *verismo* of considerable crudity (only in part alleviated even in the hands of so sophisticated and fastidious a conductor as Herbert von Karajan), but its impact has made it a lasting favourite.

Chatterton

Opera in 4 Acts.
Text by Leoncavallo (written 1876).
First performance: Rome (Teatro Nationale) March 10, 1896.

La Bohème

Opera in 4 Acts.
Text by Leoncavallo after Murger.
First performance:
Venice, May 6, 1897. Paris 1899.

I Medici (1893)
Der Roland von Berlin (1904)
Maia (1910)
Malbruk (1910)
I zingari (1912)
La reginetta delle rose (1912)
Are you there (1913)

Zazà

Opera in 4 Acts.
Text by Leoncavallo.
First performance:
Milan, November 10, 1900.

La candidata (1915)
Goffredo Mameli (1916)
Prestami tua moglie (1916)
A chi la giarettiera (1919)
Edipo re (1920)
Il primo bacio (1923)
etc.

Below: *Ruggiero Leoncavallo.*

FRANCO LEONI

(b. Milan 24.10. 1864; d. London 8.2.1949)

Leoni, a younger contemporary of Puccini » and like him a
pupil of Ponchielli », settled in England in 1896 and produced
operas during the first decades of the century. Although he lived
and died so recently, he seems a mysterious figure: there is
disagreement about the date of his death and he does not appear
in leading books of reference (including *Grove*, 1954). Even the
date of the premiere of his most famous opera is variously given
as 1905 and 1907, though the former is favoured. Leoni belongs
to the Puccini school: his music is sometimes said to be little
more than imitation Puccini, but it has a pleasant lyric quality
and is theatrically effective.

L'Oracolo

Opera in 1 Act.
Text by Camillo Zanoni after a play by C. B. Fernald.
*First performance: London (Covent Garden) June 28, 1905. New York
(Metropolitan) 1915.*

Notes:

The complex plot is reasonably clearly deployed, with pleasing
musical highlights and good opportunities for the singers. There
are well-turned set pieces and ensembles. The part of Cim-Fen
was created by the great baritone Antonio Scotti, who sang it
first at Covent Garden, later at the Metropolitan, and
subsequently throughout America for the rest of his career. It
was the part in which he gave his farewell performance in 1933.

Below: *Richard Van Allan during the recording of Leoni's* L'Oracolo.

Raggio di Luna (1888)
Rip van Winkle (1897)
Ib and Little Christina (1901)
Trigana (1908)

Francesca da Rimini (1914)
La Terra del Sogno (1921)
etc.

92

ALBERT LORTZING
(Berlin 23.10.1801; d. Berlin 21.1.1851)

Although he received some music lessons as a boy, Lortzing's main experience came from travelling with his parents, who were keen amateur singers. Their leather business failed in 1812, so they turned professional, performing in Breslau, where young Lortzing was able to listen to opera rehearsals and performances and to continue his private studies. The family wandered all over Germany for various engagements, with Lortzing taking juvenile roles and composing instrumental music and songs. In 1823 he married an actress and pursued a similar existence. His first attempt at opera was a serious subject, but he had a natural bent for comedy and most of his future works were in the lighter Rossini »/Donizetti » vein, with a strong Germanic flavour. His first work of this kind, *Die beiden Schützen* (1837) was produced in Leipzig and was immediately taken up by opera houses in Berlin, Munich and Prague; but his real success came with *Zar und Zimmermann* (also 1837). This opera became popular after a Berlin performance in 1839, played in no less than 18 German opera houses the following year, and has remained one of the most frequently performed light operas in the repertoire. After three more modest successes, Lortzing wrote what is usually considered his best work, *Die Wildschütz* (1842), a well-constructed piece with a strong sense of parody, Mendelssohn and Handel » being among the models used. In a more romantic vein, with echoes of Weber », was *Undine* (1845), which was followed by a return to the comic vein in *Der Waffenschmied* in 1846. Lortzing wrote 14 operas; he deserves his fame for producing a distinct type of German comic opera that brackets him with Nicolai ».

Zar und Zimmermann
Comic opera in 3 Acts.
Text by Lortzing, based on the play 'Le Bourgmestre de Sardam' by Mélesville, Merle and Boirie.
First performance: Leipzig (Municipal Theatre) December 22, 1837. Berlin 1839; London (Gaiety) (in English) 1871.

Undine
Opera in 3 Acts.
Text by Lortzing, based on a story by Friedrich de la Motte and his libretto written for E. T. A. Hoffmann.
First performance: Magdeburg, April 21, 1845.

Der Waffenschmied
Comic opera in 3 Acts.
Text by Lortzing, based on the comedy 'Liebhaber und Nebenbuhler in einer Person' by Friedrich Wilhelm von Ziegler.
First performance: Vienna (Theater an der Wien) May 31, 1846.

Ali Pascha von Janina (1828)
Die beiden Schützen (1837)
Die Caramo (1839)
Hans Sachs (1840)
Casanova (1841)
Der Wildschütz (1842)
Zum Grossadmiral (1847)
Rolands Knappen (1849)
Die Opernprobe (1851)
Regina (1899)
etc.

JEAN-BAPTISTE LULLY

(b. Florence 28.11.1632; d. Paris 22.3.1687)

Born Giovanni Battista Lulli, he Gallicised his name and beca.
a naturalised Frenchman. From poor beginnings, Lully rose to
pre-eminent position in French music and became a favourite o.
Louis XIV. While serving in the kitchens of the king's cousin,
Mlle de Montpensier, he was discovered to be a musician and
from that time rose rapidly. He became a member of the famous
Vingt-Quatre Violons du Roi (the '24 violins') and eventually
led the group, adding wind and other instruments and achieving
standards that led to the greatly enhanced independence of his
own orchestral writing. Lully even formed a special band for his
favourite musicians, Les Petits Violons, outshining the original
'24'. He was greatly given to intrigue and high living and was
frequently involved in scandal; but he was also dedicated to his
art and took immense pains over the production as well as the
composition of his operas. He virtually founded the French
operatic style, Italian-based but with unmistakable French
characteristics. Lully's long association with the poet Philippe
Quinault, a follower of Corneille, ensured him a steady stream
of excellent libretti; and between 1662 and 1671 he collaborated
with Molière in a series of comédie-ballets of outstanding
quality. He created the form of sinfonia or *ouverture* (or 'French
overture') in the form 'slow-quick-slow', the slow sections
majestic, the middle allegro in fugal form, which became known
as the 'Lully overture' and was used by most of the later Baroque

Below: *A design for the scenery for Lully's* Armide *in 1686 — after
Jean Berain.*

omposers, including Bach and Handel ». He was also a prolific and successful composer of church music; and it was one of these works that indirectly brought about his death. He was an exponent of the then embryonic art of the conductor, beating time by banging the end of a staff on the floor. While thus directing a performance of a *Te Deum* he crushed his toe; gangrene set in and he eventually died.

Lully wrote many operas. Much of their music is conventional, stylised and lacking in true variety, but he was genuinely gifted, highly intelligent — and always had an eye to the main chance. Thus, he succeeded where others might have failed. The king's patronage was invaluable, not only for Lully himself but for the whole of French opera of the time, for Louis ordained that all operas produced at the Académie Royale de Musique should be printed at public expense and so preserved. Lully's importance in the evolution of Baroque music, especially French music, was immense. But his influence was as much political as musical, and it is, perhaps, for this reason that his music has survived less well than his reputation.

Alceste, ou le Triomphe d'Alcide
Opera in Prologue and 5 Acts.
Text by Philippe Quinault after Euripides.
First performance: Paris (Opéra) January 19, 1674.

Notes:
The subject is the same as that of Handel's » *Admeto* and Gluck » *Alceste* a century later. There are variations, of course, in the development, including a kind of sub-plot with 'mirror characters', leading to some by-play, and a good deal of reference to affairs of the day with some unsubtle flattery of King Louis.

Isis
Opera in Prologue and 5 Acts.
Text by Philippe Quinault.
First performance: Saint-Germain, January 5, 1677. Paris 1677.

Armide et Renaud
Opera in Prologue and 5 Acts.
Text by Quinault after Tasso.
First performance: Paris (Opéra) February 15, 1686.

Cadmus et Hermione (1673)
Thésée (1675)
Atys (1676)
Isis (1677)
Psyché (1678)
Bellérophon (1679)
Proserpine (1680)

Persée (1682)
Phaéton (1683)
Amadis de Gaule (1684)
Roland (1685)
Achille et Polyxène (1687)
etc.

BOHUSLAV MARTINŮ
(b. Polička 8.12.1890; d. Liestal, Switzerland 29.8.1959)

A leading Czech composer of the first half of the 20th century, Martinů, after revealing a precocious talent for music, entered the Prague Conservatoire in 1906 but was twice expelled because other interests prevented him from meeting the official requirements. He became a member of the Czech Philharmonic Orchestra in 1913, continuing his studies. During World War I he returned to Polička, and afterwards came back to Prague to study with Josef Suk. By this time he had written his first published works. In 1923 he went to Paris, where he became a pupil of Albert Roussel. He found Paris stimulating but encountered difficulties. He married in 1931 and lived in penury for some time, being saved only when, faced with heavy bills for his wife's hospitalisation, he won the $1000 Coolidge Prize with his String Sextet (1932). Martinu remained in Paris, making slow headway, until the Hitler war drove him and his wife to America, where Koussevitsky performed his *Concerto grosso* in Boston and commissioned a symphony. After the war he went briefly to Prague but returned to America in 1948 to continue teaching. For the last two years of his life he lived in Switzerland. Martinů composed operas throughout his career: the first, *The Soldier and the Dancer*, appeared in 1928; the last, *The Marriage* (after Gogol) was presented by NBC television in 1953. *Juliette*, probably his most significant opera and the only one recorded, is generally regarded as an important landmark.

Juliette (or The Key to Dreams)
Opera in 3 Acts.
Text by Georges Neveux after his play 'Juliette ou la Clef des Songes'.
First performance: Prague, 1938.

Notes:
Georges Neveux was much influenced by Surrealism. *Juliette*, like his other well-known work, *Le Voyage de Thésée*, has no plot that one can define and analyse; it is more nearly a sequence of poetic and symbolic evocations, shifting between dream and reality. To try to impose a 'story line' on it is to obscure rather than illuminate its imaginative provenance. Author and composer are at one in avoiding any form of literalism, let alone dramatic realism.

The Soldier and the Dancer (1928)
The Miracle of Our Lady (1934)
The Suburban Theatre (1936)
The Marriage (1953)
etc.

Left: *Bohuslav Martinu*

PIETRO MASCAGNI
(b. Leghorn 7.12.1863; d. Rome 2.8.1945)

Like Leoncavallo », with whom he is indissolubly linked by fate and convenience, Mascagni wrote one opera which achieved huge and instant success and thereafter failed to repeat it. But that does not mean that he spent the rest of his life doing inferior work; some of his later pieces, notably the charming and disarming *L'Amico Fritz*, though not so blatantly effective as *Cavalleria Rusticana*, must be accounted in every other way superior. He was yet another of those who took to music against parental wishes: intended by his father for a career in law, he went in some secrecy to the Instituto Cherubini, which led to a short-lived family row. A nobleman then sponsored him at the Milan Conservatoire, where he studied under Ponchielli » and others. Mascagni was not a good student, and soon left to join a travelling opera company, finally marrying and settling down to earn a living by teaching. He won an important competition with *Cavalleria Rusticana* in 1889 and established himself as a success with its production in Rome the following year. His later operas, though not challenging its success, brought fame enough to make him prosperous, content and complacent. He was also a successful conductor.

Cavalleria Rusticana
Opera in 1 Act.
Text by Guido Menasci and Giovanni Targioni-Tozzetti after Giovanni Verga.
First performance: Rome (Teatro Costanzi) May 17, 1890. Stockholm 1890; Philadelphia 1891; London (Shaftesbury Theatre) 1891.

Below: *A scene from Mascagni's* Cavalleria Rusticana, *the work by which its composer is best remembered.*

L'Amico Fritz
Opera in 3 Acts.
Text by P. Suardon (N. Daspuro and others) after the novel by Emile Erckmann and Alexandre Chatrian.
First performance: Rome (Teatro Costanzi) October 31, 1891. London (Covent Garden) 1892; New York (Metropolitan) 1894.

Iris
Opera in 3 Acts.
Text by Luigi Illica.
First performance: Rome (Teatro Costanzi) November 22, 1898. Milan (La Scala) (revised) 1899; New York (Metropolitan) 1908.

Lodoletta
Opera in 3 Acts.
Text by Gioacchino Forzano.
First performance: Rome, April 30, 1917. New York (Metropolitan) 1918.

Le Maschere (1901)   *Pinotta (1932)*
Isabeau (1911)   *Nerone (1935)*
Il Piccolo Marat (1921)   *etc.*

JULES MASSENET
(b. Montaud, nr. Saint-Etienne 12.5.1842; d. Paris 13.8.1912)

Massenet entered the Paris Conservatoire at the age of 11, studied composition with Ambroise Thomas » and won the Prix de Rome in 1863. After a period in Rome he returned to Paris, married in 1866, and had his first opera, *La Grand'-tante* produced at the Opéra-Comique in 1867. He had his first real success with *Hérodiade* in 1881, and his greatest triumph with *Manon* at the Opéra-Comique in 1884. From 1878 to 1896 he was Professor of Composition at the Paris Conservatoire. Compared to such composers as Berlioz », Debussy » and

Below: *Placido Domingo in the title role in* Le Cid.

Ravel », Massenet was a rather conventional writer, but he was a leader of French opera in the traditional vein, producing a mixture of lyrical sweetness and dramatic fervour that makes his works peculiarly French and, in their period, eminently stageable. He increasingly came under Wagnerian influence. A fluent and prolific writer, he has suffered a critical reaction; but currently fresh interest is being shown in his works and recordings are gradually becoming available.

Don César de Bazan
Opera in 2 Acts.
Text by Adolphe Philippe d'Ennery and Jules Chantepie.
First performance: Paris (Opéra-Comique) November 30, 1872.

Le Roi de Lahore
Opera in 2 Acts.
Text by Louis Gallet.
First performance: Paris (Opéra) April 27, 1877.

Hérodiade
Tragic Opera in 4 Acts.
Text by Paul Milliet and Henri Grémont (Georges Hartmann), based on a story by Flaubert.
First performance: Brussels (Théâtre de la Monnaie) December 19, 1881.

Manon
Tragic Opera in 5 Acts.
Text by Henri Meilhac and Philippe Gille, based on Prévost's novel 'Manon Lescaut'.
First performance: Paris (Opéra-Comique) January 19, 1884. Liverpool 1885; New York 1885.

Le Cid
Opera in 4 Acts.
Text by Adolphe d'Ennery, Louis Gullet and Edouard Blau.
First performance: Paris (Opéra) November 30, 1885.

Notes:
The opera was enthusiastically received and was performed 53 times in little more than one year. It was regularly heard in France until World War I. America first heard it in New Orleans in 1890 and it was seen at the Metropolitan, New York, in 1897, with three members of the original cast: Jean and Edouard de Reszke and Pol Plancon.

Esclarmonde
Romantic Opera in Prologue, 4 Acts and Epilogue.
Text by Alfred Blau and Louis de Gramont.
First performance: Paris (Opéra-Comique) May 14, 1889.

Notes:

In this intensely romantic work, Massenet broke new ground in descriptive orchestral writing. His admiration for Wagner » is reflected in his use of important leitmotifs throughout the work, representing Magic, the Tournament, Esclarmonde, Roland, Possession, and so on. It is a richly inspired score with fine opportunities for the singers, and only difficulties in staging due to its ambitious nature have kept it out of the opera houses.

Werther

Lyric Drama in 4 Acts.
Text by Edouard Blau, Paul Milliet and Georges Hartmann, based on the novel by Goethe.
First performance: Vienna (Imperial Opera) February 16, 1892. Paris (Opéra) 1893; New York (Metropolitan) 1894; London (Covent Garden) 1894.

Thaïs

Opera in 3 Acts.
Text by Louis Gallet, based on the novel by Anatole France.
First performance: Paris (Opéra) March 16, 1894. New York 1907; London (Covent Garden) 1911; New York (Metropolitan) 1917; Milan (La Scala) 1942.

Notes:

The opera is known to most through its lovely symphonic intermezzo, the Méditation, which is simply a superb violin solo with harps, its melody later taken up by an invisible chorus.

La Navarraise

Lyric episode in 2 Acts.
Text by Jules Clarétie and Henri Cain.
First performance: London (Covent Garden) June 20, 1894. Paris (Opéra-Comique) 1875; New York (Metropolitan) 1921.

Notes:

This rather gruesome little piece is said to be Massenet's reaction to the *verismo* school of Italian opera and, specifically, to the success of Mascagni's » then sensational *Cavalleria Rusticana*. Massenet's two short scenes, divided by an intermezzo, are full of rapid action and musical power; the work is considered effective, if not one of the composer's masterpieces.

Cendrillon

Opera in 4 Acts.
Text by Henri Cain, based on Perrault's story.
First performance: Paris (Opéra-Comique) May 24, 1899.

Le Jongleur de Notre Dame

Opera in 3 Acts.
Text by Maurice Lena.
First performance: Monte Carlo, February 18, 1902. Paris (Opéra-Comique) 1904.

Above: *Janet Baker as Charlotte in* Werther *at the London Coliseum.*

Chérubin
Opera in 3 Acts.
Text by Francis de Croisset and Henri Cain.
First performance: Monte Carlo, February 14, 1905. Paris (Opéra-Comique) 1905.

Ariane
Opera in 2 Acts.
Text by Catulle Mendès.
First performance: Paris (Opéra) October 31, 1906.

Thérèse
Opera in 2 Acts.
Text by Jules Clarétie.
First performance: Monte Carlo, February 7, 1907. Paris (Opéra-Comique) 1911; London (Covent Garden) 1919.

Don Quichotte
Opera in 5 Acts.
Text by Henri Cain based on Cervantes' novel.
First performance: Monte Carlo, February 19, 1910.

La Grand' Tante (1867)
L'Adorable Bel-Boul (1874)
Bérengère et Anatole (1876)
Le Mage (1891)
Le Portrait de Manon (1894)
Sapho (1897)
Grisélidis (1901)

Marie-Magdeleine (1903)
Bacchus (1909)
Roma (1912)
Panurge (1913)
Cléopatre (1914)
Amadis (1922)
etc.

GIAN CARLO MENOTTI

(b. Cadegliano 7.7.1911)

During the 1940s and 1950s, the operas of Menotti achieved near-sensational worldwide acclaim. This was due to two factors: one political, the other artistic. The political motif was introduced in Menotti's first full-length opera, *The Consul*, which eloquently and poignantly expressed the human condition when confronted with the indifference, insensitivity and outright brutality of political systems and bureaucracies. Artistically, attention was focused on an approach to opera that blended *Puccini* »-like emotionalism with a kind of naturalism (some-times naïve, but theatrically effective) that, if not anti-opera, was at any rate anti-Grand Opera. Italian by birth—he emigrated to America early in his life, before he had made an impact in music—Menotti has the characteristic Italian warmth of expression. On the other hand, his best work is overtly, sometimes even self-consciously, contemporary in its stripping away of old traditions. The result caused considerable furore. His later work has not extended the elements that gave him his original success. Much of his appeal is sentimental (but so is part of Puccini's) and a good deal of it lies in the way in which it presents characters with whom ordinary people can immediately identify, unencumbered by too many 'operatic' distractions. That is perhaps an over-simplification, but it contains a kernel of truth. Musically, Menotti's operas are not distinguished; but they are unfailingly effective, and the music fits the drama.

Apart from *The Consul*, Menotti's best known stage works are *Amelia at the Ball*, *The Medium*, *The Telephone*, *Amahl and the Night Visitors*, *The Saint of Bleecker Street* and *Maria Golovin*. He has been closely associated with the international music festival at Spoleto.

Amelia al Ballo

Opera in 1 Act.
Text by Menotti (originally in Italian).
First performance: Philadelphia (in English—tr. G. Meade) April 1, 1937. New York (Metropolitan) (in English) 1938; San Remo (in Italian) 1938; Berlin 1947.

The Medium

Opera in 2 Acts.
Text by Menotti.
First performance: Columbia University (Brander Matthews Theatre) May 8, 1946. New York 1947; London (Aldwych) 1948; Paris 1968.

Notes:
Menotti has written that in spite of its subject and somewhat strange action, this is an opera of ideas, contrasting the world of reality, which Baba cannot understand, and a supernatural one in which she cannot believe. Menotti wrote the libretto as he always does (he also wrote that for Samuel Barber's *Vanessa*) and, as always, text and music are convincingly fused. The subject was suggested to him by a séance which he attended in

Above: *From a BBC-2 TV production of* Amahl and the Night Visitors.

Salzburg in 1936. For the first New York production of *The Medium*, Menotti wrote a short, comic, curtain-raiser, *The Telephone*, which is often given as a kind of prelude. It has been recorded thus in America, but has never appeared in the English catalogue.

The Consul
Opera in 3 Acts.
Text by Menotti.
First performance: Philadelphia, March 1, 1950.

Amahl and the Night Visitors
Opera in 1 Act (originally for television).
Text by Menotti
First performance (television): New York (NBC), December 24, 1951. Florence 1953; BBC Television 1967; Hamburg (State Opera) 1968.

Notes:
Menotti has told how, in Italy, it was not Santa Claus but the Three Kings who brought presents to children at Christmas. Later, in America, when he was asked for a Christmas television opera by NBC, he was at first at a loss for a subject: then he remembered his childhood with his brother and how they would wait for the Kings. Also he does not mention, but it is recorded elsewhere, that he himself had an infirm leg that was cured after a visit to a shrine. Thus *Amahl*, like *The Medium*, had its origins in a personal experience.

The Old Maid and the Thief (1939)
The Island God (1942)
The Telephone (1947)
The Saint of Bleecker Street (1954)
The Unicorn the Gorgon and the Manticore (1956)

Maria Golovin (1958)
Labrynth (1963)
The Last Savage (1963)
etc.

103

GIACOMO MEYERBEER

(b. Berlin 5.9.1791; d. Paris 2.5.1864)

Meyerbeer (born Jakob Liebmann Beer), is characterised as a 'controversial figure'. His reputation, exaggeratedly inflated during his lifetime, was savagely deflated as fashion changed and old jealousies combined with sudden 'discoveries' of the emptiness of his music to reduce him to something like a caricature. He was a Jew, rich, and successful, all ingredients likely to invite hostility. Meyerbeer composed the grandest of Grand Opera in Paris at a time when that form of entertainment was inordinately popular. His operas are full of brilliant spectacle, extravagant setting, and set pieces rewarding for the top international singers of the day. He showed his musical gifts early; his family (unusually) encouraged them from the outset. His father was a banker and the son inherited a fortune from a relative named Meyer, on that account changing his original name to Meyerbeer. In spite of precocious talent, he did not achieve early success, being thoroughly conscientious and taking time to acquire experience and technique. He was a student in Germany with Weber », and after hearing Hummel play in Vienna retired for further piano study before resuming his public career. He studied vocal composition in Italy for a while and produced operas both there and in Germany, though without making a mark. In 1824 he went to Paris for a performance of one of his operas and made the French capital his headquarters for the rest of his life. After his first huge success in Paris with *Robert le Diable* in 1831, he was set for fashionable success and fortune. His frequent librettist was Eugène Scribe, himself a significant figure in the French theatre. He became known and accepted as a French composer, though in 1842 he became General Music Director of Berlin at the instigation of the King of Prussia and represented German music at the International Exhibition in London in 1862. Meyerbeer's operas no doubt contain elements of empty rhetoric, of a too facile eclecticism, of wilful extravagance and sundry other faults and failings. But there remains much in them of true quality, giving lasting pleasure.

Robert le Diable

Opera in 5 Acts.
Text by Eugène Scribe.
First performance: Paris (Opéra) November 21, 1831.

Les Huguenots

Opera in 5 Acts.
Text by Eugène Scribe and Emile Deschamps.
First performance: Paris (Opéra) February 29, 1836. Cologne (I.F. Castelli) 1837;
New Orleans 1839; London (Covent Garden) (in German) 1842.

Le Prophète

Opera in 5 Acts.
Text by Eugène Scribe.
First performance: Paris (Opéra) April 16, 1849. London (Covent Garden) 1849;
New Orleans 1850.

Dinorah (Le Pardon de Ploërmel)

Opera in 3 Acts.
Text by Jules Barbier and Michael Carré.
First performance: Paris (Opéra-Comique) April 4, 1859.

L'Africaine

Opera in 5 Acts.
Text by Eugène Scribe.
First performance: Paris (Opéra) April 28, 1865 (posthumous).

Jephthas Gelühde (1812)
Wirt und Gast (1913)
Romilda e Costanza (1817)
Semiramide riconosciuta (1819)
Emma de Resburgo (1819)
Margherita d'Anjou (1820)

L'Esule di Granata (Almanzor)
  (1822)
Il crociato in Egitto (1824)
Ein Feldlager in Schleisen (1844)
L'Étoile du Nord (1854)
etc.

Below: *The Florence Opera production of Giacomo Meyerbeer's*
posthumously performed opera L'Africaine.

ITALO MONTEMEZZI
(b. Vigasio 4.8.1875; d. Verona 15.5.1952)

Originally trained as an engineer in Milan, Montemezzi took up music after some initial setbacks and obtained his diploma at the Milan Conservatoire in 1900. He produced his first opera, *Giovanni Gallurese,* at Turin in January 1905; its success was such that he could look forward to a prosperous future. His second opera, *Hellera,* also produced in Turin, was not so successful, but his third, *L'Amore dei tre re,* opened at La Scala, Milan, in April, 1913, and established his reputation. It has become his most enduring composition. Montemezzi spent ten years from 1939 in America, continuing to compose and conduct, returning to Italy in 1949. As a composer he was attracted neither to the learned nor the *verismo* schools: he wished, he declared, only to create an atmosphere in which his characters could work out their dramatic personalities.

L'Amore dei tre re
Opera in 3 Acts.
Text by Sem Benelli after his own tragic poem.
First performance: Milan (L a Scala) April 10, 1913. L ondon (Covent Garden) 1914; New York (Metropolitan) 1914.

Notes:
Symbolic meanings have been read into the opera: Fiora represents Italy; Archibaldo the hated invader; Manfredo the heir whose hand was used in bribery; and Avito the true prince.

CLAUDIO MONTEVERDI
(b. Cremona ?.5.1567; d. Venice 29.11.1643)

Monteverdi was one of the most important figures in the history of opera and in the overall evolution of Western music. Much of his output, especially his operatic work, has been lost, but the more one knows of his music the more certain one is of his position. Monteverdi was the son of a physician. He was a choirboy at Cremona Cathedral, where he was a pupil of Marc' Antonio Ingegneri, and during this period published his first compositions. He served the ducal court at Mantua and in 1594/5 married Claudia Cataneo; she died in 1607 leaving him with two young children. In 1613 he went to Venice, where he was elected *maestro di cappella* at St Mark's. He took holy orders in 1630.

Monteverdi composed much church music and his many madrigals are among the finest ever written. But only three complete operas have survived, plus one or two works which are not true operas. To call him the last madrigal composer and the first opera composer says something important about him, although neither is historically correct. The composers of the Florentine school, including Caccini, Cavalli » and Peri » (whose *Euridice*, which Monteverdi probably heard, is sometimes referred to as the first true opera) called themselves the Camerata. They wished to return dramatic music to the old Greek principles, with declamation for a single voice in what they called *stile recitative*. This was altogether too rigid and formal, though important as an evolutionary movement. It fell to Monteverdi to breathe the spirit of genius into the emergent ideals, to make the idiom flexible, genuinely creative and truly expressive. This he did in a series of masterpieces; we can only lament that so little has survived. In addition to true operas, Monteverdi wrote pioneering works classified as 'opera-ballet', which inhabit a kind of hinterland between true opera and the dance drama.

La Favola d'Orfeo

Opera in Prologue and 5 Acts.
Text by Alessandro Striggio.
First performance: Mantua, February 24 (?) 1607.

Notes:
Modern revivals of *Orfeo* began with the version prepared by Vincent d'Indy in 1905. Other important productions were those by the late Sir Jack Westrup at Oxford in 1925 (London 1929); Respighi's of 1934; and Hans Redlich's in 1936 in Zurich. More recently there have been Raymond Leppard's production at Sadler's Wells in 1965 and the recent presentations by Kent Opera. *Orfeo* was revived in New York in 1960, Leopold Stokowski conducting.

L'Arianna

Opera in Prologue and 8 Scenes.
Text by Ottavio Rinuccini.
First performance: Mantua, May 28, 1608.

Notes:
All that has survived of this opera is the great 'Lament', which became enormously popular throughout Italy as soon as it appeared.

Below: *The English National Opera production of Monteverdi's Orfeo.*

Above: *The effective staging of Monteverdi's* Il Ritorno d'Ulisse *in Peter Hall's production at Glyndebourne, first seen in 1972.*

Il Ballo delle Ingrate
Opera-ballet.
Text by Ottavio Rinuccini.
First performance: Mantua, June 4, 1608.

Notes:
This is not really an opera, though it might be called an opera in embryo. It is an entertainment of a kind suitable for the wedding celebrations that took place in the Mantuan ducal family, Gonzaga, in 1608. The poet Ottavio Rinuccini was the librettist of the earliest known operas, Peri's *Dafne* (which has not survived) and *Euridice*. *Il Ballo* includes the mythological figures Venus, Cupid and Pluto: the central episode is a dance sequence. Hans Redlich regards this as an 'unmistakable descendant of the French *ballet de coeur'* and an ancestor of the modern opera-ballet such as Stravinsky's » *Pulcinella* from Pergolesi ».

Il Combattimento di Tancredi e Clorinda
Dramatic cantata.
Text by Tasso.
First performance: Venice 1624.

Notes:
Like *Il Ballo*, this is not an opera, though it has enough operatic elements to justify its inclusion. It concerns the Christian knight Tancredi and the Saracen maid Clorinda, a female warrior of courage and resource. Challenged by Tancredi (she is dressed as a man, in armour), she is mortally wounded in the course of the fight but forgives him and asks for Christian baptism, which he gives her. In the Preface to this piece Monteverdi outlined some of his theories, most notably those which led to his great innovations of *pizzicato* and *tremolo* to heighten emotion, altering the entire instrumental spectrum. Both this work and *Il Ballo* appeared in Monteverdi's *Eighth Book of Madrigals*.

Il Ritorno d'Ulisse in Patria

Opera in Prologue and 5 Acts.
Text by Giacomo Badoaro.
First performance: Venice (Teatro San Cassiano) February 1641.

Notes:
The original version of the opera was not published until 1923, when it appeared in Vienna. Doubts were voiced about its authenticity; but is now generally accepted as the work of Monteverdi, from both internal and external evidence. The score is now usually presented in the 1942 edition of Luigi Dallapiccola, in which the Prologue is omitted and the original five Acts reduced to three. There was an earlier (concert) edition by Vincent d'Indy. Many subsequent revivals have taken place, including Erich Kraack's adaptation at Wupperthal in 1959. Raymond Leppard's version at Glyndebourne in 1972 was also notable. (Recorded in 1979.)

L'Incoronazione di Poppea

Opera in Prologue and 3 Acts.
Text by Giovanni Busenello.
First performance: Venice (Teatro SS. Giovanni e Paolo), late 1642.

Notes:
Monteverdi was 75 when he wrote this opera, a feat compared to Verdi's » with *Falstaff*. It is generally recognised as his supreme masterpiece. There have been many modern productions, including one by Raymond Leppard. Roger Norrington's Kent Opera production in 1974 is generally recognised as being as near as possible to Monteverdi's original.

Below: *Delia Wallis as Poppea and Robert Ferguson as Nero in the Sadler's Wells production of* The Coronation of Poppea.

DOUGLAS MOORE
(b. Cutchogue, N.Y. 10.8.1893; d. Greenport, Long Island 25.7.1969)

The American composer Douglas Moore was educated at Yale, served in the US Navy during World War I, and then went to Europe to study with Vincent d'Indy, Ernest Bloch and Nadia Boulanger. Returning to America, he held a succession of musical appointments and in 1934 won a Guggenheim Fellowship. During all this time he composed and made considerable progress, evolving a personal idiom that was tuneful and basically romantic, with a strong foundation of American folk music. Moore wrote in all forms. His best-known operas are *The Ballad of Baby Doe* and *The Devil and Daniel Webster*, which appears to have had a wider appeal than the Pulitzer Prize-winning *Giants in the Earth* (1950). He also wrote the operettas *The Headless Horseman* and *The Emperor's New Clothes*, and the chamber opera *White Wings*.

The Devil and Daniel Webster
Folk Opera in 1 Act.
Text by Stephen Vincent Benét.
First performance: New York (Martin Beck Theater) May 18, 1939.

Notes:
This is often considered to be Moore's most successful opera. The text is based on Stephen Vincent Benét's famous short story that appeared in *The Saturday Evening Post* in 1936. Author and composer collaborated in 1937-38 to produce this musical version. Using everyday speech, it is a folk opera by virtue of its simple musical expression, which captures the spirit of the square-dance, early New England music-making and the brave spirit of pioneering America. It is totally American in outlook and style, owing nothing to European models, and is frequently performed. Alfred Frankenstein called it 'as artful, eloquent and effective a statement of the principles of American democracy as has ever been written'.

The Ballad of Baby Doe
Opera in 2 Acts.
Text by John Latouche.
First performance: Central City, Co., July 7, 1956. New York 1958.

Notes:
The story is taken from a true incident in Leadville, Colorado, dating from the 1880s to the 1930s. Horace Tabor, the richest man in Colorado in the 1880s, whose fortune was founded on silver, took as his second wife Elizabeth Baby Doe. She had left her husband and he had divorced his wife, Augusta, a situation fraught with social peril in those days. Horace lost his fortune in the silver 'collapse' of the 1890s, dying three years later. On his deathbed he urged his wife never to leave the Matchless Mine on which his fortune had been founded — and with dog-like fidelity she lived beside it in a wooden hut until she froze to death in

1935. The opera is a direct representation of these events. The recording, originally made in 1958 under the auspices of the Koussevitzky Music Foundation, was restored in 1976 for the American Bicentennial and the concurrent centenary of the State of Colorado.

Below: *Douglas Moore's* The Ballad of Baby Doe.

Carry Nation
Opera in 2 Acts.
Text by William North Jayme.
First performance: Lawrence (University of Kansas) 1966. New York City Opera 1968.

Notes:
The opera is based on the story of Carry Nation (1846-1911) who, at the age of 53, began to campaign against drinking and gambling establishments in Kansas and later led a 'saloon-smashing' campaign throughout America, also visiting England. She became disliked as a 'self-righteous meddler', but died confident that she had done all she could for the cause of prohibition.

White Wings (1935)
The Headless Horseman (1937)
The Emperor's New Clothes (1948)

Giants in the Earth (1950)
etc.

WOLFGANG AMADEUS MOZART

(b. Salzburg 27.1.1756; d. Vienna 5.12.1791)

This is no place to enlarge further upon the unique and incomparable genius of Mozart, nor upon the details of his short unhappy life; except perhaps to say that he was probably the nearest we have come to the ideal of a perfect artist. His creative force was supremely unified: virtually everything he wrote, in whatever form and on whatever scale, is unmistakably by the same hand. Mozart wrote a great deal of bread-and-butter music; by no means all of his output consists of immortal masterpieces. But even his lesser work is nearly always impeccably written and contains at times flashes of inspiration only possible to the highest order of talent.

Mozart lived for only 36 years, but crowded into them an immense amount of creative activity. His was not a happy life — he never had a truly satisfying relationship, having married his wife Constanze Weber only after unsuccessfully courting her

Below: *Mozart wrote no less than 22 operas during his brief life.*

sister Aloysia, a singer—and during his childhood was not always wisely exploited by his father; this no doubt contributed to his later difficulties. He appears to have been a somewhat feckless and unreliable man; one reason why he found it hard, throughout his life, to obtain regular employment in official positions, for which he regularly applied. However, what may appear as personal faults were closely bound up with that sense of the unrealisable ideal of which his music eloquently speaks.

Mozart possessed a potent dramatic sense which gives his operas and other works a particular stamp. He wrote some 22 operas, as well as a number of other dramatic works for voices, and at least six of them are among the supreme masterpieces of the musical theatre. In his other music, notably the concertos, the operatic style can be seen to be operative, showing once again the total unity and integration of his genius. All the major operas and some of the lesser ones and fragments are now well represented on record.

Bastien und Bastienne
Songspiel in 1 Act.
Text by Friedrich Wilhelm Weiskern (from the French) with additions by J. H. F. Müller.
First performance: Vienna, October 1768.

La Finta Semplice
Opera buffa in 3 Acts.
Text by Marco Coltellini after Carlo Goldoni.
First performance: Salzburg, May 1, 1769.

Mitridate, ré di Ponto
Opera seria in 3 Acts.
Text by Vittorio Amadeo Cigna-Santi.
First performance: Milan (Teatro Regio Ducal) December 26, 1770.

Notes:
Mozart was only 14 when he addressed himself to this formidable subject, based on Racine.

Ascanio in Alba
Opera in 2 Acts.
Text by Abbate Giuseppe Parini.
First performance: Milan (Teatro Regio) October 17, 1771.

Il Sogno di Scipione
Dramatic Serenade.
Text by Pietro Metastasio.
First performance: Salzburg, April 29, 1772.

Lucio Silla
Opera seria in 3 Acts.
Text by Giovanni da Gamerra.
First performance: Milan (Teatro Regio Ducal) December 26, 1772.

La Finta Giardiniera
Opera buffa in 3 Acts.
Text by (probably) Ranieri de Calzabigi, revised Marco Coltellini.
First performance: Munich (Court Theatre) January 13, 1775.

Il Ré Pastore
Drama with music in 2 Acts.
Text by Metastasio after Tasso, revised Giambattista Varesco.
First performance: Salzburg, April 23, 1775.

Notes:
The pastoral setting is charming, and a string of arias do not significantly advance the 'action' but make a thoroughly diverting impression.

Zaïde
German Singspiel (unfinished).
Text by Johann Andreas Schachtner.
First performance: c. 1780.

Notes:
There are alternative endings: in one, the lovers are found to be brother and sister; in the other, the one generally used, Allazim softens the Sultan's heart and remains as his adviser while the lovers depart in peace. The work clearly anticipates the setting of *Die Entführung aus dem Serail*. No overture or finale exists: Symphony No 32 in G (K.318) is used for the former (some authorities think it was intended as such by Mozart); the March (K.335, No 1) for the latter. The gaps in the libretto are filled by adapted dialogue.

Idomeneo, rè di Creta
Opera seria in 3 Acts.
Text by Giambattista Varesco after Antoine Danchet.
First performance: Munich (Court Theatre) January 29, 1781. Vienna 1786; Rotterdam 1880; Glasgow (in English) 1934; Tanglewood, Mass. 1947.

Below: *The English Opera Group production of Mozart's* Idomeneo.

Die Entführung aus dem Serail

Comic Singspiel in 3 Acts.
Text by Christoph Friedrich Bretzner revised by Gottlieb Stephanie, Jr.
First performance: Vienna (Burg Theatre) July 16, 1782. London (Covent Garden) (as The Seraglio — W. Dimond) November 24, 1827; New York 1860.

L'Oca del Cairo

Opera buffa (unfinished).
Text by Giovanni Battista Varesco.
First performance: 1783.

Above: Der Schauspieldirektor, *again by the English Opera Group.*

Lo Sposa Deluso (ossia la Rivalità di tre Donne per un Solo Amante)

Opera buffa (unfinished).
Text by (possibly) Da Ponte.
First performance: 1783.

Der Schauspieldirektor

Comedy in 1 Act.
Text by Gottlieb Stephanie Jr.
First performance: Vienna, February 7, 1786.

Le Nozze di Figaro

Commedia per musica (opera buffa) in 4 Acts.
Text by Lorenzo da Ponte after Beaumarchais.
First performance: Vienna (Burg Theatre) May 1, 1786. Prague 1786; London (Haymarket) 1812; New York (in English) 1824.

Don Giovanni

Drama giocoso (opera buffa) in 2 Acts.
Text by Lorenzo da Ponte.
First performance: Prague (Opéra) October 29, 1787. Vienna (Burg Theatre)
1788; London (Haymarket) 1817; New York (Park Theatre) 1826.

Così fan tutte

Opera buffa.
Text by Lorenzo da Ponte.
First performance: Vienna (Burg Theatre) January 26, 1790. Prague 1791;
Frankfurt (in German) 1791; London (Haymarket) 1811; New York (Metropolitan)
1922.

Die Zauberflöte (The Magic Flute)

German Opera in 2 Acts.
Text by Emanuel Schikaneder (and possibly C. L. Giesecke).
First performance: Vienna (Theater auf der Wieden) September 30, 1791. Prague
1792; London (Haymarket) (in Italian) 1811; New York (in English) 1833.

Notes:
Both Mozart and the librettist Schikaneder were Freemasons
and members of the same Lodge. Masonry was at that time
outlawed under the Empress Maria Theresa, so Schikaneder,
with Mozart's active support, used his text to promote the
Masonic cause by representing the rites and beliefs on stage in
the guise of a species of pantomime. It has often been argued,
probably with justification, that the characters referred to
various leading personages and affairs of the day, most notably
an identification of the Queen of the Night with Maria Theresa.
Whether this is true or not, the genius of Mozart remains
supreme: into the apparent hocus-pocus of much of the libretto,
he poured an incomparable flow of great music. *The Magic
Flute* stands, and will always stand, as a monument to the
human spirit and to human aspiration.

La Clemenza di Tito

Opera seria in 2 Acts.
Text by Caterino Mazzolà after Metastasio.
First performance: Prague (National Theatre) August 6, 1791. London (King's
Theatre) 1806.

Below: Die Zauberflöte, *at the Royal Opera House, Covent Garden.*

Above: *Ilya Repin's portrait of Mussorgsky.*

MODEST MUSSORGSKY
(b. Karevo, Pskov, 21.3.1839; d. St Petersburg 28.3.1881)

The most profoundly Russian and powerfully gifted of all
Russian composers (apart from Tchaikovsky »), Mussorgsky
did not find his way in music (or even into it at all) until he
became associated with Dargomizhsky » and the ubiquitous
Balakirev in the late 1850s. He came of a wealthy landowning
family and served in the Imperial Army, sending in his papers in
1858 in order to concentrate on music. He developed more
according to his own natural genius than to any systematic
tuition. After the decline of his family fortunes following the
freeing of the serfs in 1861, he subsisted on a modest salary from
government employment, but dissipation gradually undermined
his health and damaged his talent and he died in poverty. His
achievements were great (though only partially recognised
during his lifetime), and might have been greater but for drink
and loose living. He was never robust in health and of a highly
nervous disposition; thus his life pattern was to some degree
predestined. Mussorgsky always had great sympathy with the
common people and sought in his music accurately to reproduce
the inflexions and accentuations of their speech. In this he
anticipated, and to a fair extent inspired, similar efforts by such
later composers as Falla » in Spain and Janáček » in Moravia.
Mussorgsky achieved this both in solo songs and in opera. The

117

sympathy and the gift were partly inherited, partly acquired: although he came of a prosperous family, his maternal grandmother had been a serf.

Boris Godunov

Opera in Prologue and 4 Acts.
Text by Mussorgsky after Pushkin's drama and the 'History of the Russian Empire' by Nikolai Mikhailovich Karamazin.
First performance: St Petersburg (Imperial Opera), February 8, 1874. St Petersburg (Imperial Opera) (R-K version), 1896. Paris (Opéra) (R-K) 1908; New York (Metropolitan) (R-K in Italian) 1913; L ondon (Drury L ane), (R-K) 1913; L eningrad (original version) 1928; L ondon (Sadler's Wells) (original version, in English) 1935.

Notes:

Mussorgsky was, as Professor Gerald Abraham has observed, 'completely a dramatic composer'. In his greatest opera *Boris Godunov* (one of the greatest ever written), the dramatic and lyric elements in his genius meet in magnificent confrontation, superbly balanced in opposition.

Khovanshchina

Opera in 5 Acts.
Text by Mussorgsky and Vladimir Stassov.
First performance: St Petersburg (Kononov Hall), February 21, 1886. Paris (Théâtre des Champs-Élysées) (ed. Stravinsky and Ravel), 1913; London (Drury Lane) 1913; New York (Metropolitan) 1931.

Notes:

The later and unfinished *Khovanshchina* represents a supreme fusion of drama and lyricism little less than that ot *Boris Godunov*. The 'editing' of the latter and completion of the former by Rimsky-Korsakov, in each case leading to an alien sophistication and 'civilising' process, has tended to blur the harsh outlines and ethnic truth of Mussorgsky's art and vision. On the other hand, it is easy to be too hard on Rimsky: whatever else he did, it was probably because of him that Mussorgsky's masterpieces obtained a firm foothold: 'undiluted' Mussorgsky was too much for contemporary audiences; the grind of his exposed harmonies and the often brutal truth of his declamation is decidedly uncomfortable. Rimsky made it palatable.

Sorochintsy Fair

Unfinished Opera.
Text based on Gogol. Various versions by Sakhnovsky (1913), Cesar Cui (1917), Tcherepnin (1923), Shebalin (1931).
First performance: St Petersburg (Comedia Theatre) (original form), December 30, 1911.

Notes:

The opera is set in Sorochinsk, Ukraine, in the 19th century. The score is full of evocative Russian folk songs and dances. In certain respects, *Sorochintsy Fair* looks forward to *Petrouchka*.

OTTO NICOLAI
(b. Königsberg 9.6.1810; d. Berlin 11.5.1849)

Above: *Helen Donath and Trudeliese Schmidt as Fraus Fluth and Reich.*

Nicolai's active and successful career was brought to an abrupt end when he died from a stroke at the early age of 39. He had a very unhappy childhood but was helped by various patrons who took charge of him. One of them sent him to Rome as organist to the Prussian Embassy, which allowed him to continue his studies. He was appointed to the Court in Vienna in 1841 and the following year founded the Philharmonic concerts. In Berlin he became director of the Cathedral choir in 1847 and officiated at the Court Opera. As a composer Nicolai was prolific and competent; but nothing he wrote came near to the lasting success of his opera *The Merry Wives of Windsor*. It is a sparkling piece, not least its ebullient overture, which has long delighted many who do not know the pleasures of the opera itself.

Die Lustigen Weiber von Windsor (The Merry Wives of Windsor)
Opera in 3 Acts.
Text by Hermann von Mosenthal, after Shakespeare.
First performance: Berlin (Hofoper) March 9, 1849; London (Her Majesty's) (in Italian) 1864; New York (Metropolitan) 1900.

Rosmonda (Enrico II d'Inghilterra) (1839)
Il Templario (1840)
Odoardo e Gildippe (1841)
Odoproscritto (1841)
Die Heimkehr des Verbannten (1844)
etc.

JACQUES OFFENBACH

(b. Cologne 20.6.1819; d. Paris 5.10.1880)

After studying at the Paris Conservatoire, without much enthusiasm, and pursuing an early career as an orchestral musician, conductor and cello virtuoso, Offenbach tried to establish himself as a composer of operetta. Finding it difficult to get his works staged, he established his own theatre, Les Bouffes-Parisiens, in 1855. He gradually established a reputation both in France and abroad (his works appeared regularly in London and were a considerable inspiration to composers like Sullivan »; and in Vienna, where they influenced Suppé and Strauss ») and had his first great success with the satirical *Orphée aux Enfers (Orpheus in the Underworld)*. Although he wrote around 100 operettas, many starring Hortense Schneider, including such lasting classics as *La Belle Hélène*, *Geneviève de Brabant*, *La Grande Duchesse de Gérolstein*, *La Vie Parisienne* and *La Périchole*, his ultimate ambition was to produce a grand opera. His final days were spent in writing *Les Contes d'Hoffmann*, but he died before he could . hear the first performance. The music of all Offenbach's operettas is a blend of frivolous gaiety (the famous Can-Can from *Orpheus* is an obvious example) and tender lyricism—as in the Letter Song from *La Périchole*. Much of his work, some of it hastily written but nearly always containing some excellence, remains neglected: we tend to hear the same handful of popular pieces performed in London and elsewhere in the kind of pantomimic productions that Offenbach himself frequently sanctioned in his lifetime. There is a great need to hear the principal works in their original Bouffes-Parisiens styling, and for a further exploration of the less frequently heard works like *Les Brigands* and *Geneviève de Brabant*. This is most likely to come about through authentic

Below: *The English National Opera production of* Orpheus.

Above: La Vie Parisienne, *successfully revived in London.*

recordings. The ballet *Gaité Parisienne*, arranged by Rosenthal in 1938, offers a good chance to capture the flavour of Offenbach's music. His one full-length ballet, *Le Papillon* (with its once popular Valse de Rayons, frequently used as an Apaché Dance), has also been recorded.

Le Mariage aux Lanternes
Opérette in 1 Act.
Text by Jules Dubois (Marcel Carré and Léon Battu) (revised version of 'Le Trésor à Mathurin').
First performance: Paris (Bouffes-Parisiens) October 10, 1857. Vienna (Carl) 1858; London (Lyceum) 1860; London (Gaiety) 1871; Vienna (Theater an der Wien), 1889.

Orphée aux Enfers
Opéra-bouffon in 2 Acts.
Text by Hector Crémieux and Ludovic Halévy.
First performance: Paris (Bouffes-Parisiens) October 21, 1858. Berlin 1860; Vienna 1861; London (Haymarket) (in English) 1865. Revised version in 4 Acts, Paris (Gaité) 1874; London (Royalty) 1876; Vienna (Carl) 1892.

La Belle Hélène
Opéra-bouffe in 3 Acts.
Text by Henri Meilhac and Ludovic Halévy.
First performance: Paris (Variétés) December 17, 1864. Vienna 1865; London 1866; London (Gaiety) 1871.

Barbe-Bleu
Opera-bouffe in 3 Acts.
Text by Henri Meilhac and Ludovic Halévy.
First performance: Paris (Variétés) February 5, 1866. London 1866; Vienna (Theater an der Wien) 1866; New York 1870.

La Vie Parisienne
Opéra-bouffe in 4 Acts.
Text by Henri Meilhac and Ludovic Halévy.
First performance: Paris (Palais-Royal) October 31, 1866. Vienna 1867; London 1872.

La Grande-Duchesse de Gérolstein

Opéra-bouffe in 3 Acts.
Text by Henri Meilhac and Ludovic Halévy.
First performance: Paris (Variétés) April 12, 1867. Vienna 1867; London 1867.

Robinson Crusoë

Opéra-comique in 3 Acts.
Text by Eugène Cormon and Hector Crémieux, based on Defoe.
First performance: Paris (Opéra-Comique) November 23, 1867. London (Camden Festival) 1973; London (Sadler's Wells) 1976.

La Périchole

Opéra-bouffe in 3 Acts.
Text by Henri Meilhac and Ludovic Halévy, based on Prosper Mérimée's 'La Carosse du Saint Sacrement'.
First performance: Paris (Variétés) October 6, 1868. Vienna (Theater an der Wien) 1869; London (Princess') 1870. Expanded to 3 Acts in 1874.

La Fille du Tambour-Major

Opéra-comique in 3 Acts.
Text by Henri Charles Chivot and Alfred Duru.
First performance: Paris (Folies-Dramatiques) December 13, 1879. Vienna (Theater an der Wien) 1880; London (Alhambra) 1880.

Above: *Joan Sutherland sings the triple lead to Placido Domingo's Hoffmann in* The Tales of Hoffmann.

Les Contes d'Hoffmann (The Tales of Hoffman)

Opéra in a Prologue, 3 Acts and an Epilogue.
Text by Jules Barbier and Michel Carré, based on stories by Ernst Theodor Amadeus Hoffmann (1776-1822).
First performance: Paris (Opéra-Comique) February 10, 1881. Vienna (Ringtheater) 1881; New York 1882; Vienna (Theater an der Wien) 1883; Berlin 1905; London (Adelphi) 1907; London (Covent Garden) 1910.

Notes:

It was Offenbach's ambition to write a grand opera, but he died in 1880 with only a piano score completed and the first act scored for orchestra. The first auditions had been held at his house in 1879, and he had heard some of the music rehearsed; he wrote to the Director of L'Opéra-Comique: "Hurry up and stage my opera, I haven't much time left and my only wish is to attend the opening night". There were many delays and his last wish was unfulfilled. He died with the score in his hands. The orchestration was completed by Ernest Guiraud. Because of the opera's length, the Venetian scene was omitted for the première and the famous Barcarolle was added to Act 3. The opera was tampered with in subsequent performances, recitatives were added and the order of events frequently changed, and only in fairly recent times have attempts been made to return to Offenbach's original conception.

Pépito (1853)
Oyayaie (1855)
Les Deux Aveugles (1855)
Le Violoneux (1855)
Ba-ta-clan (1855)
Tromb-al-Cazar (1856)
Geneviève de Brabant (1859)
La Chanson de Fortunio (1861)
Un Mari à la porte (1869)
Les Brigands (1869)
Vert-Vert (1869)

Le Roi Carotte (1872)
Pomme d'api (1873)
La Jolie Parfumeuse (1873)
Madame l'Archiduc (1874)
La Créole (1875)
Le Voyage dans la lune (1875)
Le Docteur Ox (1877)
Madame Favart (1878)
Belle Lurette (1880)
etc.

CARL ORFF
(b. Munich 10.7.1895)

Orff's entire musical life has been centred on Munich, where he was born, and where he founded the Günter Schule in 1925. It is difficult to define the ingredients that make up his music: his style remains obstinately individual, distinctive, and, in its way, original. He has had substantial influence on aspects of contemporary musical life. Briefly, his aim was to by-pass the Romantic Age, and its obsession with harmony, and return music to its very roots. It is hard to put his works into any specific category: most have a theatrical background, yet only two or three of them could be called operas. His most famous work *Carmina Burana* is not strictly an opera, being written as a scenic cantata, but it was often staged. We include here only those compositions that may properly be called operas.

Der Mond
Fairy-tale opera in five scenes.
Text by Orff after the Brothers Grimm.
First performance: Munich, February 5, 1939. New York 1956.

Above: *The German composer Orff, best known for* Carmina Burana.

Die Klüge

Opera in 6 scenes.
Text by Orff after the Brothers Grimm.
First performance: Frankfurt, February 20, 1943. London 1959.

Notes:

Die Klüge, otherwise known as *The King and the Wise Woman* has often been produced with puppets. Orff himself insists that the costumes and masks must be fanciful.

Antigonae

Tragedy in 1 Act.
Text by Friedrich Hölderlin after Sophocles.
First performance: Salzburg, August 9, 1949.

Notes:

In this work Orff has made a successful attempt to recreate the drama of ancient Greece with its fusion of music, drama and dance, in modern terms. The textures are spare, the instrumentation (six pianos, four harps, nine double basses, six flutes, six oboes, six (muted) trumpets, and a battery of kettledrums and other percussion) skilfully used and highly effective. It is a large work, its single act lasting over three hours; and that, coupled with the extravagant instrumentation, has not helped make it popular. But it more than worth extended exploration.

FERNANDO PAER

(b. Parma 1.6.1771; d. Paris 3.5.1839)

A composer of Italian birth who became French by adoption, Paer studied music in Parma and by the age of 20 was established as a conductor in Venice. He married the singer Riccardi and in 1798 was invited to Vienna, where she was singing at the Court Opera, and produced his opera *Camilla*

..ere. He was an opera conductor in Dresden from 1803 to 1806, where he produced his *Sargino* (1803)—a work full of charming melodic invention—and *Leonora*—an Italian version of Gaveaux's opera on which Beethoven's » *Fidelio* was also based. Beethoven was an admirer of Paer's music, and his own score shows some sign of Paer's influence. In 1806 Paer accompanied Napoleon to Warsaw and Posen and settled in Paris in 1807 as his court composer. In this position he began to make a substantial fortune, continuing under Louis Philippe and as singing teacher to the Empress Marie Louise. He succeeded Spontini » as musical director of the Theatre Italien in 1812, his considerable influence waning somewhat with the arrival of Rossini » on the scene. In his heyday he composed some fifty works for the theatre. His Italian operas were fluent and attractive; his operas to German and French librettos sometimes more ambitious but generally less successful, although his most popular work was *Le Maître de Chapelle* produced in 1821. Other operas bore titles which clearly reflect his adherence to literary fashions of his time—*Il nuovo Figaro* (after Beaumarchais), *Idomeneo* and *La sonnambula*.

Sargino
Opera in 3 Acts.
Text by
First performance: Dresden, May 26, 1803.

Leonora
Opera in 2 Acts.
Text by Jean Nicolas Bouilly.
First performance: Dresden, October 1804.

Le Maître de Chapelle
Opera in 2 Acts.
Text by Sophie Gay, based on Duval's comedy 'Le Souper Imprevu'.
First performance: Paris, March 29, 1821. London (Covent Garden) 1845; New York 1852.

Notes:
The opera appears to be a send-up of Paer's growing rival Rossini, then so much in vogue, and the overture is reminiscent of *The Thieving Magpie*. The opera remained popular at the Opéra-Comique in Paris into the 20th century and was still being heard in London to the end of the 19th.

Orphée et Euridice (1791)	*Il nuovo Figaro (1794)*
Circe (1792)	*I molinari (1794)*
Il tempo fa giustizia a tutti (1792)	*Il matrimonio improviso (1794)*
Laodicea (1793)	*Idomeneo (1794)*
I pretendenti burlati (1793)	*Ero e Leandro (1794)*
Ora fa tutto (1793)	*Rossana (1795)*

Cinna (1795)	I fuorusciti di Firenze (1802)
L'intrigo amoroso (1795)	Una in bene ed una in male (1805)
L'orfana riconosciuta (1796)	Sofonisba (1805)
L'amante servitore (1796)	Numa Pompilio (1809)
Il principe di Taranto (1797)	Agnese de Fritz-Henry (1809)
La virtù al cimento (Griselda) (1798)	Didone abbandonata (1811)
	I Baccanti (1813)
Camilla (1799)	L'Oriflamme (1814)
Il morto vivo (1799)	L'eroismo in amore (1815)
La testa riscaldata (1800)	La primavera felice (1816)
La sonnambula (1800)	Blanche de Provence (1821)
Ginevra degli Almieri (1800)	La Marquise de Brinvilliers (1831)
Poche, ma buone (1800)	Un Caprice de femme (1834)
Achille (1801)	etc.

GIOVANNI PAISIELLO
(b. Taranto 8.5.1740; d. Naples 5.6.1816)

A talented, industrious producer of *opera buffa*, Paisiello won and deserved considerable contemporary fame. He is reputed to have written over 100 operas, including *Il Barbiere di Siviglia*; ousted eventually by Rossini's version », written to the same text. After studying at the Conservatorio Sant' Onofrio, Paisiello began to compose choral music. He set out on his true path with *Il ciarlone* (1764) and over the years produced comic operas at Bologna, Modena and Parma, before settling in Naples. In 1776 he was offered, and accepted, a lucrative post at St Petersburg by the Empress Catherine. After eight years he began to make his way back to Italy where he became *maestro di cappella* to Ferdinand IV, and continued to produce operas, both *buffa* and *seria*. His official position was threatened with the temporary overthrow of the Royal State in 1799, but he soon regained it when the Royal House was restored.

Il Barbiere di Siviglia
Opera in 2 Acts.
Text by Giuseppe Petrosellini after Beaumarchais's 'Le Barbier de Séville'.
First performance: St Petersburg, October 26, 1782. Subsequently many performances throughout Europe.

Below: *A scene from Paisiello's* Barbiere di Siviglia *at Salzburg.*

The libretto is substantially the same as that used by Rossini for his *Barbieri*. At that time Paisiello's piece was still immensely popular and Rossini encountered opposition for having been so presumptuous as to set the text of an old favourite. He made a gesture by asking the ageing Paisiello for permission, but it still took a little time for the Rossini version to win the greater lasting popularity.

Nina, ossia La pazza per amore (Nina, or the Lunatic from Love)

Comic Opera in 3 Acts.
Text by Giuseppe Carpani and G. B. L orenzi after Marsollier.
First performance: Naples (Cæserta Palace) June 25, 1789 (private). Florence (Teatro Fiorentino) 1790.

L'idole cinese (1767)	*Nina (1789)*
La Frascatana (1774)	*La locanda (1791)*
La serva padrona (1781)	*I giuochi d'Agrigento (1792)*
Il re Teodoro in Venezia (1784)	*Proserpine (1803)*
Pirro (1787)	*etc.*
L'amor contrastato (La molinara) (1788)	

GIOVANNI BATTISTA PERGOLESI
(b. Jesi 4.1.1710; d. Pozzuoli 16.3.1736)

Pergolesi was one of those fragile geniuses who reveals a rare talent, but dies before it has time to mature. He was little appreciated in his own lifetime (he is said to have been once hit on the head by an orange hurled by a member of an irate audience during the first performance of his *opera seria*, *L'Olimpiade* in January, 1735). Yet he shot to fame almost immediately after his death at the age of 26. Suddenly his works were performed everywhere, but little consolation for Pergolesi who was buried in a pauper's grave. There is some mystery about his early life; even more about his compositions. Many works have been attributed to him without convincing evidence, mostly in the instrumental and choral fields. But enough is established as authentic to secure him his place. In the opera field, Pergolesi's lasting memorial is the delightful comedy *La serva padrona*. However, the work upon which Pergolesi's fame chiefly rests is his *Stabat Mater*, which he composed in the Capuchin monastery at Pozzuoli, where he went at the end of 1735, poor of health, knowing he had not long to survive.

La serva padrona

Intemezzo in two parts.
Text by Gennaro Antonio Federico.
First performance: Naples (Teatro San Bartolommeo) August 28, 1733.

Notes:
The delightful, sparkling overture is very familiar. The little opera became, later in the century, a piece in the *'Guerre des Buffons'* in Paris, where the Franco/Italian operatic war was raging. *La serva* achieved a great number of acclaimed performances, first at the Opéra and then at the Comédie-Française.

Salustia (1731)	*La contadina astuta (1734)*
Lo frate nnammorato (1732)	*L'Olimpiade (1735)*
Il prigionier superbo (1733)	*Flaminio (1735)*
Adriano in Siria (1734)	*etc.*

JACOPO PERI
(b. Rome 20.8.1561; d. Florence 12.8.1633)

Peri is credited with having written the first opera, in the modern sense, to have survived. His *Euridice* appeared in 1600 (published 1601), just before a setting of the same subject by Giulio Caccini. Both were written for the marriage of Henry IV of France and Marie de Médicis in 1600. Caccini's opera was not given complete until 1602 and Peri's *Dafne*, which would otherwise have been the first opera, has not survived. Peri was a pupil at the church of San Lorenzo, Florence. and later became *maestro di cappella* to the Médici family. He was a singer and lutanist as well as a composer. He belonged to that group of musicians and poets known as the Camerata who, in the belief that they were restoring the Greek principles of music and drama, produced the earliest forms of opera, virtually by accident. Like Peri, most were little more than amateurs, but their work, although soon superseded, was important in that it paved the way for future developments. They aimed to present dramatic action in a naturalistic way, the musical settings designed to adhere as closely as possible to speech. Their monodic style (the *stile rappresentativo*) had serious limitations; but it sowed seeds that were to grow into formidable trees.

Euridice
Opera in Prologue and 5 Scenes.
Text by Ottavio Rinuccini.
First performance: Florence (Pitti Palace) October 6, 1600 (with some items by Caccini).

Notes:
The action is carried forward by solo voices in the new *stile rappresentativo*. Rinuccini omits the condition that Orpheus must not look at Eurydice or she must return to Hades: Orpheus's song alone secures the release and return. At the first performance Peri himself sang the name part.

AMILCARE PONCHIELLI

(b. Paderno Fasolaro, Cremona 31.8.1834; d. Milan 16.1.1886)

Hardly a major composer, even where opera is concerned, Ponchielli was nevertheless a skilful and industrious one. He studied at the Milan Conservatoire from 1843 until 1854 and two years later produced his first opera *I promessi sposi*, which he then revised and re-presented. In 1881 he was appointed *maestro di cappella* at Bergamo and composed a famous hymn to the memory of Garibaldi. The only opera of Ponchielli's that is still widely remembered is *La Gioconda*, and largely because of the orchestral excerpt 'Dance of the Hours', and the tenor aria 'Cielo e mar!'

La Gioconda

Opera in 4 Acts.
Text by Arrigo Boito (under the anagrammatic pseudonym Tobia Gorrio) after Victor Hugo's 'Angelo'.
First performance: Milan (La Scala) April 8, 1876. London (Covent Garden) 1883; New York (Metropolitan) 1883.

Notes:
La Gioconda is a large-scale Grand Opera; somewhat crude but full of dramatic spirit. It is similar to Meyerbeer » in its coloured spectacle and spates of concerted song and dance. Each Act has its separate title.

Il Figliuol Prodigo

Opera in 3 Acts.
Text by Angelo Zanardini.
First performance: Milan (La Scala) December 26, 1880.

I promessi sposi (1856)	*Il figliuol prodigo (1880)*
La Savoiarda (1861)	*Marion Delorme (1885)*
Roderico (1863)	*I Mori di Valenza (1914)*
I Lutuani (1874)	*etc.*

Below: *A production at Verona of Ponchielli's opera* La Gioconda.

FRANCIS POULENC

(b. Paris 7.1.1899; d. Paris 30.1.1963)

Above: *Francis Poulenc, photographed during the early '30s.*

Poulenc received a classical education but his interest in music led to piano lessons with Ricardo Viñes. He acquired a theoretical knowledge of music from various sources. By the time he joined the Army in 1918, he had written one or two compositions inspired by Erik Satie. After the War, continuing to idolise Satie, he became one of the group of French composers known as 'Les Six'—the others being Auric, Durey, Honegger, Milhaud   and Tailleferre—which also led to his meeting and being influenced by Jean Cocteau. Poulenc's musical activity was largely outside the theatre, and all his music retained a very individual style and an unschooled freshness of outlook, veering between the light, frivolous, satirical vein that he inherited from Satie and the deep seriousness of his religious works. His few operas reveal the different sides of his nature. A comédie-bouffe *Le Gendarme Incompris* was written in 1920; then no further opera until the brilliantly satirical *Les Mamelles de Tirésias* in 1947, a piece frequently produced and recently heard in London. *Les Dialogues des Carmélites* (Milan 1957) was a complete contrast, a profound and serious work. An interesting 'operatic monologue' *La Voix Humaine*, text by Cocteau, is a 45-minute soprano solo at one end of a telephone.

Les Mamelles de Tirésias
Opéra-bouffe in 2 Acts.
Text by Guillaume Apollinaire.
First performance: Paris (Opéra-Comique) June 3, 1947. New York 1953; Aldeburgh 1958.

Notes:
The surrealistic plot concerns a husband and wife who change sex. He produces 40,000 children before he reverts to manhood —and advises the audience to follow his example.

Les Dialogues des Carmélites
Opera in 3 Acts.
Text by Georges Bernanos, based on Gertrude von le Fort's novel 'Die letzte am Schafott' (1931) and a film scenario.
First performance: Milan (La Scala) January 26, 1957. San Francisco 1957; London (Covent Garden) 1958.

Notes:
The opera tells of the Carmelite nuns of Compiègne who defied the revolutionary tribune of 1794 and went to the guillotine.

La Voix Humaine
Tragédie lyrique in 1 Act.
Text by Jean Cocteau.
First performance: Paris (Opéra-Comique) February 6, 1959. New York (Carnegie Hall) 1960; Edinburgh Festival 1960.

Notes:
The piece dramatises a telephone conversation between a jilted young woman and her lover.

Below: *Poulenc (right) with Lennox Berkeley.*

SERGEI PROKOFIEV
(b. Sontsovka 23.4.1891; d. Moscow 5.3.1953)

A remarkable child prodigy, Prokofiev studied composition at the St Petersburg Conservatoire under Rimsky-Korsakov » and Liadov (as did Stravinsky »). After the Russian Revolution he travelled abroad and in 1922 settled in Paris, which remained his home base until 1933 when he returned to Russia as a permanent citizen: being obliged by the authorities to make a firm decision as to where he wanted to settle. His music has a spiky brittleness but with a particular kind of lyricism that keeps trying to escape. During his Russian years, Prokofiev tried, but did not always succeed, to obey the official directive of simple, direct music for the people. But he was too much of an artist and creator to be bound by this and inevitably he fell foul of the party line. Prokofiev's dramatic gift was always strong and he composed a number of operas and ballets of the highest quality. The range of his operas is wide (from the fantastic *Love of Three Oranges* to the epic *War and Peace*). At his best, Prokofiev remains one of the foremost figures of 20th-century music.

Above: *Examples of Soviet theatrical art: Rabinovich's designs for* The Love of Three Oranges *by Sergei Prokofiev, first produced in Chicago in 1921.*

The Love of Three Oranges
Opera in Prologue and 4 Acts.
Text by Prokofiev after Carlo Gozzi.
First performance: Chicago, December 30, 1921. New York, 1922; Milan (La Scala) 1947; Edinburgh 1962.

Notes:
The whole opera is a play, not so much on words, as on the traditions of the *commedia dell'arte*, as in Gozzi's original. The best known music is undoubtedly the Orchestral Suite Prokofiev made from it.

The Gambler

Opera in 4 Acts.
Text by Prokofiev based on Dostoyevsky's story.
First performance: Brussels, April 29, 1929. New York 1957. Edinburgh 1962.

War and Peace (Viona y Mir)

Opera in 13 Scenes.
Text by Prokofiev and Mira Mendelson after Tolstoy.
First performance: (orig. version, cut) Moscow, June 7, 1945. ('Final version')
Leningrad, April 1, 1955; Florence, 1953; New York (NBC TV) 1957; London
(Sadler's Wells) 1972; Australia (Sydney Opera) 1973.

Notes:

The opera went through several stages of evolution. At first it was mostly concerned with personal matters; but the Hitler war was raging and Russia was again under the invader. So Prokofiev was urged to insert more martial and patriotic material. The result is a mixture of two opposing elements. In the first part (Peace) we have a picture of a slightly decadent, aristocratic Russian society warmed by personal involvements. The second part (War) shows that society's break-up under invasion. Some see the patriotic music in Part 2 as simply a response to the needs of the moment which are no longer valid. But that response is a universal feeling, especially in Russia. To make an opera out of Tolstoy's huge novel was a near impossible task yet Prokofiev and his collaborator achieved it. *War and Peace* is as richly generated an opera as any to come out of Russia since *Boris Godunov*.

Betrothal in a Monastery (The Duenna)

Opera in 4 Acts.
Text by Prokofiev and Mira Mendelson based on Sheridan's 'The Duenna'.
First performance: Leningrad, November 3, 1946.

Notes:

The idea for this sparkling *opera buffa* was suggested by Mira Mendelson in 1940. She was then a student and had collaborated in a production of Sheridan's play. (She was later to become Prokofiev's wife and collaborated with him on several projects. She wrote some verses for this opera.) Prokofiev wrote the libretto himself, staying close to Sheridan's text, which had in any case been intended for operatic production and included popular 18th-century airs. In general the composer bends the emphasis towards the two pairs of lovers and slightly away from the more obvious satire and humour. The score is full of colourful music, with many dances and festivities in the Spanish manner. The opera went into rehearsal at the Stanislavsky Music Theatre in 1941; but the German invasion of Russia prevented public production, which had to wait until 1946.

The Story of a Real Man
Opera in 4 Acts.
Text by Prokofiev and Mira Mendelson after Boris Polevoi's novel.
First performance: (private) Leningrad (Kirov Theatre) December 3, 1948.

Notes:

This opera has had little success and has not been published.
Prokofiev wrote it at a time when he was under censure from
official critics, and hoped it would restore his fortunes. He filled
it with 'clear, melodic episodes' and 'interesting authentic folk
songs of the Russian north' (Nestyev). The style was popular
and simplified; the result (predictably) was unimpressive. The
story from an 'inspiring' novel of the time dealing with the war,
was a little too self-consciously 'heroic'. It concerns the exploits
of a valiant Soviet flyer in the war who is shot down behind
enemy lines, crawls back, though seriously wounded, has his leg
amputated, loses the will to carry on and is revived by the
example of an old Bolshevik Commissar. At the same time it
deals with the life of the Russian people under war conditions,
but does not do this with any great conviction—hence the
opera's hostile reception. As well as folk material, two numbers
from the arrangements Prokofiev issued as Op. 104, the score
includes some items from his music for the film *Ivan the
Terrible*. A sick, disillusioned man at the time of its composition,
Prokofiev seems to have approached it as therapeutic . . . maybe
identifying himself subconsciously with the 'hero', the 'real
man'.

L'Ange de Feu (The Flaming Angel)
Opera in 5 Acts.
Text by Prokofiev after Valery Bruisoff's novel.
*First performance: (concert) Paris (Théâtre des Champs-Elysées) November 25,
1954. (Stage) Venice, September 14, 1955; London (Sadler's Wells), 1965.*

Notes:

The opera had a chequered career. Prokoviev hoped that Mary
Garden would produce it in Chicago after *The Love of Three
Oranges*; but she resigned as director before anything could
come of it. Bruno Walter showed some interest in Berlin in 1926;
but to no avail. Koussevitzky gave some parts in Paris, but after
that the score was lost and surfaced in Paris during the 1950s,
after Prokofiev's death.

Right: *Prokofiev's challenging
gaze, caught in this portrait by
Shukhayev, epitomised his whole
personality.*

134

GIACOMO PUCCINI
(b. Lucca 22.12.1858; d. Brussels 29.11.1924)

Puccini's father died while he was still a child, but his mother arranged a special Royal grant to help with her son's musical education and in 1880 he entered the Milan Conservatoire where he studied under Bazzini and Ponchielli ». The latter encouraged Puccini to enter his first opera (*Le Villi*) into a competition: even though it was beaten by Mascagni's » entry (*Cavalleria Rusticana*), Puccini's effort was eventually produced, in 1884, and led to a commission to write another opera from the publisher Ricordi—the unsuccessful *Edgar*. In 1893, however, Puccini scored his first major success at Turin with *Manon Lescaut*, and from then established himself as the most prominent and popular opera composer of his time. He might not have possessed the depth and range of Verdi », but he did have a sure touch for the theatre and an unfailing ability to match dramatic situations with appropriate music and memorable melody. His style is frankly emotional, often sentimental, sometimes melodramatic, seldom fastidious; yet he found a distinctive idiom within a conventional framework. Even if his music sometimes sounds old-fashioned and his later experiments, designed to catch up with modern ideas, are not always viable, his operas remain supremely convincing and obstinately indestructible. In short: it is easy to criticise Puccini, but impossible not to enjoy him.

Le Villi
Opera in 1 Act (new version in 2 Acts).
Text by Ferdinando Fontana.
First performance: Milan (Teatro dal Verme) May 31, 1884. Turin (Teatro Reggio) (2 Acts) December 26, 1884; New York (Metropolitan) 1908.

Notes:
The story is the same as that used by Adam for the ballet *Giselle* and James Loder's play with music *The Night Dancers*. This, Puccini's first opera, was a modest success on its original production (especially in the 2 Act revision); but it is not much heard outside Italy.

Edgar
Opera in 4 Acts (new version in 3 Acts).
Text by Ferdinando Fontana after Alfred de Musset's 'La coupe et les lèvres'.
First performance: Milan (La Scala) April 21, 1889. Ferrara (3 Acts) February 28, 1892.

Notes:
Edgar has never made much headway. Puccini himself appeared to think little of it, judging by various tart remarks he made. There are hints in the score of the Puccini to come, but the libretto has been universally condemned as preposterous rubbish, even by operatic standards.

Above: *Beverly Sills as Manon in Puccini's version of Prévost's* Manon Lescaut.

Right: *Giacomo Puccini.*

Manon Lescaut

Opera in 4 Acts.
Text by Marco Praga, Domenico Oliva and Luigi Illica after Abbé Prévost's novel.
First performance: Turin (Teatro Regio) February 1, 1893. London (Covent Garden) 1894; New York (Metropolitan) 1907.

Notes:

Manon Lescaut was Puccini's first success and soon achieved worldwide acclaim. Early commentators remarked on the opera's 'symphonic structure'. Although this was misunderstood at the time, it was to become characteristic of Puccini's operas.

Below: *The Bohemian Parisian setting of Puccini's* La Bohème.

La Bohème

Opera in 4 Acts.
Text by Giuseppe Giacosa and Luigi Illica, after Henri Murger's novel.
First performance: Turin (Teatro Reggio) February 1, 1896. Manchester 1897;
London (Covent Garden) 1897; New York 1898; New York (Metropolitan) 1900.

Notes:

La Bohème is unquestionably a masterpiece, but is also different from Puccini's other operas in the way it combines a taut, economical conversational style with Puccini's natural lyricism and emotional ripeness. This combination not only sets *La Bohème* firmly among the modern operas but also among the Romantic ones. Like Puccini's earlier works it is built on symphonic principles, but significantly advancing them. Each Act is in fact a 'Movement', worked out and developed with consummate skill. A significant achievement.

Tosca

Opera in 3 Acts.
Text by Giuseppi Giacosa and Luigi Illica, after Sardou's play.
First performance: Rome (Teatro Costanzi) January 14, 1900. New York (Metropolitan) 1901.

Notes:

With *Tosca* Puccini approached more deliberately the *verismo* style much in favour at the time. There is great care for natural detail. The opera is certainly melodramatic, with passions being more insistent than the characters as individuals. The sexual confrontations are crude but, on the other hand, there is much lyric surge and melodic power; plus several instances of genuine dramatic interplay. It may not possess the subtlety and ease of *La Bohème* but, nonetheless, *Tosca* remains true Puccini.

Madama Butterfly

Opera in 3 Acts.
Text by Giacosa and Illica after David Belasco's play on John Luther's story.
First performance: Milan (La Scala) February 17, 1904. London (Covent Garden)
1905; New York (Metropolitan) 1907.

Notes:

The first performance of *Madama Butterfly* was a famous fiasco; but Puccini revised it within ten months and it reopened at Brescia conducted by Toscanini. It was a total success, and has remained so. Puccini's use of Japanese tunes to create atmosphere was once regarded as a talking point; today it is seen as a not entirely successful device, the opera's other qualities being more interesting and memorable. *Madama Butterfly* was originally a 2-Act opera, but Act 2 was divided into two parts, making it in effect a 3-Act opera.

Above: *A Covent Garden production of the ever-popular* Madama Butterfly, *first performed there in 1905 with Emmy Destinn in the leading role.*

La Fanciulla del West

Opera in 3 Acts.
Text by Guelfo Civinini and Carlo Zangarini after David Belasco's play 'The Girl of the Golden West'.
First performance: New York (Metropolitan) December 10, 1910. London (Covent Garden) 1911; Milan (La Scala) 1912.

Notes:

A highly successful opera, in which Puccini made some experiments with more modernistic technique. Certainly, *La Fanciulla* contains less 'hit numbers' than many other Puccini operas, but he had an alert mind that picked up much going on around in the musical world and the technique to make profitable use of it.

La Rondine

Opera in 3 Acts.
Text by Giuseppe Adami from the German of Alfred Maria Willner and Heinrich Reichert.
First performance: Monte Carlo, March 27, 1917. Bologna 1917; Rome 1918; New York (Metropolitan) 1928; England (Opera Viva) 1966.

Notes:

La Rondine was commissioned as an operetta by a Viennese publisher in 1912, but was not completed until the end of World War I. It contains a good deal of light music and some waltzes, but could scarcely be called an operetta. It was also a total failure, perhaps because it was outside Puccini's normal and natural style. Although he could handle comedy his natural bent was for emotionally dark-hued lyricism.

Il Trittico

Three 1 Act Operas.
Texts: Il tabarro: Giuseppe Adami after Didier Gold; Suor Angelica *and* Gianni Schicchi: *Giovacchino Forzano.*
First performance: New York (Metropolitan) December 14, 1918.

Notes:

Puccini always wanted the three 1 Act operas that make up *Il Trittico* to be given together as a single evening's entertainment. They are well contrasted: *Il tabarro* is a piece of Grand Guignol in the *verismo* style; *Suor Angelica* is supposed to be mystical but hardly goes better than the sentimental; *Gianni Schicchi* is a piece of comedy that some regard as Puccini's masterpiece. In fact it has long been popular on its own. *Il tabarro* has also made a favourable independent impression. Only *Suor Angelica* has made no headway

Turandot

Opera in 3 Acts (unfinished by Puccini).
Text by Giuseppe Adami and Renato Simoni after Gozzi.
First performance: Milan (La Scala) April 25, 1926. Buenos Aires 1926; New York (Metropolitan) 1926; London (Covent Garden) 1927.

Notes:

Puccini died before he had completed the score of *Turandot*. It was finished by Franco Alfano, using sketches left by Puccini for a great love duet. Toscanini once again conducted the first performance, and at the point where Alfano took over, stopped the performance, turned to the audience, and announced: 'Here the Master's work ends'. The oriental atmosphere is less obviously evoked than in *Madama Butterfly* and the melodic sweep and harmonic structure are as far 'advanced' as Puccini ever went.

HENRY PURCELL
(b. London 1659; d. London 21.11.1695)

Purcell was England's greatest composer between the death of William Byrd and the rise of Edward Elgar. Had he not died at the age of 36 and had he lived in a more ordered and sophisticated musical environment he would certainly have achieved much more — especially where opera was concerned. In vocal music Purcell was caught between the French and Italian influences in an age of transition, by the requirements of a thoroughly secularised Church. Also he was hampered by poor libretti and enfeebled stage convention. In his instrumental music, however, he could break free and establish his own style. Purcell held a number of official positions after the Restoration and in 1967 succeeded his master John Blow » as organist of Westminster Abbey. He soon became a noted and successful composer for church and theatre, and wrote much ceremonial music for Royal and State occasions.

Dido and Aeneas
Opera in Prologue and 3 Acts.
Text by Nahum Tate after Virgil.
First performance: London (Mr Josias Priest's Boarding School for Girls, Chelsea) December 1689.

Notes:
Purcell's only true opera, *Dido and Aeneas* remains a landmark. The overture (lacking the Prologue music) is in the French (Lully) style and sets the true tones of the tragedy.

The Prophetess
Play with music.
Text by Thomas Betterton, based on Beaumont & Fletcher.
First performance: London (Dorset Gardens Theatre) April/May 1690.

King Arthur, or The British Worthy
Drama with music in Prologue, 5 Acts and Epilogue.
Text by John Dryden.
First performance: London (Dorset Gardens Theatre) summer 1691. New York 1808; Cambridge 1928.

Notes:
This is one of the most elaborate of Purcell's 'non-operas' or, at best, 'semi-operas'. It is more in the line of a stage play with extended musical numbers. The original score was lost after the first performance, but reconstructions have been made for subsequent performance. There is some superb music embedded in this, as in other works of a similar kind, notably *The Fairy Queen* (see below). Dryden was of course a major poet and dramatist; but the conventions of the Restoration theatre prevented the emergence of a fully realised work.

Above: *An English Opera Group production of Purcell's* King Arthur.

The Fairy Queen
Drama with music in Prologue and 5 Acts.
Text by (probably) Elkanah Settle from Shakespeare's 'A Midsummer Night's Dream'.
First performance: London (Dorset Gardens Theatre) May 1692. Cambridge 1920.

Notes:
Much the same may be said of this as of *King Arthur* (above). The music consists mostly of songs and masque-like pieces at the ends of the acts. Nothing of Shakespeare's original text was retained, not even the words of his songs. The result is a hotch-potch; but with some marvellous music. The score of this also was lost but was later recovered, following a once famous advertisement. The Cambridge production of 1920 was the first since its original première.

The Indian Queen
Play with music.
Text by John Dryden and Robert Howard.
First performance: London (Drury Lane) 1695

Notes:
This is, like *The Tempest* (see below), even more nebulously referred to as an 'opera'. It is mostly a matter of incidental music integrated into the drama, though much of it is excellent.

The Tempest
Play with music.
Text by (?) Shadwell after Shakespeare.
First performance: London (Dorset Gardens) 1695.

SERGEI RACHMANINOV
(b. Oneg, Novgorod 1.4.1873; d. Beverly Hills, California, 28.3.1943)

Known mainly for his Second Symphony and Second Piano Concerto, Rachmaninov's vocal and operatic music is much less appreciated; yet his music for voices contains some of his best, most authentic work. He studied at the Moscow Conservatoire with Nikolai Sverev, and continued his studies with Tanayev and Arensky. In 1892 he won the Gold Medal for composition and soon became in demand all over the world as a conductor and particularly as a pianist. He visited the US for the first time in 1909, but returned to Moscow the following year and stayed there until 1917, when the Revolution drove him away for ever. He settled in America but returned to Europe for frequent visits. Rachmaninov completed three operas (the first, *Aleko* written while he was still a student).

Aleko
Opera in 1 Act.
Text by V. I. Nemirovich-Danchenko after Pushkin's 'The Gypsies'.
First performance: Moscow, May 9, 1893.

Notes:
The opera, though admired by Tchaikovsky », did not make much headway after its early performances and was in fact disliked by Rachmaninov himself later in his life. The big *scena* for Aleko was one of the triumphs of Chaliapin; otherwise revivals have been few and mostly amateur.

The Miserly Knight
Opera in 1 Act.
Text after Pushkin.
First performance: Moscow, January 24, 1906.

Notes:
This effective 1 Act piece about a miserly knight strongly tested and provoked by a greedy and unscrupulous son and an equally unprepossessing and totally dishonest usurer, was originally intended for Chaliapin, though apparently he never actually sang it. The story is again by Pushkin and has a sharp edge of satire and irony finely matched by Rachmaninov's setting, which is taut, economical and perfectly structured.

Francesca da Rimini
Opera with Prologue, 2 Scenes and Epilogue.
Text by Modest Tchaikovsky after Dante and Pushkin.
First performance: Moscow, January 24, 1906.

Notes:
This opera's lack of success is blamed on the libretto by Tchaikovsky's brother. The music, however, contains some of the composer's best writing, including a lengthy orchestral prologue which, on stage, is rather inclined to unbalance the work, however effective the music.

JEAN-PHILIPPE RAMEAU
(b. Dijon 25.9.1683; d. Paris 12.9.1764)

The son of a church organist at Dijon, Rameau received his first musical training at home. He was intended for the law and attended a Jesuit college, but as soon as his true gifts were recognised he studied music seriously and was sent to travel in Italy in the best musical circles. He soon returned to France, where he was was appointed organist first at Avignon and then at Clermont-Ferrand before going to Paris in 1705. Finding little success in Paris, he returned to Dijon and took over his father's post as organist. He subsequently worked at Lyons before returning to Clermont-Ferrand. In 1722 he again left for Paris, where his theoretical *Traité de l'harmonie* was published. This gained him some notoriety and brought his name to the attention of musical circles. He now began to make his mark in the theatre and came to occupy a two-fold position: first with Couperin, as one of the great French clavecinistes who were greatly to influence the later French composers; second, as a major figure in French baroque opera who, before Gluck », laid the foundations of true music drama. In the latter he was handicapped by poor libretti and by the stultifying conventions of the time. Although he was an admirer of Lully », especially in the matter of recitative, he offended the contemporary 'Lullistes' by introducing elements of French naturalism into the predominantly severe Italian style of Lully. Rameau increased the range and scope of the orchestra in opera and he also wrote, in the custom still prevailing, the hybrid form of opera-ballet as well as true opera. The former works do not really come within our scope; but we include brief references for guidance, and as they contain fine examples of Rameau's expressive style.

Below: *Rameau's first opera was* Hippolyte et Aricie *in 1733.*

Hippolyte et Aricie
Tragédie in Prologue and 5 Acts.
Text by Abbé Simon Joseph de Pellegrin.
First performance: Paris (Opéra) October 1, 1733.

Notes:
Hippolyte et Aricie was Rameau's first attempt at serious opera. It had been preceded by the *opéras-comique* and the lyric tragedy *Samson*, which were unsuccessful. *Hippolyte* aroused the opposition of the 'Lullistes' (Rameau was to suffer a similar experience in reverse when Pergolesi's » *La Serva Padrona* was given in Paris and the notorious *'guerre des bouffons'* broke out between the supporters of the new light Italian style·and the French classicists, represented by Rameau). After his death, Rameau's art was vindicated; but the confrontation had disturbed him. *Hippolyte et Aricie* thus became something of a spearhead, although the actual 'war' came a little later.

Les Indes Galantes
Ballet héroique in 3 Acts.
Text by Louis Fuzelier.
First performance: Paris (Opéra) August 23, 1735.

Castor et Pollux
Tragédie in 5 Acts.
Text by Pierre Joseph Justin Bernard.
First performance: Paris (Opéra) October 24, 1737.

Notes:
Castor and Pollux was highly successful. It contains a good deal of Rameau's finest and most 'experimental' music. It achieved more than 250 performances in Paris in less than 50 years and was frequently given at the Paris Opéra up to World War II.

Les Fêtes d'Hébé
Ballet in 3 Acts.
Text by Antoine Gautier de Montdorge.
First performance: Paris (Opéra) May 21, 1739.

Le Temple de la Gloire
Fête in 5 Acts.
Text by Voltaire.
First performance: Versailles November 27, 1745.

Zoroastre
Tragédie in 5 Acts.
Text by Louis de Cahusac.
First performance: Paris (Opéra) December 5, 1749.

L'Endriague (1723)
L'Enrôlement d'Arlequin (1726)
La Robe de dissention (1726)
Les Courses de Temple (1734)
Dardanus (1739)

Pandore (1740)
Les Festes d'Hymen (1744)
La Guirlande (1751)
etc.

MAURICE RAVEL
(b. Ciboure 7.3.1875; d. Paris 28.12.1937)

Sometimes loosely paired with Debussy », Ravel was different in almost every respect. In some ways he is closest in creative evolution to the poet W. B. Yeats; both began in the style of the late Romantic era, and each developed in the post-1918 years a more 'modernist' technique. There the parallel ends, but it is worth noting if only because it tends to highlight a direction taken by thought and feeling, and therefore art, following World War I. It had begun before that, of course: Schoenberg », Stravinsky » and Richard Strauss » had each in his way set the death seal on the Romantic movement (although Strauss was to return to something like it). After 1920 Ravel's music became more economical, more concise, more intellectual; but it still remained the production of the same creative faculty that had produced the romantically inclined, more indulgent and luxurious earlier works. Ravel's early life and training produced no conflicts. His family moved to Paris immediately after his birth; he had piano lessons as a child and went eventually to the Paris Conservatoire in 1889. Always a fastidious composer, Ravel wrote comparatively little, but through his transcriptions from one medium to another he made many of his works go a long way. If we disregard a very early operatic project on *Shéhérazade*, a subject which always fascinated him and on

Below: *Ravel's* L'Heure Espagnole *at the Royal Opera House.*

which he later wrote a fine song cycle, Ravel composed two small operas, *L'Heure espagnole* and *L'Enfant et les sortilèges*.

L'Heure Espagnole

Opera in 1 Act.
Text by Franc-Nohain (Maurice Legrand).
First performance: Paris (Opéra-Comique) May 19, 1911. London (Covent Garden) 1919; Chicago 1920; New York 1920; Milan (La Scala) 1929 (with Conchita Supervia).

Notes:
Although it is about Spain and uses Spanish idioms, *L'Heure Espagnole*, like Bizet's » *Carmen*, is not Spanish music but French music set in Spain. It is full of sophisticated wit and subtlety. A musical comedy, Ravel called it, and so it is: superior comedy and superior music.

L'Enfant et les Sortilèges

Opera in 2 Parts.
Text by Colette.
First performance: Monte Carlo, March 21, 1925. Paris (Opéra-Comique) 1926; San Francisco 1930.

Notes:
This opera is difficult to present. It requires a large cast for such a short work, and is so virtually untranslatable that much would be lost in the process. Colette's scenario began as a theme for a ballet submitted to the Paris Opéra. It was then sent to Ravel, who was serving at the time on the Front in World War I. He turned it into an opera and completed it in 1924. It is a moral fairy-story in which the books, toys and furniture that a bad boy has ill-treated turn against him. They only relent when he shows some kindness to an injured squirrel.

NIKOLAI RIMSKY-KORSAKOV
(b. Tikhvin, Novgorod, 18.3.1844; d. St Petersburg 21.6.1908)

Rimsky-Korsakov began his professional life as an officer in the Russian Imperial Navy and remained so until he was 30. All the time, however, he studied music and began composing. His first symphony, written mostly while he was away on service duty, was a considerable success when Balakirev conducted it in the St Petersburg Music School in December 1865. Rimsky-Korsakov resigned from the navy in 1873, though he had been appointed professor of composition at the St Petersburg Conservatoire two years earlier. He lived to be a powerful and lasting influence on Russian musical life. He was a great master of orchestration and also had a reputation for editing and 'completing' other

...mposers' operas, notably those of Mussorgsky » and Borodin
. Rimsky-Korsakov himself composed 17 operas, mostly on
Russian historical or legendary themes. Many brought out the
fantastic, often humorous side of the Russian character, but
they have not been all that widely appreciated outside Russia.

Above: *Nikolai Rimsky-Korsakov.*

The Maid of Pskov (Pskovityanka)
Opera in 4 Acts.
Text by Rimsky-Korsakov after Lev Alexandrovich Mey's play.
*First performance: St Petersburg (Maryinsky Theatre) January 13, 1873. 2nd
revision, St Petersburg (Panayevsky Theatre) April 18, 1895. Paris, 1909;
London (Drury Lane), 1913.*

Mlada
*Opera-Ballet by Rimsky-Korsakov, Borodin, Cui, Mussorgsky, Minkus
(unfinished).*
Text by V. A. Krilov.
First performance: None recorded (compl. 1872).

A May Night (Msiskaya Noch)
Opera in 3 Acts.
Text by Rimsky-Korsakov after Gogol.
*First performance: St Petersburg (Maryinsky Theatre) January 21, 1880. London
(Drury Lane) 1914; Oxford (in English) 1931.*

Notes:
This was Rimsky-Korsakov's second opera. He wrote operas in
three categories, the 'Peasant', the 'Heroic' and the 'Fantastic',
this one falling into the first. The role of the Mayor was
originally created by Stravinsky's father.

The Snow Maiden (Snegurochka)
Opera in Prologue and 4 Acts.
Text by Rimsky-Korsakov after N. Ostrovsky's play.
*First performance: St Petersburg (Maryinsky Theatre) February 10, 1882. New
York (Metropolitan) 1922; London (Sadler's Wells) 1933.*

Notes:
This is one of Rimsky-Korsakov's 'fantastic' operas and is
perhaps the most lyrical and varied. As well as writing often in a
broadly folk style, Rimsky-Korsakov also introduces some
genuine Russian folk tunes. He was enchanted by Ostrovsky's
fairy-tale of the coming of spring, and wrote the score in an
unusually short time.

Mlada
Opera (see Mlada above).
Text adapted from Krilov's for ballet-opera (1872).
First performance: St Petersburg (Maryinsky Theatre) November 1, 1892.

Notes:
Mlada began as a composite opera-ballet by Rimsky-Korsakov,
Cui, Mussorgsky », Borodin » and Minkus, but it never made
much headway. In 1892 Rimsky-Korsakov recast the libretto
and set it himself.

Christmas Eve (Notch Pered Rozhdestvom)
Opera in 4 Acts.
Text by Rimsky-Korsakov after Gogol.
First performance: St Petersburg (Maryinsky Theatre) December 10, 1895.

Sadko
Opera in 4 Acts.
Text by Rimsky-Korsakov and V. I. Belsky.
First performance: Moscow (Solodovnikov Theatre) January 7, 1898.

The Tsar's Bride (Tsarskays Nevesta)
Opera in 4 Acts.
Text by I. F. Tumenev after L. A. Alexandrovich.
First performance: Moscow (Solodovnikov Theatre) November 3, 1899.

Notes:
This tale of a luckless girl whose love is overwhelmed by the
courtship of Tsar Ivan the Terrible is full of typically Russian
inconsistencies and incomprehensibilities, but it is a vital and
stimulating piece. The Tsar's theme which acts as a kind of
leitmotif is an authentic Russian folk theme.

Above: The Tale of Tsar Saltan *at the Bolshoi Theatre, with Petrov.*

The Tale of Tsar Saltan (Skazka o Tsarie Saltanie)

Opera in 4 Acts.
Text by V. I. Belsky after Pushkin.
First performance: Moscow (Solodovnikov Theatre) November 3, 1900. London 1933; New York 1937.

Pan Voyevoda

Opera in 4 Acts.
Text by I. M. Tumenev.
First performance: St Petersburg (Conservatoire) October 16, 1904.

The Legend of the Invisible City of Kitezh and the Maiden Fevronia (Skazhanie o nevidimom gradie Kitezh i dieve Fevronie)

Opera in 4 Acts.
Text by V. I. Belsky after Pushkin.
First performance: St Petersburg (Maryinsky Theatre) February 20, 1907.

The Golden Cockerel (Zolotoy Petushok) (Coq d'Or)

Opera in 3 Acts.
Text by V. I. Belsky.
First performance: Moscow (Solodovnikov Theatre) October 20, 1909.

Notes:
For some peculiar reason the censors refused to sanction the first performance of this, Rimsky-Korsakov's last opera, and it was not given until after the composer's death. Its magnificent coloured spectacle and dramatic point have long made it a popular international success. The Orchestral Suite is also a popular favourite.

Mozart and Salieri (1898)   *Kashchey the Immortal (1902)*
Servilia (1902)

GIOACCHINO ROSSINI

(b. Pesaro 29.2.1792; d. Passy (Paris) 13.11.1868)

Rossini, like Bellini » and Donizetti », was one of the three b
names in Italian opera in the early part of the 19th century. H
joined a theatre as accompanist and singer at the age of 13. At 15
he had already started to compose and went to the Liceo
Musicale in Bologna, where he studied counterpoint with Padre
Mattei and cello with Cavedagni. In 1808 his cantata *Il pianto
d'armonia sulla morte d'Orfeo* won first prize there, and two
years later his first comic opera *La cambiale di matrimonio* was
produced at the Teatro San Moisè in Venice. From then Rossini
went from success to success; his progress was triumphant as
opera after opera spread his fame throughout Europe . . . and
filled his purse. He was best known for his *buffa*, or comic,
operas; but he also had successes in the field of Italian *opera
seria* and in the loose tradition of French grand historical opera.
A tendency to work too hastily and leave things to the last
moment, so that he had to pillage his own works for inspiration,
hardly dented his reputation. Then, at the age of 37, Rossini
virtually retired from composing and spent the rest of his days
enjoying himself. He lived in Bologna and Paris, had a mistress
(Olympe Pellissier), and entertained his friends lavishly.
Although he composed no more operas, Rossini still wrote a few
more works, including his *Stabat Mater* and the *Petite Messe
solennelle*. Also, he was active in the encouragement of singing
and took seriously his duties as Director of the Bologna Liceo,

Below: *Gioacchino Rossini (1792-1868) — an early portrait.*

til 1847 when he was forced to leave due to political upheaval. He left Bologna, lived for a time in Florence, but returned to Paris in 1855 and spent the rest of his life there.

La Cambiale di matrimonio (The Marriage Market)

Comic Opera in 1 Act.
Text by Gaetano Rossi.
First performance: Venice (Teatro San Moisè) November 3, 1810.

Notes:
Rossini's first comic opera, composed when he was 18, already sets his typical tone and style. The story, wildly unbelievable, concerns Slook, a Canadian tycoon, who is in England looking for a bride. He makes a marriage contract with Fanny, but she is in love with Eduardo, so Slook magnanimously releases her. The piece is a rarity nowadays, and the only complete recording, commissioned by the publishing firm of Ricordi, has long been unobtainable.

L'Inganno Felice (The Happy Deceit)

Comic Opera in 1 Act.
Text by Giuseppe Foppa.
First performance: Venice (Teatro San Moisè) January 8, 1812.

La Scala di seta (The Silken Ladder)

Comic Opera in 1 Act.
Text by Gaetano Rossi after Planard's 'L'Echelle de soie'.
First performance: Venice (Teatro San Moisè) May 9, 1812.

Notes:
This little piece has a famous overture which is generally thought to include the first appearance of the 'Rossini crescendo'.

Il Signor Bruschino

Comic Opera in 1 Act.
Text by Giuseppe Foppa.
First performance: Venice (Teatro San Moisè) January 1813.

Notes:
A typically involved plot of mistaken identities and frustrated love affairs—a true operatic farce made digestible by some delightful music in Rossini's most jovial vein, as typified by the popular overture.

Tancredi

Opera Seria in 3 Acts.
Text by Gaetano Rossi after Tasso and Voltaire.
First performance: Venice (Teatro La Fenice) February 6, 1813.

L'Italiana in Algeri (The Italian girl in Algiers)

Comic Opera in 2 Acts.
Text by Angelo Anelli.
First performance: Venice (Teatro San Benedetto) May 22, 1813.

Notes:
Rossini wrote this work at top speed, completing the score in less than a month. Its style and structure are based on the *commedia dell'arte* instead of formal operatic practice. It was an immediate success and reveals Rossini's genius in full flood.

Il Turco in Italia (The Turk in Italy)

Comic Opera in 2 Acts.
Text by Felice Romani.
First performance: Milan (La Scala)·August 14, 1814. London (King's Theatre) 1821; New York 1826.

Notes:
The opera is these days given in 3 Acts instead of the original 2. There is no other change in the structure or story.

Elisabetta, Regina d'Inghilterra

Opera Seria in 2 Acts.
Text by Giovanni Schmidt.
First performance: Naples (Teatro San Carlo) October 4, 1815. London 1818; Paris 1822.

Notes:
In this opera, Rossini made two innovations: he supported the recitatives with orchestral accompaniment, and wrote out the vocal ornaments. For the overture, he 'borrowed' his own overture from the opera *Aureliano in Palmira* (1813). Indeed, two years after writing *Elisabetta* he purloined the same overture for his *Il Barbiere di Siviglia*. Also, one of Elisabetta's arias has a striking similarity to one in *Il Barbiere*.

Torvaldo e Dorliska

Comic Opera in 2 Acts.
Text by Cesare Sterbini.
First performance: Rome (Teatro Valle) December 26, 1815.

Il Barbiere di Siviglia (The Barber of Seville)

Comic Opera in 2 Acts.
Text by Cesare Sterbini after Beaumarchais.
First performance: Rome (Teatro Argentina) February 20, 1816. London (Haymarket) 1818; New York (in English) 1819.

Notes:
The first performance of *The Barber* was a failure, partly

Above: *Henriette Sontag was a famous Rosina, in London 1828.*

because of the popularity of Paisiello's » opera on the same subject. But other reasons contributed to its failure: the bad production, and many signs of carelessness in the score. By the next night all the problems had been ironed out, and *The Barber* was launched upon its happy way.

Otello, ossia il Moro di Venezia

Opera in 3 Acts.
Text by Marchese Francesco Berio di Salsa after Shakespeare.
First performance: Naples (Teatro del Fondo) December 12, 1816. London 1822; New York 1826.

La Cenerentola, ossia La Bontà in Trionfo

Comic Opera in 2 Acts.
Text by Jacopo Ferretti after Etienne's French libretto.
First performance: Rome (Teatro Valle) January 25, 1817. London (Haymarket) 1820; New York 1826.

Notes:

La Cenerentola is full of rich Rossini humour and brilliant vocal writing, with sparkling ensembles. The name part is written for a *coloratura* contralto, a rare specimen. As with Rosina in *The Barber*, originally for mezzo, the part has often been appropriated by sopranos; but today the tendency is to return to Rossini's original conception.

153

La Gazza Ladra (The Thieving Magpie)

Opera in 3 Acts.
Text by Giovanni Gherardini after d'Aubigny and Caigniez' French melodrama
'La Pie Voleuse'.
First performance: Milan (La Scala) May 31, 1817. London (King's Theatre) 1821;
New York (in French) 1831.

Mosè in Egitto (Moses in Egypt)

Opera in 4 Acts.
Text by Andrea Leone Tottola.
First performance: Naples (Teatro San Carlo) March 5, 1818. Revised version in
French with text by G. L. Balochi and V. J. E. de Jouy, as Moïse et Pharon, Paris
(Opéra) March 26, 1827.

Notes:

Rossini substantially revised and re-wrote the opera for Paris, and it is the later version which is usually heard, though to an Italian text. The famous prayer, 'Dal tuo stellato soglio' did not appear in the first performance but was added for the Naples revival a year later.

La Donna del Lago (The Lady of the Lake)

Opera in 2 Acts.
Text by A. L. Tottola after Sir Walter Scott.
First performance: Naples (Teatro San Carlo) September 24, 1819. London
(King's Theatre) 1823; New York (in French) 1829.

Semiramide

Opera seria in 2 Acts.
Text by Gaetano Rossi after Voltaire.
First performance: Venice (Teatro La Fenice) February 3, 1823. London
(Haymarket) 1824; New York (Metropolitan) 1893.

Notes:

Wagner's jibe about *Semiramide* exhibiting the worst traits of Italian opera was no doubt a piece of special pleading. It might not be a masterpiece; but it does contain a marvellous chance for soprano-contralto combination. Melba and Sofia Scalchi sang it at the Metropolitan in 1893, and Sutherland and Simionato in 1962. Rossini, never a slouch, wrote the opera in three weeks.

Le Siège de Corinthe (The Siege of Corinth)

Opera in 3 Acts.
Text by Alexandre Soumet and Luigi Balocchi.
First performance: Paris (Opéra) October 9, 1826.

Notes:

The Siege of Corinth is a French revision of an Italian *opera seria*, *Maometto II*, produced in Naples in 1820. The story concerns the siege of Greeks by the Turks in 1459.

Le Comte Ory

Opera in 2 Acts.
Text by Eugène Scribe and Charles Gaspard Delestre-Poirson.
First performance: Paris (Opéra) August 20, 1827. London (King's Theatre) 1828.

Notes:
With the exception of *Guillaume Tell* (produced the following year) this is Rossini's only truly French opera—the others being adaptations of earlier Italian works. It has been a great favourite in France but neglected elsewhere until the Glyndebourne revival under Vittorio Gui in 1954.

Guillaume Tell (William Tell)

Opera seria in 3 Acts.
Text by Victor Joseph Étienne de Jouy and Hippolyte Louis Florent Bis, after Schiller.
First performance: Paris (Opéra) August 3, 1829. London (Drury Lane) 1830. New York (in English) 1831.

Notes:
The overture is an eternal favourite and a fine piece. The opera itself is perhaps too long, but being Rossini's last opera, he probably intended it to be his masterpiece, however long.

L'equivoco stravagante (1811)
Demetrio e Polibio (1812)
La Pietra del paragone (1812)
L'occasione fa il ladro (1812)
Aureliano in Palmira (1813)
Sigismondo (1814)
La gazzetta (1816)
Armida (1817)
Adelaida di Borgogna (1817)
Ermione (1819)
Ricciardo e Zoraide (1818)

Edoardo e Cristina (1819)
Bianca e Faliero (1819)
Maometto II (1820)
Matilde de Shabran (1821)
Zelmira (1822)
Il viaggio a Reims (1825)
Adino (1826)
Moïse (1827)
Robert Bruce (1846)
etc.

CAMILLE SAINT-SAËNS
(b. Paris 9.10.1835; d. Algiers 16.12.1921)

A child prodigy, Saint-Saëns began serious musical study at seven and in 1848 went to the Paris Conservatoire as an organ scholar, and studied under Benoist and Halévy   . In 1853 he was appointed organist at the Saint-Merry church, Paris; in 1857 he was appointed to the Madeleine. He was a prolific composer who, although largely traditional and conservative in his own work, was a champion of new French music. He travelled widely and was immensely successful, a fact which led to some jealousy. An impeccable craftsman with a near infallible sense of form and apt orchestration, Saint-Saëns composed 12 operas, of which only *Samson et Dalila* has survived with any degree of international recognition.

Samson et Dalila

Opera in 3 Acts.
Text by Ferdinand Lemaire.
First performance: Weimar (Court Theatre) (in German) December 2, 1877.
Paris 1890.

Notes:
Because of its biblical subject, the opera was banned by the French authorities and was first produced in Germany. It was finally presented in France in 1890. It was for long a popular favourite in the world's opera houses, attracting many of the leading singers of the day: Kirkby Lunn appeared in the 1909 Covent Garden revival; Caruso at the Metropolitan in 1915.

Above: Samson et Dalila *produced at the Paris Opéra in 1976.*

Ascanio

Opera in 5 Acts.
Text by Louis Gallet after Dumas and Paul Meurice's 'Benvenuto Cellini'.
First performance: Paris (Opéra) March 21, 1890.

La Princesse jaune (1872)
Le Timbre d'argent (1877)
Étienne Marcel (1879)
Henry VIII (1883)
Proserpine (1887)
Phryné (1893)

Frédégonde (1895)
Les Barbares (1901)
Hélène (1904)
L'Ancêtre (1906)
Déjanire (1911)
etc.

ANTONIO SALIERI

(b. Legnano 18.8.1750; d. Vienna 7.5.1825)

Salieri's principal claim to fame is the saga of his intrigues against Mozart ». It was once said he poisoned him, but that theory has long been discredited. Salieri was, in many ways, a generous and helpful man, and after Mozart's death helped his son. Yet he deliberately undermined Mozart's chances and reputation. He composed much in the style of the day, with skill but no marked originality. His many operas were quite successful but are now forgotten. Beethoven » dedicated his Op.12 violin sonatas to

Salieri and also consulted him on small matters of music, even calling himself at one time 'Salieri's pupil'.

La Fiera di Venezia
Opera in 3 Acts.
Text by Gaston Boccherini.
First performance:
Vienna (Hoftheater) 1772.

Below: *Antonio Salieri (1750-1825) was a dominant figure in the Italian opera of his time, a rival of Mozart's. Title page of* Tarare, *Paris 1787.*

Le donne letterate (1770)
Armida (1771)
La moda (1771)
Il barone de Rocca Antica (1772)
La secchia rapita (1772)
La locandiera (1773)
La calamita de' cuori (1774)
La finta scema (1775)
Delmita e Daliso (1776)
Europa riconosciuta (1778)
La partenza inaspettata (1779)
Il talismano (1779)
La dama pastorella (1780)
Der Rauchfangkehrer (1781)
Semiramide (1782)
Les Danaïdes (1784)
Il ricco d'un giorno (1784)

La grotta di Trofonio (1785)
Prima la musica e poi le parole (1786)
Les Horaces (1786)
Tarare (1787)
Il pastor fido (1789)
Il mondo alla rovescia (1795)
Eraclito e Democrito (1795)
Palmira, regina di Persia (1795)
Il Moro (1796)
Falstaff (1799)
Cesare in Farmacusa (1800)
Angiolina (1800)
Annibale in Capua (1801)
Die Negersclaven (1804)
etc.

Above: *Alessandro Scarlatti, who lived and worked mainly in Naples.*

ALESSANDRO SCARLATTI
(b. Palermo 2.5.1660; d. Naples 24.10.1725)

One of the most important figures in the evolution of opera, Alessandro Scarlatti may, with justice, be called the founder not only of the Neapolitan school of opera but of the entire classical style in concerted music as brought to perfection by Haydn ≫, Mozart ≫ and ultimately Beethoven ≫. He began his professional life in Rome, where his family moved when he was 12. Restrictions of the church hampered his operatic composing, but he continued to write operas for patrons in other cities. In all he composed some 115 operas, most of which contain music of great beauty but not all of which survive. In addition he wrote important chamber cantatas. Scarlatti's operatic innovations came through his 'ensemble of perplexity'—a device whereby several people sing at the same time about the same thing. Ultimately, this led to the quartets, quintets and sextets of later composers such as Donizetti ≫, Bellini ≫ and Rossini ≫, and Verdi ≫ and Wagner ≫ in their turn. Scarlatti's son, Domenico, is famed for his rich series of harpsichord sonatas but he does not figure in operatic history.

L'Honestà ne gli Amori
Opera in 3 Acts.
Text by Felice Parnasso.
First performance: Rome (Palazzo Bernini) February 6, 1680.

l Pompeo
Opera seria in 3 Acts.
Text by Niccolo Minato.
First performance: Rome (Teatro Colonna) January 25, 1683.

Gli equivoci in Amore, overa la Rosaura
Opera in 3 Acts.
Text by Giovanni Battista Lucini.
First performance: Rome (French Embassy, Palazzo della Cancelleria) December, 1690.

Pirro e Demetrio
Opera in 3 Acts.
Text by Adriano Morselli.
First performance: Naples (Teatro San Bartolomeo) January 28, 1694.

Flavio Cuniberto
Opera in 3 Acts.
Text by Matteo Noris.
First performance: Rome (Teatro Capranica) 1696.

La Donna Ancora e Fedele
Opera in 3 Acts.
Text by Domenico Filippo Contini.
First performance: Naples (Teatro San Bartolomeo) 1698.

Gli equivoci nel sembiante (1679)
Psiche (1683)
Turno Aricino (1704)
Lucio Manlio (1705)
Il gran Tamerlano (1706)
Mitridate Eupatore (1707)
Il trionfo dell libertà (1707)

Tigrane (1715)
Carlo,re d'Alemagna (1716)
Il trionfo dell'onore (1718)
Cambise (1719)
Griselda (1721)
La virtù negli amore (1721)
etc.

ARNOLD SCHOENBERG
(b. Vienna 13.9.1874; d. Los Angeles 13.7.1951)

It is impossible to exaggerate the importance of Schoenberg and his work. He showed early musical ability and studied for a while with Alexander von Zemlinsky (whose sister he married), but was otherwise self-taught. He worked for a time in cabaret and operetta while advancing his own compositions, and held several teaching posts in Germany and Austria until Nazi policies forced him to leave for America, where he spent the rest of his life, teaching and composing. Schoenberg was an inspiring teacher, and among his famous pupils were Alban Berg » and Anton Webern. Schoenberg began composing in a post-Wagnerian manner, pushing chromaticism to its limits, in works such as *Verklärte Nacht*, *Gurrelieder* and the symphonic

Above: *Schoenberg's* Moses und Aron *at Covent Garden in 1965.*

poem *Pelléas und Mélisande.* His first Chamber Symphony (1906) was a key work, creating a considerable furore when it appeared. He finally rejected tonality with his Three Pieces for piano, Op.11 (1908), and confirmed this with the Three Orchestral Pieces, Op.16. He then moved over to serialism. Although he did not invent it, he made it his own, and the leading force in modern music. He wrote a large amount of music in various forms, including two operas, the comedy *Von Heute auf Morgen* and the powerful! *Moses und Aron*; he completed the text shortly before his death. There is also *Erwartung*, styled a 'monodrama' for single voice and orchestra which is sometimes described as an opera, and *Die glückliche Hand*—a 'drama mit Musik' (1910-13).

Von Heute auf Morgen (From Today to Tomorrow)
Opera in 1 Act.
Text by 'Max Blonda' (Gertrud Kolisch, Schoenberg's second wife).
First performance: Frankfurt February 1, 1930. Naples 1953; Holland Festival 1958.

Notes:
Although written in the 12-tone style and often complex, the work is expressive and enjoyable, with some highly effective scoring.

Moses und Aron
Opera in 3 Acts.
Text by Schoenberg.
First performance: Hamburg Nordwestdeutsche Rundfunk (broadcast) March 12, 1954.

Notes:
Schoenberg began work on his opera in 1931 and finished Act 2 in 1932. He did not return to it for nearly 20 years. The text to Act 3 was finished but was never set to music.

FRANZ SCHUBERT
(b. Vienna 31.1.1797; d. Vienna 19.11.1828)

As one of the greatest songwriters of all time, it might be expected that Schubert would turn his hand to writing opera; indeed, he did, but success in the theatre constantly eluded him. Although some of his narrative songs contradict the contention, it has often been said that Schubert lacked dramatic sense and, whether by mischance or misjudgment, he never found a libretto that give him the proper inspiration or produced an effective work for the stage. As the theatre was the one medium that could bring real wealth and fame to a composer in Schubert's time, his failure in this realm was of real concern. Between 1814 and 1827 he produced a number of dramatic scores, fragments and sketches, never losing the hope of operatic success. He composed or began 17 stage works in all, but the only opera to be properly staged in his lifetime was the singspiel *Die Zwillingsbrüder*, commissioned by the Kärntnerthor Theater, which managed seven performances. Others have since been given isolated performances, but with the exception of one or two pleasant overtures, and the incidental music to *Rosamunde*, Schubert's stage works are still neglected. They may never find a place in the theatre, unless substantially edited and rewritten, but they contain delightful music which is well worth hearing.

Das Teufels Lustschloss
Opera in 3 Acts.
Text by Auguste von Kotzebue.
No known performances.

Der Vierjährige Posten
Singspiel in 1 Act.
Text by Theodor Körner.
First performance: Dresden, September 23, 1896.

Claudine von Villa Bella
Singspiel in 3 Acts.
Text by Goethe.
First performance (Act 1): Vienna (Gemeindehaus Wieden) April 26, 1913 (Acts 2 and 3 were lost in a fire).

Below: *Franz Schubert had little success with his 15 stage works.*

Die Freunde von Salamanka
Singspiel in 2 Acts.
Text by Johann Mayrhofer.
First performance (extracts): Vienna (Musikvereinssaal) December 19, 1875.
Halle, May 6, 1928.

Notes:
The Act 2 duet (No. 12) 'Gelagert unter'm hellen Dach' is immediately familiar as the melody upon which Schubert based the delightful variations of the 4th movement of his Octet, written some nine years later.

Die Bürgschaft
Opera in 3 Acts.
Text by unknown.
First performance: Vienna (Wiener Schubertbund) March 7, 1908.

Die Zwillingsbrüder
Singspiel in 1 Act.
Text by Georg von Hofmann, based on 'Les Deux Valentins'.
First performance: Vienna (Kärntnerthor Theater) June 14, 1820.

Alfonso und Estrella
Opera in 3 Acts.
Text by Franz von Schober.
First performance (abridged): Weimar, June 24, 1854 (conducted by Franz Liszt).

Notes:
Schubert thought the overture unsuitable for the work and, intending to write another, used the original for the first performance of *Rosamunde* in 1823.

Die Verschworenen
Singspiel in 1 Act.
Text by I. F. Castelli, based on Aristophanes' comedies 'Ecclesiazusae' and 'Lysistrata'.
First performance: (concert) Vienna (Musikvereinsaal) March 1, 1861; (stage) Frankfurt am Main, August 29, 1861.

Note:
The name of the opera was later changed, by order of the censor, to *Der Häusliche Krieg.*

Fierrabras
Opera in 3 Acts.
Text by Joseph Kupelweiser, based on the old French romance 'Fierrabras' and the legend 'Eginhard und Emma'.
First performance: (abridged concert performance) Vienna (Theater in der Josefstadt) May 7, 1835; (stage) Vienna (Redoutensaal) February 9, 1858.

DMITRI SHOSTAKOVICH
(b. St Petersburg 25.9.1906; d. Moscow 9.8.1975)

Shostakovich is the most important Soviet composer after Prokofiev ≫; but whereas half Prokofiev's creative life was spent in the West, Shostakovich was at all times intimately involved with Soviet musical activities. He entered the St Petersburg Conservatoire in 1919, studying with Steinberg, Nikolaiev and Glazunov. By 1925, when he left the Conservatoire, he had already shown his hand as a prolific and original composer. He made an immediate impression with his brilliant and witty First Symphony and continued to develop at a great pace. Throughout his life, Shostakovich tended to conflict with the official 'line', especially during the years of Stalin's dictatorship; despite the familiar acts of obeisance and apparent penance, there was always, as in the famous case of the Fifth Symphony and its "reply to just criticism", a certain sense of irony and irreverence concealed behind the formal gesture. He is best known for his series of symphonies—15 in all—and for an even longer series of string quartets, the medium to which he became most closely attached in his later years. He wrote, like his Soviet contemporaries, a number of 'official' works which, though entirely sincere, are no better and no worse than anyone else's. Shostakovich wrote two operas, both of which

Below: *Shostakovich's* The Nose *at the English National Opera.*

got him into trouble with the authorities, totally contrasted though they are. He left an unfinished project for an opera on Gogol's *The Gamblers*; since this was undertaken in 1942, its abandonment had nothing to do with failing health or approaching death: the increasing grind and tension of the war years, no doubt, had something to do with it. Although the two operas he completed show great merits, along with some less convincing features, it seems likely that symphony and string quartet rather than opera suited Shostakovich's creative gifts best.

163

The Nose
Opera in 3 Acts.
Text by Y. Preis after Gogol.
First performance: Leningrad, January 18, 1930.

Notes:
This brilliant and brittle satire was produced successfully when 'advanced' music was not banned in the Soviet Union. Later critics decided it was a bad joke, inaugurating a period of increasingly abrasive relationships between Soviet composers and critics. The opera dropped out of circulation and, although subsequently revived, has not become fully established, although there was a 1979 production at the English National Opera.

Katerina Ismailova (Lady Macbeth of Mtsensk)
Opera in 4 Acts.
Text by Shostakovich and Y. Preis after Nikolai Leskov.
First performance: Leningrad, January 22, 1934. Moscow 1934; Cleveland 1935; Dusseldorf 1959.

Notes:
The opera caused a famous furore. In 1934 it was warmly praised, but by 1936 the changing political climate led to Shostakovich being denounced as, among other things, bourgeois, formalist, muddled, discordant, incomprehensible and (oddly) 'leftist'. At this time, rehearsals for the Fourth Symphony—with its honourable relationships to both Mahler (Sixth Symphony) and Stravinsky (*Rite of Spring*)—were in progress. Shostakovich immediately withdrew it, replacing it a year later with the more conventional Fifth Symphony. For some years there were rumours of a revised version of the opera, but it eventually appeared with only minor musical and textual changes. Shostakovich's first title was that of Leskov's story, *Lady Macbeth of the District of Mtsensk*; this title continued in use abroad, although *Katerina Ismailova* was the title given when the composer re-edited the work in 1956.

BEDŘICH SMETANA
(b. Litomyšl 2.3.1824; d. Prague 12.5.1884)

Smetana was a musical prodigy, giving his first public piano recital at the age of eight, although at first his parents opposed any idea of a musical career, only yielding when his determination became clear. He went to Prague to study, on a pittance, but after initial hardships was fortunate in securing a post as music master to the family of Count Leopold Thun, on the recommendation of the director of the Conservatoire, J. B. Kittl,

Above: *Smetana led the way in creating Czechoslovakian opera.*

in 1844. He was involved in the abortive Czech uprising against
Austrian rule in 1848, married his childhood sweetheart, the
pianist Kateřina Kolařová, and founded a music school with the
financial help of Liszt, who greatly influenced his development. In 1856 Smetana went to Sweden, where he taught at
Göteborg and became conductor of the Philharmonic Society.
When his wife's health failed, he decided to return to Prague: she
died at Dresden on the way home, in 1859, and he returned to
Sweden for a short time, after marrying Bettina Ferdinandova in
1860. After touring for a year or two, he settled finally in Prague
in 1863, founding another school for national music. In 1864 the
Czech National Theatre was established and he began to write
for it the series of operas on which his principal fame rests,

beginning with *The Brandenburgers in Bohemia*. All Smetana's operas are on Czech national subjects. For this reason, and also because they depend for their full meaning on the original language, they found difficulty in crossing national frontiers, though they had great success at home. But one, *The Bartered Bride*, became an international success, and others, notably *Dalibor*, slowly gained a wider hearing as musical horizons expanded. Smetana's orchestral music, especially the cycle of symphonic poems *Má Vlast*, is widely popular, and his piano music, owing a good deal to Liszt, has also made some headway. He became deaf in 1874, a shattering experience which found musical expression in the string quartet *From My Life*, but continued to compose until he lost his reason, spending the last year of his life in an asylum.

The Brandenburgers in Bohemia (Braniboři v Čechách)

Opera in 3 Acts.
Text by Karel Sabina.
First performance: Prague (Czech Theatre) January 5, 1866.

Notes:

This, Smetana's first patriotic opera, has been likened to *Boris Godunov* in subject matter, though the libretto is flawed and Smetana had not yet found his mature voice.

The Bartered Bride(Prodaná nevěsta)

Opera in 3 Acts.
Text by Karel Sabina.
First performance: Prague (Czech Theatre) May 30, 1866. Revised final version 1869. Chicago 1893; London (Drury Lane) 1895 (in German).

Notes:

The Bartered Bride is a 'folk opera' of the best kind, full of delightful tunes and national dances, with the famous overture setting the mood. But at first it was regarded in Prague as too 'Wagnerian' and not truly nationalistic in spirit.

Dalibor

Opera in 3 Acts.
Text by Joseph Wenzig (in German —trans. Ervín Špindler).
First performance: Prague (National Theatre) May 16, 1868. Vienna (in German) 1892; Chicago 1924.

Notes:

The parallel with *Fidelio* is almost too obvious to remark. 'Rescue' operas were popular everywhere, especially in an atmosphere of oppression and foreign dominance. An alternative ending has Dalibor executed before the attack, in which Milada is killed.

Libuše

Opera in 3 Acts.
Text by Joseph Wenzig (in German —trans. Ervín Špindler).
First performance: Prague (Czech National Theatre) June 11, 1881. Vienna 1924.

Notes:

Libuše was written for the opening of the Czech National Theatre in 1881. Smetana regarded it as a 'festive tableau' rather than an opera, and wanted it to be given only on those occasions for which, because of its close connection with Czech history and national aspirations, it was particularly fitted.

The Two Widows (Dvě vdovy)

Opera in 2 Acts.
Text by Emanuel Züngel after P. J. F. Malefille.
First performance: Prague (Czech National Theatre) March 27, 1874. New version with recitutives, Prague 1878; Hamburg 1881.

Notes:

The opera is a lively comedy in what Smetana himself called 'a distinguished salon style'. It has a number of Mozartean affinities, although its early hearers again complained of Wagnerisms.

The Kiss (Hubička)

Opera in 2 Acts.
Text by Eliška Krásnohorská after Karolina Světlá.
First performance: Prague (Czech National Theatre) November 7, 1876.

Tjemství (The Secret) (1878)   *Viola (1924)*
Čertova stěna (The Devil's Wall) (1882)   *etc.*

GASPARO SPONTINI

(b. Maiolati 14.11.1774; d. Maiolati 24.1.1851)

Spontini was the son of poor peasants and was initially intended for the priesthood, but an uncle's help enabled him to study music. In 1791 he went to the Conservatoire de' Turchini at

Below: *Spontini believed his masterpiece was* Olympie *(1819).*

Naples. He produced his first opera, *I puntigli delle donne*, in Rome in 1796, and thereafter produced a series of operas, mostly in Naples and Paris. He held a number of official appointments, including court composer to the Empress Joséphine in Paris, where he first went in 1803. He was Napoleon's favourite composer, and in 1807 his opera *La Vestale* scored a triumphant success in Paris: it has remained his one lasting work. He was called to the court of Friedrich Wilhelm III in Berlin in 1820; but after that monarch's death his position became impossible, partly because of Spontini's quarrelsome and litigious behaviour. He returned to Paris in 1842, after being threatened with imprisonment in Berlin, visited various continental centres, and returned to his home town where he died three years after becoming deaf. He composed many operas; but only *La Vestale* has maintained a tenuous hold.

La Vestale

Opera in 3 Acts.
Text by Etienne de Jouy.
First performance: Paris (Opéra) December 16, 1807. Milan (La Scala) 1824; London (King's Theatre) 1926; New York (Metropolitan) 1925.

Notes:
The libretto was originally written for Boïeldieu » and later rejected by Méhul. The score contains some famous numbers and brought Spontini instant fame. In the following 50 years it was given at the Paris Opéra 213 times and was produced in most of the world's major opera houses. It was a vehicle for the art of the late Maria Callas, who sang it at La Scala in 1955. Spontini himself claimed that he should be regarded as the successor to Gluck » rather than as the rival of Cherubini ». The subject also recalls Bellini », as does the emotional tone of several of the set pieces.

Agnes von Hohenstaufen

Opera in 3 Acts.
Text by Ernst Raupach.
First performance: Berlin (Court Opera) June 12, 1829. (Act 1 alone, May 28, 1827).

Notes:
This was Spontini's last completed opera. A re-write of his earlier opera on an English subject, *Milton*, did not materialise except in fragments. Ernst Raupach was official librettist to the Berlin Opera, and together he and Spontini set to work on an operatic work based on German medieval history. True to his reputation for thoroughness, Spontini embarked upon an intensive study of the period. The subject was a new departure for him, but he was not deterred. The long Act 1 was given by

itself before the opera was completed. The complete opera was produced to coincide with the wedding celebrations of Prince Wilhelm, who later became Emperor Wilhelm I of the newly-united Germany. Spontini was not satisfied with its original form: accordingly, the Baron von Lichtenstein and others reworked the libretto and Spontini himself revised the musical score. The new version was given on December 6, 1837.

Li puntigli delle donne (1796)
Adelina Senese (1797)
L'eroismo ridicolo (1798)
L'isola disabitati (1798)
Chi più guarda meno vede (1798)
Teseo reconosciuto (1798)
La finta filosofa (1799)
La fuga in maschera (1800)
I quadri parlante (1800)
Gli Elisi delusi (1800)
Sofronia ed Olindo (1800)
Il finto pittore (1800)

Gli amanti in cimento (1801)
Le metamorfosi di Pasquale (1802)
La Petite Maison (1804)
Milton (1804)
Julie (1805)
Fernand Cortez (1809)
Pélage (1814)
Les Dieux rivaux (1816)
Olympie (1819/21)
Nurmahal (1822)
Alcidor (1825)
etc.

Above: *Johann Strauss, whose* Die Fledermaus *is the apex of Viennese operetta.*

JOHANN STRAUSS
(b. Vienna 25.10.1825; d. Vienna 3.6.1899)

The son of a famous composer and orchestra leader, also named Johann Strauss, who tried at first to dissuade his son from following in his footsteps. Music was too much in the family blood, however, and soon young Strauss was running an orchestra; and eventually, when his father died, he took over his orchestra. He became renowned as a composer of music for the ballroom, especially for his fine concert waltzes which were admired by composers such as Brahms and Wagner » and made him an international figure. Initially, Strauss was not very interested in the theatre, and it was his wife who persuaded him to try his hand. His first attempt, *Die Lustigen Weiber von Wien* written in 1869, came to nothing because Strauss could not get the actress he wanted for the leading part. *Indigo* in 1871 was a moderate success, and *Karneval in Rom* in 1873 was a failure. Then, a year later, a splendid libretto inspired him to write *Die Fledermaus*—possibly the greatest Viennese operetta of all time. In spite of many other attempts, Strauss did not achieve this quality again until *Der Zigeunerbaron*. Again Strauss hit a rich vein with, in some ways, an even more substantial score than *Die Fledermaus*. His final success was *Wiener Blut* but by then he was old, and left the completion of the score to other hands and did not live to see the first performance.

Indigo und die Vierzig Räuber
Operetta in 3 Acts.
Text by Maximilian Steiner.
First performance: Vienna (Theater an der Wien) February 10, 1871.

Karneval in Rom (Der Carneval in Rom)
Operetta in 3 Acts.
Text by Josef Braun.
First performance: Vienna (Theater an der Wien) March 1, 1873.

Die Fledermaus
Operetta in 3 Acts.
Text by Carl Haffner and Richard Genée, based on the comedy 'Le Reveillon' by Henri Meilhac and Ludovic Halévy.
First performance: Vienna (Theater an der Wien) April 5, 1874. Berlin 1874; Paris 1875; London 1876; New York 1879; Vienna (Opera) 1894.

Below: Die Fledermaus *at the Royal Opera House.*

Cagliostro in Wien

Operetta in 3 Acts.
Text by F. Zell and Richard Genée.
First performance: Vienna (Theater an der Wien) February 27, 1875.

Prinz Methusalem

Operetta in 3 Acts.
Text by Carl Treumann.
First performance:
Vienna (Carltheater) January 3, 1877.

Blinde Kuh

Operetta in 3 Acts.
Text by Rudolf Kneisel.
First performance: Vienna (Theater an der Wien) December 18, 1878.

Der Spitzentuch der Königin

Operetta in 3 Acts.
Text by Heinrich Bohrmann-Riegen and Richard Genée.
First performance: Vienna (Theater an der Wien) October 1, 1880.

Left: Eine Nacht in Venedig; *an English National Opera production.*

Eine Nacht in Venedig

Operetta in 3 Acts.
Text by F. Zell and Richard Genée.
First performance: Berlin (Friedrich-Wilhelm Städtisches Theater) October 3, 1883. Vienna (Theater an der Wien) 1883. New version by Hubert Marischka and Erich Korngold, Vienna (State Opera) 1923. London 1944.

Der Zigeunerbaron

Operetta in 3 Acts.
Text by Ignaz Schnitzer, based on the novel 'Saffi' by Maurus Jókai.
First performance: Vienna (Theater an der Wien) October 24, 1885.

Ritter Pasman

Operetta in 3 Acts.
Text by Lajos Dóczy.
First performance: Vienna (Hofoperntheater) January 1, 1892.

Der Waldmeister

Operetta in 2 Acts.
Text by Gustav Davis.
First performance: Vienna (Theater an der Wien) December 4, 1895.

Wiener Blut

Operetta in 3 Acts.
Text by Victor Léon and Leo Stein. Score completed by Adolf Müller, Jr.
First performance: Vienna (Carltheater) October 25, 1899.

Notes:
Strauss was asked in 1899 to write this opera, but was unwell and no longer had strength for the effort. But he helped to select the music from his once popular but now neglected pieces; the

waltz 'Wiener Blut', written in 1873, was used as the main theme. The task of putting the score together was left to Adolf Müller, Jr (a composer himself, and musical director at the Theater an der Wien) who worked well with librettists Léon and Stein. Opening four months after Strauss's death, it was a total failure. Staged again in 1901 it was a popular success and has remained a close rival to the composer's best operettas.

Der lustige Krieg (1881) *Jabuka (1894)*
Simplizius (1887) *Die Göttin der Vernunft (1897)*
Fürstin Ninetta (1893) *etc.*

RICHARD STRAUSS
(b. Munich 11.6.1864; d. Garmisch-Partenkirchen 8.9.1949)

One of the last major composers to reach the hearts and minds of the larger public—and certainly one of the last German composers to do so—Strauss was also among the last prolific composers of opera. He has been called a man who began as a 'progressive' and ended as a 'conservative'; but the fact that those words need placing in quotes shows that they are not essentially relevant. Richard Strauss had a long life and was active to its end: he survived long enough to see the collapse and destruction of the Germany he knew and loved. He was a musician through and through; the son of a horn player and a prodigy who had published compositions to his credit from the age of ten. His earliest influences stemmed from both Brahms and Wagner » —and also from Mozart ». He held many conducting and directing appointments in Germany, becoming conductor of the Berlin Philharmonic Orchestra in 1894, and was always a prolific composer in all forms, including opera. His career was interrupted but not seriously affected by two World Wars. He married Pauline de Ahna, the singer who had taken the lead in his first opera, *Guntram*, in 1894, and they remained together until Strauss's death in 1949; Frau Strauss died in 1950. Strauss's operas are rich and varied. The most significant single fact in the series is his close collaboration with his librettist, the poet Hugo von Hofmannsthal, who wrote all Strauss's texts from *Elektra* (1906) to *Arabella* (1930). Hofmannsthal's death in 1929 was a severe blow, but it did not prevent Strauss from continuing to write opera: Stefan Zweig, and then Josef Gregor, became his collaborators. A valuable insight into the collaboration between Strauss and Hofmannsthal comes from their letters, issued in English as *The Correspondence between Richard Strauss and Hugo von Hofmannsthal*, translated by Hanns Hammelemann and Ewald Osers (Collins, London, 1961). Even if Strauss frequently seemed to share the German failing of being unable to distinguish between a commonplace idea and a genuinely powerful one, he knew a good libretto

Above: *Richard Strauss in an 1898 portrait when he was aged 34.*

when he saw it: the quality of Hofmannsthal's text is an integral part of the quality of Strauss's operas.

Guntram
Opera in 3 Acts.
Text by Strauss.
First performance: Weimar (Court Opera) May 10, 1894. Revised 1940.

Salome
Opera in 1 Act.
Text from Oscar Wilde's play, translated into German by Hedwig Lachmann.
First performance: Dresden (Court Opera) December 9, 1905. Manhattan Opera (in French) 1909; London (Covent Garden) 1910.

Notes:
The subject and its treatment not unnaturally caused trouble in the early days: the opera was banned in England at one time and was withdrawn after one performance at the Metropolitan, New York. The Dance of the Seven Veils in particular gave offence, and the whole opera was regarded as degraded and obscene. However, it soon surmounted these difficulties, the vividness and dramatic point of the music overriding puritanical objections.

Elektra
Opera in 1 Act.
Text by Hugo von Hofmannsthal after Sophocles.
First performance: Dresden (Court Opera) January 25, 1909. New York (Manhattan Opera) (in French) 1910; London (Covent Garden) 1910.

Notes:
The harsh dissonances and 'cruelty' of *Elektra* have long since been accepted. Many have seen in this opera and in *Salome* an accurate representation of the disintegration that was overtaking Europe at the time, reaching its apotheosis in 1914.

Der Rosenkavalier (The Knight of the Rose)
Opera in 3 Acts.
Text by Hugo von Hofmannsthal.
First performance: Dresden (Court Opera) January 26, 1911. London (Covent Garden) 1913; New York (Metropolitan) 1913.

Notes:
The most popular and frequently performed German opera written this century, *Der Rosenkavalier*'s enduring appeal rests on three principal factors: a profusion of memorable melody, including the famous waltz sequences; an unmistakable style and elegance; and the marvellously drawn figure of the Marschallin, so full of emotional grace and generous humanity. It also has that aura of nostalgia which, especially nowadays, has an irresistible appeal. Nor should one forget the genuine comic elements.

Ariadne auf Naxos
Opera in Prologue and 1 Act.
Text by Hugo von Hofmannsthal.
First performance: Vienna (State Opera) October 4, 1916. London (Covent Garden) 1924; New York 1934.

Notes:
This is the second, restructured version. Originally the opera section was designed to go with a shortened performance of Molière's *Le Bourgeois Gentilhomme*, for which Strauss had written some splendid incidental music. However, the idea proved impractical: the mixing of a play and an opera put an unacceptable strain on theatre resources and audience endurance alike. The original was given in Stuttgart on October 25, 1912, and at once the impracticalities were apparent. It was played quite widely in that form, and has been occasionally revived. There are some who think it the better of the two; among them Sir Thomas Beecham, who conducted the first London performance at His Majesty's in 1913. But the second version was generally accepted, if not as definitive. Recordings are always of

Above: Ariadne auf Naxos *was first staged at Covent Garden in 1924.*

the second version. The orchestra is reduced, from the inflation of much of Strauss, to a mere 39 players.

Die Frau ohne Schatten (The Woman Without a Shadow)
Opera in 3 Acts.
Text by Hugo von Hofmannsthal.
First performance: Vienna (State Opera) October 10, 1919. Salzburg 1932; San Francisco 1959; London 1966.

Notes:
Die Frau ohne Schatten is the most complex and 'difficult' of the Strauss/Hofmannsthal operas. The text, taken from Hofmannsthal's own play, is full of symbolism. Central to the theme is the purification of the two couples: the excessively proud and remote on one side; the too earthy and acquisitive on the other. But it goes much deeper than that. Strauss's music, too, is complex and ambitious.

Intermezzo
Opera in 2 Acts.
Text by Richard Strauss.
First performance: Dresden (State Opera) November 4, 1924. New York 1963; Edinburgh Festival 1965.

Die Ägyptische Helena (The Egyptian Helen)
Opera in 2 Acts.
Text by Hugo von Hofmannsthal.
First performance: Dresden (State Opera) June 6, 1928. New York 1967.

Arabella
Opera in 3 Acts.
Text by Hugo von Hofmannsthal.
First performance: Dresden (State Opera) July 1, 1933. London (Covent Garden) 1934; New York (Metropolitan) 1955.

Notes:

Arabella does not quite repeat the success of *Der Rosenkavalier*. It has many of the same ingredients, including waltzes, but lacks, in its more frivolous tone, the overall charm and depth of its famous predecessor. There are some fine character sketches and some lovely musical passages. *Arabella* was the last of the Strauss/Hofmannsthal collaborations. In July 1929, Hofmannsthal's son, Franz, committed suicide, and Hofmannsthal himself died of a stroke on the day of the funeral.

Daphne
Opera in 1 Act.
Text by Josef Gregor.
First performance: Dresden (State Opera) October 15, 1938. New York 1960.

Notes:

Strauss, like Nietzsche, was devoted to the ideal of Greek classical mythology. This late opera was one result of that devotion. It is a splendid, somewhat neglected, piece.

Die Liebe der Danae (The Love of Danae)
Opera in 3 Acts.
Text by Josef Gregor.
First performance: Salzburg August 14, 1952. London (Covent Garden) 1953.

Notes:

The opera was written in 1938-40 and planned for production in 1944. But after the plot on Hitler's life, all German theatres were closed: although there was a dress rehearsal before an audience, it was eight years before it was produced, at Salzburg. The recording is of that performance.

Capriccio
Opera in 1 Act.
Text by Clemens Krauss.
First performance: Munich (State Opera) October 28, 1942. New York (Juilliard School) 1954; London (Covent Garden) 1953; Glyndebourne 1963.

Notes:

Capriccio was Strauss's last opera, though it was produced before *Die Liebe der Danae*. Although it is in one Act, *Capriccio* lasts for more than two hours without a break. It is concerned principally with arguments over the relative importance of words and music in opera, cunningly linked to human entanglements.

Feuersnot (1901)   *Friedenstag (1938)*
Der schweigsame Frau (1935)

IGOR STRAVINSKY

(b. Oranienbaum, St Petersburg 17.6.1882; d. New York 6.4.1971)

The agile and active mind of Stravinsky acted as something of a catalyst in modern music. No man, with the possible exception of Wagner », exercised a greater influence over his age; no musical faculty was more receptive to what was going on around it and what had preceded it. Stravinsky's neo-classicism not only embraced a contemporary style of great vigour and clarity, but also entailed a delving into the past and a creative transmutation of what he found there. The son of a bass singer at the Imperial Russian Opera, Stravinsky became a pupil of Rimsky-Korsakov » in 1907, when he already had a number of

Above: *Igor Stravinsky, a truly international composer.*

compositions to his credit. But there is no doubt that his developing style was greatly influenced by that master's teaching and example, most notably in the ballet *The Firebird*, with which Stravinsky began his long association with Diaghilev and the Ballets Russes. The famous furore in Paris over *The Rite of Spring* occurred in 1913, and between the wars came the period of neo-classicism—sometimes dubbed 'Back to Bach'— with Stravinsky in the van. His constantly questing musical intelligence did not remain for long in one creative groove; yet through all the apparent changes of direction, he remained totally and unmistakably himself. His music is as immediately recognisable as any ever written. He long represented the opposite pole to Schoenberg » in modern music, as an opponent of serialism, but in the latter part of his career he again changed direction and embraced with total conviction a form of serialism nearer to Webern than that of Schoenberg himself.

Intensely Russian by temperament and sympathies, Stravinsky was for the first part of his life a deep-dyed nationalist in the line of Mussorgsky », Glinka » and Tchaikovsky »; yet he was at the same time music's great cosmopolitan, whose magpie mind ranged over the entire spectrum of the art in search of material. Although essentially a man of the theatre, Stravinsky's major contribution was to the ballet rather than opera. He wrote one full-scale opera, *The Rake's Progress*, and one opera-buffa, *Mavra*. To these may be added *Le Rossignol*, an early work later made into a ballet, and the 'opera-oratorio' *Oedipus Rex*; as well as the television opera *The Flood*. Other works for the theatre, apart from the ballets proper, like *L'Histoire du Soldat, Renard* and *Perséphone*, fall into no clearly defined category. They can hardly be classed as opera, though they are often characterised as such for want of any better description; if only because with the exception of *L'Histoire du Soldat*, they contain singing parts. Stravinsky's fertile imagination often produced works which do not come within any traditional definition.

Le Rossignol (The Nightingale)
Opera in 3 Acts.
Text by Stravinsky and Stepan Nikolayevich Mitusov after Hans Andersen.
First performance: Paris (Opéra) May 26, 1914. London (Drury Lane) 1914; New York (Metropolitan) 1926.

Mavra
Opera buffa in 1 Act.
Text by Boris Kochno after Pushkin.
First performance: Paris (Opéra) June 3, 1922. Berlin 1928; London (BBC) 1934.

Notes:
This preposterous tale, based on Pushkin's *The House at Kolomna*, appealed to Stravinsky as a vehicle for an operatic skit. He was much attracted to the traditional Russo-Italian style of opera and, further, wished to demonstrate the falsity of certain 'picturesque' ideas about Russia, particularly to those of his French friends who were taken in by the 'tourist-office orientalism' of certain influential Russians. *Mavra* is dedicated 'to the memory of Tchaikovsky, Glinka, and Pushkin'. The music is deliberately *demodé*.

Renard
Burlesque for the stage.
Text by Stravinsky; French version by C. F. Ramuz.
First performance: Paris (Opéra) June 3, 1922 (double bill with Mavra*). New York (concert) 1923; London (BBC) 1935.*

Notes:
Renard, based on Russian folk tales, was intended for the

Princess de Polignac's private theatre, along with Falla's » *El retablo de Maese Pedro* and Erik Satie's *Socrate*; but only Falla's work was actually given there. The score contains a part for the cembalon; Stravinsky had heard this instrument in a café in Geneva and was much taken with its sound.

Oedipus Rex
Opera-oratorio in 2 Acts.
Text by Jean Cocteau after Sophocles, translated into Latin by J. Danielou.
First performance: (as oratorio) Paris (Théâtre Sarah Bernhardt) May 30, 1927.
(Stage production) Vienna 1928; New York 1931; London (Queen's Hall) 1936.

Notes:
Oedipus Rex is not an opera in any accepted sense of the term; but it is a powerful piece of drama. If it is highly stylised, it is also highly effective. In some ways it harks back to the style and forms of Monteverdi ». It can be staged or given in concert: this makes little difference, there is virtually no 'action'. The text is in Latin and the Narrator is instructed to speak in the language of the audience.

The Rake's Progress
Opera in 3 Acts and Epilogue.
Text by W. H. Auden and Chester Kallman after Hogarth.
First performance: Venice (Teatro La Fenice) September 11, 1951.

Notes:
The Rake's Progress was Stravinsky's first and only full-scale opera. *Le Rossignol*, though in 3 Acts, is short and comparatively undeveloped. Also, *The Rake* is the first English text set by Stravinsky. At the Venice première in 1951, Elisabeth Schwarzkopf sang Anne Trulove and Jennie Tourel was Baba the Turk. Fritz Reiner was the conductor of the New York (Metropolitan) première on May 14, 1953, with a cast that later made the first recording, issued in the UK by Philips (ABL3055/7) and conducted by the composer.

(Sir) ARTHUR SULLIVAN
(b. London 13.5.1842; d. London 22.11.1900)

Arthur Sullivan was the second son of Thomas Sullivan, clarinettist and bandmaster of the Royal Military College, Sandhurst. Showing an early inclination for music, Arthur was entered as a chorister of the Chapel Royal. He sold his first composition at the age of 11 and won a scholarship to the Royal Academy of Music. While there, he composed incidental music for *The Tempest* and quickly earned recognition as a new hope for English music. Throughout his career he was to be torn

(SIR) ARTHUR SULLIVAN

Above: *Arthur Sullivan, best known for his comic operas with Gilbert.*

between the expectation that he would become a respectable, 'serious' composer and the commercial success of his comic operas. Sullivan's first venture in this field was in collaboration with F. C. Burnand, on *Cox and Box*. The famous collaboration with W. S. Gilbert started with *Thespis* in 1871 and really got under way with *Trial by Jury* in 1875. A regular succession of comic operas followed, the finest and most sparkling to come from an English composer; 'serious' composition tended to take a back seat. After the highly successful *The Mikado* in 1885, there were various quarrels between the collaborators and the partnership often seemed likely to break up, but they continued to work together until *Utopia Limited* in 1892. In the meantime, Sullivan satisfied his higher aspirations with the oratorio *The Golden Legend* and the unsuccessful grand opera *Ivanhoe* in 1890. Both Sullivan and Gilbert tried to work with other collaborators, but without much success. The Savoy operas have never lost their appeal and have rarely been surpassed. Their popularity has overshadowed the other excellent music, now being rediscovered, that Sullivan wrote.

Cox and Box

Triumviretta in 1 Act.
Text by F. C. Burnand:
First (private) performance: November 1866. Manchester (Prince's) December 17, 1866; London (private) April 27, 1867; London (St George's Hall) 1869.

Thespis

Extravaganza in 2 Acts.
Text by W. S. Gilbert.
First performance: London (Gaiety) December 26, 1871.

Notes:

This was the first collaboration between Gilbert and Sullivan, commissioned by John Hollingshead of the Gaiety Theatre. Often labelled a failure, it did in fact achieve 63 performances. The libretto has survived, though apparently lacking some dialogue and lyrics as compared to the stage performance, and was reprinted in 1911, though Gilbert died that year without being able to check the proofs. The score was lost, the only surviving elements being 'Little Maid of Arcadee', which was published in 1872 as a drawing-room ballad, and 'Climbing over rocky mountains', which Sullivan re-used in *The Pirates of Penzance*. It is possible that other items were utilised elsewhere. It is now heard in a reconstructed version, using music from Sullivan's less-known operas and some unpublished music.

Trial by Jury

Dramatic Cantata in 1 Act.
Text by W. S. Gilbert.
First performance: London (Royalty) March 25, 1875.

The Zoo

Musical Folly in 1 Act.
Text by Bolton Rowe.
First performance: London (St James's Theatre) June 5, 1875.

The Sorcerer

Comic Opera in 2 Acts.
Text by W. S. Gilbert.
First performance: London (Opéra-Comique Theatre) November 17, 1877. New York 1879.

H.M.S. Pinafore

Comic Opera in 2 Acts.
Text by W. S. Gilbert.
First performance: London (Opéra-Comique Theatre) May 25, 1878. New York 1878.

The Pirates of Penzance

Comic Opera in 2 Acts.
Text by W. S. Gilbert.
First performance: Paignton (Royal Bijou Theatre) December 30, 1879. New York (Fifth Avenue Theater) December 31, 1879; London (Opéra-Comique Theatre) April 3, 1880.

Patience
Comic opera in 2 Acts.
Text by W. S. Gilbert.
First performance: London (Opéra-Comique Theatre) April 23, 1881; (Savoy) October 10, 1881; New York 1881.

Iolanthe
Comic Opera in 2 Acts.
Text by W. S. Gilbert.
First performance: London (Savoy) November 25, 1882. New York 1882.

Princess Ida
Comic Opera in 3 Acts.
Text by W. S. Gilbert.
First performance: London (Savoy) January 5, 1884. New York 1884; London (Savoy) 1922.

The Mikado
Comic Opera in 2 Acts.
Text by W. S. Gilbert.
First performance: London (Savoy) March 14, 1885. New York 1885.

Ruddigore
Comic Opera in 2 Acts.
Text by W. S. Gilbert.
First performance: London (Savoy) January 22, 1887. New York 1887.

The Yeomen of the Guard
Comic Opera in 2 Acts.
Text by W. S. Gilbert.
First performance: London (Savoy) October 3, 1888. New York 1888.

The Gondoliers
Comic Opera in 2 Acts.
Text by W. S. Gilbert.
First performance: London (Savoy) December 7, 1889. New York 1890.

Notes:
This was the last real success of the Gilbert and Sullivan partnership. Both men were in ill health, and quarrelling over finances; their next two operas failed to achieve the old sparkle.

Ivanhoe
Opera in 5 Acts.
Text by Julian Sturgis, based on Sir Walter Scott.
First performance: London (Royal English Opera House) January 31, 1891.

Above: *Kenneth Sandford as King Paramount, despot of* Utopia Limited.

Utopia Limited
Comic Opera in 2 Acts.
Text by W. S. Gilbert.
First performance: London (Savoy) October 7, 1893. New York 1894.

The Grand Duke
Comic Opera in 2 Acts.
Text by W. S. Gilbert.
First performance: London (Savoy) March 7, 1896.

The Rose of Persia
Comic Opera in 2 Acts.
Text by Basil Hood.
First performance: London (Savoy) November 29, 1899. New York 1900.

The Contrabandista (1867)
Haddon Hall (1892)
The Chieftain (1894)

The Beauty Stone (1898)
The Emerald Isle (1901)
etc.

KAROL SZYMANOWSKI
(b. Timashkovka 6.10.1882; d. Lausanne 29.3.1937)

The first Polish composer after Chopin to make a major international reputation (the only possible exception was Moniuszko), Szymanowski was born into a cultured and wealthy landowning Polish family in the Ukraine. He showed early musical gifts which were encouraged, especially because he suffered an accident in childhood which did permanent damage to one of his legs and prevented him from carrying on a normal, active life. He entered the Warsaw Conservatoire in 1903 and lived for a time in Berlin. His family was ruined by the Russian Revolution of 1917 and thereafter he suffered much poverty, in spite of a growing reputation as a pianist and composer, until he was appointed professor of composition and later director of the Warsaw State Conservatoire. His health, never robust, finally broke down in 1936; despite treatment in France and Switzerland he died of tuberculosis in the Lausanne clinic where he had been obliged to spend his last days. Szymanowski's music is unique in various respects. His travels, especially to Africa, widened his musical horizons and influenced his development. Chopin and Scriabin, and later Richard Strauss », contributed to the original synthesis he gradually developed; but Wagner » was from the beginning a major source of inspiration. A combination of individual vision and folk cultures lies at the heart of Szymanowski's creative force. What he achieved lies outside any of the familiar schools or movements in 20th century music; this is particularly evident in his well-known first violin concerto and also in his opera *King Roger*. This, apart from the single Act *Hagith*, constitutes his only venture into operatic composition (there is also an operetta, but it was not finished and never performed).

King Roger (Król Roger)
Opera in 3 Acts.
Text by Szymanowski and Jaroslav Iwaszkiewicz.
First performance: Warsaw, June 19, 1926. London (New Opera Company) 1975.

Notes:
The central theme of the opera, the dichotomy of Christianity and paganism, is represented both by the setting, Sicily, and the opening scene in the Byzantine cathedral, with its complementary aspects of East and West. The libretto is something of a jumble; but the music is original and frequently of surpassing beauty. Szymanowski's mysticism is a permeating force, but the intellectual side of the story, and of the eponymous central character, is somewhat played down. Thus, the pantheism of the Shepherd's philosophy has a stronger impact than the Christian ideal. One suspects that the composer—not only here, but throughout his work—was more on the side of pantheism than of theism.

PYOTR ILYICH TCHAIKOVSKY

(b. Kamsko-Votinsk 7.5.1840; d. St Petersburg 6.11.1893)

Above: *Tchaikovsky was unable to resist the call of opera.*

Like several other Russian composers and writers, Tchaikovsky began as an amateur, while working in a government department. He learnt music as a child: he could play the piano competently by the age of six, and later studied with Zaremba. The turning point came in 1862, when he entered the newly-founded Conservatoire at St Petersburg, and then, three years later, went as professor of composition to the Moscow Conservatoire, itself newly-founded by Nicolas Rubinstein. Tchaikovsky became familiar with the nationalist school, 'The Five', but although he sympathised with some of their objectives, he was never one of them. His sympathies led him to the theatre, though he was not a natural dramatist in the mould of Verdi » or Wagner ». His tendency to compose episodically (as in his famous recognition of his weaknesses as a symphonist) is strongly in evidence in his theatre music, opera and ballet. Structurally, his operas may be faulted; but they are, at their best, tremendously effective, full of superb music and, as always with Tchaikovsky, unforgettable melody. A strain of genuine pathos informs many of the scenes. They are hugely popular in Russia, and at least two have gained, and retained, an international foothold. Of the others, scenes and excerpts add to the general delight given by the music of this most popular of composers. It was once the fashion to sneer at Tchaikovsky, largely because he wrote good tunes, but this is no longer the case. He stands in the world's eye as in Stravinsky's » estimation: 'the largest talent in Russia, and, with the exception of Mussorgsky's », the truest'. He wrote ten operas in

185

all: indeed, his first recognition came from opera and he persevered with the form to the end of his life. He was not always lucky, either in his subject or its handling — and still less its reception, especially early in his career; but he persevered, despite subjective doubts. He said it took heroism to refrain from writing operas, and confessed frankly that 'I don't possess this heroism'.

The Voyevode (A Dream on the Volga)
Opera in 3 Acts.
Text by Tchaikovsky and A. N. Ostrovsky, after the latter's play.
First performance: Moscow (Bolshoi Theatre) February 11, 1869.

The Oprichnik
Opera in 2 Acts.
Text by Tchaikovsky, based on the play by Ivan Ivanovich Lazhechnikov.
First performance: St Petersburg (Maryinsky Theatre) April 24, 1874.

Yevgeny Onyegin (Eugene Onegin)
Opera in 3 Acts.
Text by Tchaikovsky and Konstantin S. Shilovsky after Pushkin.
First performance: Moscow (Maly Theatre) March 29, 1879.

Notes:
This is Tchaikovsky's most popular opera; he called it 'Lyric Scenes', indicating its episodic structure. But he found exactly the right music for Pushkin's verse-novel. He appears to have begun from the famous Letter Scene and worked both ways from that.

The Maid of Orleans
Opera in 4 Acts.
Text by Tchaikovsky based on Vassily Andreyevich Zhukovsky's Russian version of Schiller's play.
First performance: St Petersburg (Maryinsky Theatre) February 25, 1881.

Notes:
The story is implausible and totally unhistorical. Schiller's drama was even worse: it ended with Joan's escape, her rescue of the French King and her death in battle. The whole Joan/Lionel entanglement is apochryphal. Tchaikovsky made a few alterations from his source material, notably in the last Act, from Jules Barbier's *Jeanne d'Arc*. The opera has taken more hard knocks from critics than it deserves. It has not, to be sure, the charm and conviction of *Eugene Onegin* or of the later *Pikovaya Dama*. Nor does the characteristic episodic treatment suit a historical drama. But the central figure of Joan appealed to Tchaikovsky and aroused his sympathy. For that alone, the opera is worth attention.

Mazeppa

Opera in 3 Acts.
Text by Tchaikovsky and Victor Petrovich Burenin after Pushkin.
First performance: Moscow (Bolshoi Theatre) February 15, 1884. Liverpool
1888; New York 1933.

Pikovaya Dama (The Queen of Spades/ Pique Dame)

Opera in 3 Acts.
Text by Tchaikovsky and Modest Tchaikovsky after Pushkin.
First performance: St Petersburg (Maryinsky Theatre) December 19, 1890.

Notes:

This opera is more dramatically structured than *Eugene Onegin* or *The Maid*. Pushkin's poem needed a good deal of modification for stage purposes; but this was skilfully accomplished. The scene by the canal in Act 3 was inserted by Tchaikovsky against his brother Modest's advice. Apparently Tchaikovsky felt that a woman was needed to fill out the Act, and the audience would want to know what became of Lisa. The emotional temper of the opera is parallel to that of the last two symphonies, which it bisects chronologically.

Yolanta (Iolanthe)

Opera in 1 Act.
Text by Modest Tchaikovsky based on Henrik Hertz's play.
First performance: St Petersburg (Maryinsky Theatre) December 18, 1892.
London (Camden Festival) 1968.

Notes:

Yolanta was originally designed as a single Act complement to *The Nutcracker*, the two to be given on the same evening. The libretto, by Modest Tchaikovsky, was based on Zvantsev's translation of Hertz's play *Kong Renés Datter*, itself derived from Hans Andersen.

Undine (1869)
Vakula the Smith (1876)
Tcherevichky (1887)

The Sorceress (1887)
etc.

GEORG PHILIPP TELEMANN

(b. Magdeburg 14.3.1681; d. Hamburg 25.6.1767)

Long-lived and enormously prolific, Telemann was largely self-taught: he studied the scores of his great contemporaries and predecessors, including Lully ». He studied languages and science at the University of Leipzig, where he went in 1700, and four years later was appointed organist of the New Church. He also founded a 'Collegium musicum' among the students. The

Above: *Georg Philipp Telemann, composer of some 40 operas.*

same year he briefly served one prince and then entered the service of another at Einstadt. Tours through Europe helped give his style a marked eclecticism with a total mastery of all forms of music. He was not an original musical thinker, but he was a thoroughly learned one. His principal fame, until the Baroque revival of the post-1945 years, centred on his association with J. S. Bach, who was appointed Cantor at Leipzig after Telemann, the first choice, had declined the offer. The two had already encountered each other during Bach's time at Weimar. Telemann was godfather to one of Bach's children. In 1721 he was appointed music director in Hamburg, remaining there for the rest of his long life. The gradual emergence of Telemann's reputation has revealed that, among other things, he produced what is in effect the first German comic opera. He wrote some 45 operas in all, but apart from *Pimpinone* little is heard of them.

Pimpinone
Intermezzo in 1 Act.
Text by Johann Philipp Praetorius.
First performance: Hamburg September 27, 1725.

Notes:
This lively little work preceded Gay's » *The Beggar's Opera* by two years and Pergolesi's » *La serva padrona*, which it more or less resembles, by eight years. Telemann's characteristic style, based upon German counterpoint and Italian aria, is here deployed with a light touch. The story concerns only two characters, a foolish old man and an alert serving wench. The plot makes the familiar point that there is no fool like an old fool. Pimpinone is at the mercy of the servant girl, Vespetta, who twists him round her little finger: after a few hilarious incidents, she marries him and takes control of the purse-strings.

Der gedultige Socrates (1721)
Der neu-modischer Liebhaber Damon (1724)
Miriways (1728)

Flavius Bertaridus König
der Longobarden (1729)
etc.

AMBROISE THOMAS

(b. Metz 5.8.1811; d. Paris 12.2.1896)

As a child, Thomas began to study music with his father. He entered the Paris Conservatoire in 1828 and won the first prize for piano in 1829 and the Prix de Rome in 1832. On returning from Rome he began to gain success in Paris at the Opéra-Comique and later at the Opéra. He wrote a little non-operatic music, including two masses and some instrumental pieces, but his fame rests upon his operas, and on *Mignon* in particular. However, like some other French composers, he had ambitions beyond his creative means: he would tackle subjects from Shakespeare, Dante and Goethe instead of concentrating on the lighter, melodious type of work for which his talents best fitted him. Thomas was appointed Chevalier of the Legion of Honour in 1845 and received the Grand Cross in 1894. He became professor of composition at the Conservatoire in 1852 and Director in 1871.

Le Caïd

Opera in 2 Acts.
Text by Thomas Sauvage.
First performance: Paris (Opéra-Comique) January 3, 1849.

Raymond, ou le Secret de la Reine

Opera in 3 Acts.
Text by Adolphe de Leuven and Joseph Bernard Rosier.
First performance: Paris (Opéra-Comique) June 5, 1851.

Mignon

Opera in 3 Acts.
Text by Jules Barbier and Michel Carré based on Goethe's 'Wilhelm Meister'.
First performance: Paris (Opéra-Comique) November 17, 1866. New York 1871; London (Sadler's Wells) 1932.

Notes:
Mignon has lost a good deal of its one-time popularity, though its charms can still excite admiration. Its decline has been largely brought about by over-exposure of its famous set numbers, which are numerous. Alternative endings have been used, one tragic.

Hamlet

Opera in 5 Acts.
Text by Jules Barbier and Michel Carré based on Shakespeare.
First performance: Paris (Opéra) March 9, 1868.

La Double Échelle (1837)
Le Perruquier de la régence (1838)
Le Panier fleuri (1839)
Le Comte de Carmagnola (1841)
Le Guerillero (1842)
Carline (1840)
Angélique et Médeor (1843)
Mina (1843)
Le Songe d'un nuit d'eté (1850)
La Tonelli (1853)
La Cour de Célimène (1855)
Psyché (1878)
Le Carnaval de Venice (1857)
Le Roman d'Elvire (1860)
Gille et Gillotin (1874)
Françoise de Rimini (1882)
etc.

VIRGIL THOMSON
(b. Kansas City 25.11.1896)

Virgil Thomson has written music of every conceivable form and style—much of it full of a simple charm too long absent from serious music. He has drawn inspiration from many popular sources, notably from Cajun folksong, to the wider fields of American folk song and jazz. He studied music with Nadia Boulanger at Harvard, where he was also Assistant Instructor from 1920-25. He was organist and choirmaster at King's Chapel, Boston, 1922-23, and in 1925 went to live in Paris where he stayed for 15 years. He became a friend of Satie, who influenced his music, and of Gertrude Stein, who wrote the libretti for two of his operas, *Four Saints in Three Acts* (1934) and *The Mother of Us All* (1946). On his return to America in 1940, Thomson became chief music critic of the *New York Herald Tribune*, where he remained until 1954, writing in an entertaining and penetrating style. In general, Thomson's perceptive knowledge of music produces a sense of timelessness in his operas, always with that sure touch of the Thomson hand: at once tender and wry, sentimental and humorous. He is particularly successful in capturing the essence of American speech in his music.

Right: *The American composer Virgil Thomson.*

Four Saints in Three Acts
Opera in 4 Acts.
Text by Gertrude Stein.
First (stage) performance: Hartford,
Connecticut (Avery Memorial Theater)
February 8, 1934. New York 1934 and
1952; Paris 1952.

Notes:
The composer has said: 'Please do not try to construe the works of this opera literally or to seek in it any abstruse symbolism. If, by means of the poet's liberties with logic and the composer's constant use of the simplest elements in our musical vernacular, something is here evoked of the child-like gaiety and mystical strength of lives devoted in common to a non-materialistic end, the authors will consider their message to have been communicated'. The four saints of the title are Saint Teresa of Avila, Saint Ignatius Loyola of 16th-century Spain, and their confidants, invented characters, Saint Settlement and Saint Chavez. A male and female compère, a small chorus of named saints and a larger chorus of un-named saints completes the cast. The compères talk to the audience about the progress of the opera, where the figures move in a landscape giving a 'panoramic view of sainthood'. From all this arises what Gilbert Chase has described as 'a lovely work—a masterpiece in originality and invention'. There is little or no logic in Stein's libretto but Thomson brings the language to life with great clarity and precision.

190

The Mother of Us All

Opera in 2 Acts.
Text by Gertrude Stein.
First performance: New York (Brander Matthews Hall, Columbia University)
May 7, 1947.

Notes:
The theme of the opera is the struggle for women's rights in America centred round the figure of Susan B. Anthony, who wrote a four-volume 'History of Women's Suffrage' and, around the 1870s, led women's marches and was frequently arrested. The opera deals with Susan B. Anthony's history and draws in such diverse characters as Daniel Webster, Andrew Johnson (17th President), John Quincy Adams (6th President), stage star Lillian Russell and Ulysses Grant (who mentions Eisenhower). These people debate the issues in a series of *non sequiturs* that defeat any synopsis. As in *Four Saints in Three Acts* there are two compères who discuss the whole proceeding; in this case two characters called Gertrude S. and Virgil T. Again the simple charms of Thomson's music make the score one of outstanding beauty and clarity.

(Sir) MICHAEL TIPPETT
(b. London 2.1.1905)

The most visionary of living English composers and a profound musical and metaphysical thinker, Tippett's achievement is remarkable by any standards. Biographical details are few and totally unostentatious. He studied at the Royal College under R. O. Morris and Charles Wood, then worked in the music department of London County Council and was music director

Below: *Tippett's* The Midsummer Marriage *at the Royal Opera House.*

at Morley College, where his performances of Purcell's »church music were extremely important, both for Purcell's reputation and for his own. Indeed, his artistic nature polarises on an ardent and individual vein of lyricism and polyphonic complexity. This has sometimes led to stylistic dichotomy; but the internal tensions which result have also produced extremely stimulating and potent music. This is frequently difficult, not because it is wilfully obscure, but in the sense in which Shelley said of Plato that he is obscure only because he is profound. Some of Tippett's earlier music was in danger of being 'difficult' beyond its profundity; but as he evolved his personal idiom and worked out his personal problems, his music clarified—although it did not necessarily become 'easy listening'. Each of his three operas is a key work in his development, and each is paralleled by other kinds of music. An ardent pacifist and a man of great spiritual insight, Sir Michael Tippett is a deeply enriching individual in everything he says or does.

The Midsummer Marriage

Opera in 3 Acts.
Text by Tippett.
First performance: London (Covent Garden) January 27, 1955.

Notes:
Tippett describes *The Midsummer Marriage* as a 'Quest' opera, in the manner of *The Magic Flute*. The text was written under the influence of T. S. Eliot's poetic drama. Mark and Jenifer, with their overtones of ancient history and mythology, are contrasted with the more earthy Jack and Bella—the 'marvellous' couple and the 'everyday' couple. When it first appeared the opera excited differing responses: the complexity of the libretto which, it was suggested, even Tippett himself did not fully understand, was contrasted with the luminous beauty of the music. The music itself was related to Tippett's contemporary works in other forms, including the Piano Concerto and the First Piano Sonata.

King Priam

Opera in 3 Acts.
Text by Tippett.
First performance: Coventry, May 29, 1962. London (Covent Garden) 1962; Karlsruhe 1963.

Notes:
As *The Midsummer Marriage* is related musically to the Piano Concerto and other works of a similar nature, so *King Priam* was related to such works as the Concerto for Orchestra and the Second Piano Sonata in a further evolution of the composer's creative force, now requiring a curbing of the former lyricism and a hardening of the structural and expressive edges.

The Knot Garden

Opera in 3 Acts.
Text by Tippett.
First performance: London (Covent Garden) December 2, 1970.

Notes:
The structure, metaphysical as well as musical, is delineated in the subheadings of the three Acts: Confrontation—Labyrinth—Charade. The opera is again complex, though in a totally different manner from *The Midsummer Marriage*. It is a play in the true sense: that is: a 'thing in itself', a self-contained piece of drama with an independent existence, not a simulation of 'real life'. The subtleties and complexities can be clarified at several points in recording, where certain effects and intentions can be realised in a way not wholly possible in the theatre. This is not an unusual situation. The influence of T.S. Eliot, whom Tippett has described as 'my artistic father', is again apparent.

RALPH VAUGHAN WILLIAMS

(b. Down Ampney, Glos., 12.10.1872; d. London 26.8.1958)

Vaughan Williams was born in Gloucestershire, son of a clergyman, educated at Charterhouse and Cambridge, and studied music at the Royal College. Later he went to Europe to study with Max Bruch and, briefly, with Maurice Ravel ». He

Below: *Portrait of Ralph Vaughan Williams by Sir Gerald Kelly.*

developed slowly, forging an individual style and technique out of various elements, the most important being English folk song and Tudor church music. He served in the army in World War I (while on active service in France, he first conceived his Pastoral symphony, often regarded as his most inwardly English work), and afterwards became professor of composition at the Royal College. Otherwise, he held no major official position, though he was always active in the organisation and encouragement of festivals and other public and private musical events. He composed a great deal of vocal music, solo and choral, and six operas. Although he was not, perhaps, a natural composer of opera, he could adapt himself to it when necessary. He represents in its purest form in music the poet W. B. Yeat's description of the English mind as 'meditative, rich, deliberate'. His first operatic piece, *The Shepherds of the Delectable Mountains*, called a 'pastoral episode', was later incorporated into his masterpiece *The Pilgrim's Progress*, both being derived from John Bunyan's book.

Hugh the Drover
Ballad opera in 2 Acts.
Text by Harold Child.
First performance: London (RCM) July 11, 1922. London (His Majesty's) 1924; Toronto 1932; New York 1952.

Notes:
Besides original, folk-song based material, Vaughan Williams incorporated a number of English folk songs direct into his score. The story, which takes place at a country fair at a small town in Gloucestershire during the time of the Napoleonic wars, concerns Hugh's love for Mary, who is already engaged to John; John's accusation, after a fight, that Hugh is a French spy; Hugh's arrest; Mary's abortive attempt to release him; the soldiers' recognition of Hugh as a well-known patriot; and the release of Hugh and Mary to enjoy freedom and love.

Sir John in Love
Opera in 4 Acts.
Text from Shakespeare's 'The Merry Wives of Windsor'.
First performance: London (RCM) March 21, 1929.

Notes:
Shakespeare's *Merry Wives* and the 'fat knight' (Vaughan Williams's original title for his opera) have afforded much grist to the operatic mill. As well as the famous productions of Verdi » and Nicolai », there are a number of others, less famous but not all deserving oblivion. Vaughan Williams bends the emphasis to his own ends here and there, and incorporates some English

folk songs and Elizabethan songs, the most famous example being the use of 'Greensleeves' at the beginning of Act 2. He omits the basket-ducking episode and makes the climax the discovery of Mistress Page behind the arras. He also places more emphasis than does Verdi on the love between Ann and Fenton. Vaughan Williams wrote the opera 'for his own enjoyment', according to his widow, and as 'the height of impertinence', according to himself.

The Poisoned Kiss (or The Empress and the Necromancer)

Opera in 3 Acts.
Text by Evelyn Sharp after Richard Garnett and Nathaniel Hawthorne.
First performance: Cambridge May 12, 1936. London 1936.

Riders to the Sea

Opera in 1 Act.
Text from play by J. M. Synge.
First performance: London (RCM) November 30, 1937. Cambridge (Arts Theatre) 1938.

Notes:
The text is an almost verbatim rendering of Synge's drama, which was inspired by an incident he witnessed on the Irish coast. It is Vaughan Williams's most successful operatic work, a small masterpiece of music drama, at once poetic and realistic.

The Pilgrim's Progress

Morality in Prologue, 4 Acts and Epilogue.
Text by John Bunyan.
First performance: London (Covent Garden) April 26, 1951.

Notes:
The Pilgrim's Progress, together with the Fifth symphony, to which it is thematically related, is absolutely central to Vaughan Williams's life work. It took more than 40 years to complete and when it was coolly received at its first performance, Vaughan Williams said that although people did not like it, and perhaps never would, it was the kind of opera he wanted to write. Although it was regarded as more or less unstageable, he was adamant that it was a work for the theatre — not the cathedral or concert hall. Vaughan Williams said that he used the name 'Pilgrim', rather than Bunyan's 'Christian', because he wanted the work to address itself to all men of all beliefs, not to Christians only. In this he followed in the footsteps of Elgar, who declared that *The Dream of Gerontius* was not to be considered in any sense sectarian.

GIUSEPPE VERDI

(b. Le Roncole, Busseto 10.10.1813; d. Milan 27.1.1901)

Italy's greatest opera composer came of poor peasant stock. He had his first lessons from the parish priest and heard his first music in the church where he became a choirboy and later organist. He was 11 when he was sent to school in Busetto, where he was befriended by Antonio Barezzi, a wealthy merchant, who took the boy into his house and promoted his further musical studies, most notably under the *maestro di cappella* at the church of San Bartolomeo. He was already beginning to compose and had several pieces performed. In 1832 he was sent to Milan but was rejected by the Conservatoire. In 1836 he married Barezzi's daughter Margherita, but during the two years 1838-40 she and her two children died. In 1839, Verdi's first opera, *Oberto*, was produced. From then on he composed opera after opera but then, duly honoured, he apparently ceased to compose for the theatre. During 1873/4 he wrote his great *Messa da Requiem* for the first anniversary of the death of the poet-patriot Alessandro Manzoni. Then, in his old age, with an astonishing burst of rejuvenated creativity, he produced his two operatic masterpieces, *Otello* and *Falstaff*.

Oberto, Conte di San Bonifacio

Opera in 2 Acts.
Text by Antonio Piazza, Bartolommeo Merelli and Temistocle Solera.
First performance: Milan (La Scala) November 17, 1839.

Un Giorno di Regno

Opera in 2 Acts.
Text by Felice Romani.
First performance: Milan (La Scala) August 5, 1840.

Notes:
A pretty impossible story. But even here, in his second opera, Verdi makes all that is to be made of it—and the result when well produced is certainly diverting.

Nabucodonosor (Nabucco)

Opera in 4 Acts.
Text by Temistocle Solera.
First performance: Milan (La Scala) March 9, 1842. London 1846; New York 1848.

Notes:
The famous Hebrew Chorus, 'Va, pensiero', was taken up as a national theme of liberation.

I Lombardi alla Prima Crociata

Opera in 4 Acts.
Text by Temistocle Solera based on a romance by Tommaso Gossi.
First performance: Milan (La Scala) February 11, 1843.

Above: *Verdi wrote his first opera in 1836 and his last in 1889.*

Notes:
In 1847 Verdi visited Paris on his way home from London. He was asked to write an opera, and decided to adapt *I Lombardi*. A new French libretto was written by Gustave Vaëz and Alphonse Royer, and the opera was presented as *Jérusalem* at the Opéra on November 26, 1847. The story was considerably altered and the setting moved from Lombardy to Toulouse.

Ernani
Opera in 4 Acts.
Text by Francesco Maria Piave after Victor Hugo's 'Hernani'.
First performance: Venice (Teatro La Fenice) March 9, 1844. London 1845; New York 1847.

I Due Foscari
Opera in 3 Acts.
Text by Francesco Maria Piave based on Byron's 'The Two Foscari'.
First performance: Rome (Teatro Argentina) November 3, 1844. London 1847.

Above: *A production of* I Lombardi *by the Budapest State Opera.*

Giovanna d'Arco
Opera in Prologue and 3 Acts.
Text by Temistocle Solera based on Schiller's 'Jungfrau von Orleans'.
First performance: Milan (La Scala) February 15, 1845.

Notes:
Verdi's setting is closer to Schiller than Tchaikovsky's » but even farther from history.

Alzira
Opera in Prologue and 2 Acts.
Text by Salvatore Cammarano based on Voltaire's play.
First performance: Naples (Teatro San Carlo) August 12, 1845.

Attila
Opera in Prologue and 3 Acts.
Text by Temistocle Solera based on Zacharias Werner's play.
First performance: Venice (Teatro La Fenice) March 17, 1846. London 1848; New York 1910.

Macbeth
Opera in 4 Acts.
Text by Piave and Andrea Maffei based on Shakespeare's play.
First performance: Florence (Teatro della Pergola) March 14, 1847. New York 1850; Dublin 1859.

Notes:
The opera was a favourite of Verdi's, who took great pains over everything: libretto, composition, production. It fell from public favour for some years, but has lately made a strong comeback. It was not the first Shakespeare play Verdi

considered; a project for *King Lear* was one of the few major plans that did not materialise. A French version of *Macbeth* was produced in Paris at the Théâtre-Lyrique in 1865, with a new text by Charles Nuitter and A. Beaumont.

I Masnadieri

Opera in 4 Acts.
Text by Andrea Maffei based on Schiller's 'Die Räuber'.
First performance: London (Her Majesty's) July 22, 1847.

Notes:
After the production of *Attila* in Venice, Verdi was supposed to go to London to produce an opera for the impresario Benjamin Lumley. But he was ill, and was ordered complete rest. He produced *Macbeth* in Florence before returning to complete *I Masnadieri* for Lumley. He was still not well, and the English climate did him no good. But the opera was produced at the command of Queen Victoria, who attended the first night with Prince Albert, Prince Louis Bonaparte and the Duke of Wellington. It was a successful evening, but it did not last and Lumley himself seems to have been disappointed.

Il Corsaro

Opera in 3 Acts.
Text by Piave based on Byron's poem.
First performance: Trieste (Teatro Grande) October 25, 1848.

Below: *Sherrill Milnes as Macbeth in Verdi's first Shakespearian opera, which has recently regained popularity.*

Notes:

After Verdi had seen the production of *Jérusalem* through, he decided to stay on awhile in Paris, and while there wrote *Il Corsaro*, originally for Francesco Lucca to publish and Lumley to stage in London. But it was given first at Trieste. Much has been made of the fact that Verdi did not attend the première: in fact he was otherwise engaged with his attentions to Giuseppina Strepponi (the singer he lived with for some years, and eventually married in 1859), with political matters, and also he had a bad cold.

La Battaglia di Legnano

Opera in 4 Acts.
Text by Salvatore Cammarano.
First performance: Rome (Teatro Argentina) January 27, 1849.

Notes:

This was another of Verdi's patriotic operas, written during the years of Italy's struggle for freedom from foreign domination. The cry 'Viva Italia!' was bound to produce a spirited reaction. It did: 'Viva Verdi!'

Luisa Miller

Opera in 3 Acts.
Text by Cammarano based on Schiller's 'Kabale und Liebe'.
First performance: Naples (Teatro San Carlo) December 8, 1849. New York 1852; London 1858.

Rigoletto

Opera in 3 Acts.
Text by Piave based on Victor Hugo's 'Le Roi s'amuse'.
First performance: Venice (Teatro La Fenice) March 11, 1851. London (Covent Garden) 1853; New York 1857.

Notes:

Rigoletto was the first opera of Verdi's 'middle period' which produced his most popular works. Its combination of melodic richness and dramatic, sometimes melodramatic, effectiveness has proved irresistible. It is hardly subtle; but it is entirely memorable, and has, from the very first performance, always achieved great popularity.

Il Trovatore

Opera in 4 Acts.
Text by Cammarano based on Antonio García Gutiérrez's play 'El trovador'.
First performance: Rome (Teatro Apollo) January 19, 1853. New York 1855; London (Covent Garden) 1855.

Right: *Luciano Pavarotti, in a scene from* Luisa Miller.

Notes:

Il Trovatore is generally thought to be absurd and incomprehensible in terms of its libretto. This is compounded by the fact that apparently the music exists virtually without reference to the dramatic situations. The sheer vitality and infectious verve of Verdi's music puts most ungenerous thoughts out of mind.

Above: *Fiorenza Cossotto in* Il Trovatore *at Covent Garden.*

La Traviata
Opera in 3 Acts.
Text by Piave based on Alexandre Dumas's 'La Dame aux camélias'
First performance: Venice (Teatro La Fenice) March 6, 1853. London (Her Majesty's) 1856; New York 1856.

Notes:

This great and enduringly popular opera had the worst possible first performance. The singers had no confidence in the opera, and thought it ridiculously 'avant-garde'. Nothing went right. Even Verdi himself suspected what would happen if the arrangements were not changed; but he was powerless to do anything about it. It was not long, however, before *La Traviata* found its rightful place in the international repertoire. Violetta is based on Dumas's Marguerite Gautier, herself based on the Parisian courtesan Marie Duplessis who died of consumption at the age of 23. Verdi saw Dumas's play in 1852, in Paris, and *La Traviata* remained a particular favourite of its composer.

Les Vêpres Siciliennes (The Sicilian Vespers)
Opera in 5 Acts.
Text by Eugène Scribe and Charles Duveyrier.
First performance: Paris (Opéra) June 13, 1855.

I Vespri Siciliani

(*Originally* 'Giovanna di Guzman': *Italian version of* 'Les Vêpres siciliennes)
Opera in 5 Acts.
Italian text by A. Fusinato.
First performance: Parma, December 26, 1855. London (Drury Lane) 1859; New York 1859.

Notes:

Verdi wrote the *Vespers* to a commission from the Paris Opéra for a work to be performed during the Great Exhibition of 1855. Both subject and librettist were pre-determined. The opera would be in the style still favoured in Paris: the kind of spectacular Grand Opera on which Meyerbeer » had risen to fame and fortune. Verdi was not happy from the start. To begin with the unscrupulous Scribe gave him a crude text barely altered from one he had sold Donizetti » and the composer had set as *Il Duca d'Alba*. But as usual, Verdi overcame the limitations of his text and poured some glorious music into his setting. The original French version was translated and played throughout Italy, reaching La Scala, Milan on February 4, 1856. Thereafter it faded from favour somewhat. The Italian version is the one nowadays usually played (and recorded), though a good case can be made for a revival of the original French.

Simon Boccanegra

Opera in Prologue and 3 Acts.
Text by Piave based on the play by Antonio Garcia Gutiérrez.
First performance: Venice (Teatro La Fenice) March 12, 1857. New York 1932.

Notes:

In 1880, 23 years after its première, Verdi took *Simon Boccanegra* in hand and re-worked a good deal of it in conjunction with his then librettist, Arrigo Boito ».

Below: *Joan Sutherland as Violetta in* La Traviata *at Covent Garden.*

GIUSEPPE VERDI

Aroldo
Opera in 4 Acts.
Text by Piave.
First performance: Rimini, August 16, 1857.

Notes:
Aroldo is, in fact, another version of the opera *Stiffelio*, which
Verdi wrote at Piave's suggestion on a text based on a French
play *Le Pasteur* by Emile Souvestre and Eugène Bourgeois and
which was produced in Trieste on November 16, 1850. The plots
are virtually identical until the last Act, though the situations
are changed. Act 3 of *Stiffelio* is cut short in *Aroldo* and a fourth
Act added.

Un Ballo in Maschera (A Masked Ball)
Opera in 3 Acts (original title 'Gustavo III').
Text by Antonio Somma based on Eugène Scribe's play.
First performance: Rome (Teatro Apollo) February 17, 1859. New York 1861;
London 1861.

Below: Un Ballo in Maschera *at the Royal Opera House, Covent Garden.*

Notes:

The story is based on the assassination of King Gustavus III of Sweden in 1792, at a masked ball. Verdi originally set the opera in Stockholm with a Swedish cast. But political unrest made the Italian authorities jib at an opera depicting the assassination of a king. They allowed its performance only provided the setting and characters were transferred to Boston, and the cast made English. In fact, an assassination attempt was made against Napoleon III when *Ballo* was to be produced in Naples; and again the cry went up — *Viva Verdi!* But it was not only the musical acumen of the crowd that was implied: the call was also a political acrostic — Vittorio Emmanuele, Re D'Italia. Nowadays some opera houses revert to the original Swedish version, but we have retained the Italian since it is generally in that form. The music remains splendidly the same.

La Forza del Destino (The Force of Destiny)

Opera in 4 Acts.
Text by Piave based on the play 'Don Alvaro, o La fuerza de sino' by Angelo Pérez de Saavedra, Duke of Rivas.
First performance: St Petersburg (Court Opera) November 10, 1862. New York 1865; London (Her Majesty's) 1867.

Notes:

La Forza is a big sprawling opera of tremendous dramatic and musical force. Verdi wrote it for the Imperial Opera in St Petersburg for their 1861/2 season. At first he proposed to use Victor Hugo's *Ruy Blas*, but decided in favour of the Spanish play, which Piave adapted with additions from Schiller's *Wallenstein's Camp*. At the end of 1869 he revised the score with the help of the librettist Antonio Ghislanzoni. It was from this revised version that the overture, one of the most popular and extended in all Verdi, was written. It is a stirring piece, often played in concerts.

Don Carlos

Opera in 5 Acts.
Text by François Joseph Méry and Camille du Locle based on Schiller's play.
(Italian translation by Achille de Luazières and Angelo Zanardini.)
First performance: Paris (Opéra) March 11, 1867. London (Covent Garden) 1867; New York 1877.

Don Carlo

Opera in 4 Acts (revised Italian version of above).
Text revised by Antonio Ghislanzoni.
First performance: Milan (La Scala) January 10, 1884.

Notes:

Don Carlos, like the *Sicilian Vespers*, was written for the Paris Opéra and was designed also on a scale to meet that city's taste.

Seventeen years later, Verdi took the opera in hand and refashioned it. He suppressed the first Act, retaining only Carlos's aria, so that the new Italian version emerged with four Acts instead of five, not entirely to its advantage. The original French version is virtually never heard these days, but the four-Act revision is often performed. The most intelligent and most frequent compromise, however, is to restore the first Act to the later revision.

Aida

Opera in 4 Acts.
Text by Camille du Locle after synopsis by Auguste Mariette (Bey) translated into Italian by Antonio Ghislanzoni.
First performance: Cairo (Opéra House) December 24, 1871. Milan (La Scala) 1872; New York 1873; London (Covent Garden) 1876.

Notes:

Verdi wrote *Aida* to a commission from the Khedive of Egypt for a work to open the new Cairo Opera House. It was not in fact used for that occasion, but found its place there as a grand opera of great colour and power. It has been argued that the story of *Aida* was borrowed from a libretto by Metastasio entitled *Nitteti*.

Otello

Opera in 4 Acts.
Text by Arrigo Boito based on Shakespeare's play.
First performance: Milan (La Scala) February 5, 1887. New York 1888; London (Lyceum Theatre) 1889.

Notes:

After *Aida* Verdi wrote no more operas for several years. It seemed, as he himself said, that his account was closed. But a meeting was arranged with Boito » who was anxious to work with Verdi on a Shakespeare project (Boito having already written a Shakespeare libretto, on *Hamlet*, for Franco Faccio). Verdi became interested, and his miraculous late burst of creativity was set in motion. Boito's texts for *Otello* and *Falstaff* are generally considered the best ever provided for an Italian composer.

Falstaff

Opera in 3 Acts.
Text by Arrigo Boito based on Shakespeare's 'Merry Wives of Windsor' and 'Henry IV'.
First performance: Milan (La Scala) February 9, 1893. London (Covent Garden) 1894; New York 1895.

Notes:

Apart from the early and unsuccessful *Un giorno di regno*, Verdi wrote no comedy until *Falstaff*. There were one or two comic scenes in his operas, but nothing to suggest that he had in him a

Above: Don Carlos *at the Royal Opera House, Covent Garden.*

great comic masterpiece. His life's work up to *Otello* appeared as a long succession of tragic dramas, frequently magnificent in power and expressiveness. Then Boito put this into his hands: he recognised it as unusual, and set to work, at first saying he was writing it simply for his private pleasure. He led Italian opera forward into new domains. He created a marvellous conversational style and found a declamation in which the Italian language was matched with its perfect musical equivalent.

ANTONIO VIVALDI
(b. Venice 4.3.1678; d. Vienna ?.7.1741)

For much of his life, Vivaldi was music director of the Conservatore dell'Ospidale della Pieta in Venice, a music school for girls, where he produced a great profusion of instrumental works. He himself had his early training from his father and later from Giovanni Legrenzi in Venice. He took holy orders in 1703 and because of his red hair became known as *'il prete rosso'* ('red priest'). Later in his life he travelled much in Europe; but his last years were not happy. He allowed ambitious schemes to distort his judgement and in the end he died in poverty in Vienna, where he had settled in 1739, hopeful of making a great success but finding time and circumstance against him. As an opera composer, Vivaldi does not occupy anything approaching the position he holds in the instrumental field. He was prolific and ambitious, and his operas were produced in many Italian cities; but those that survive today — a scant 18 or so — are patchy, and too often marked by haste and careless workmanship, sometimes imposed by the demands of his patrons. Their chief merit, however, lies in their splendid individual numbers.

Orlando
Opera in 3 Acts.
Text by Grazio Braccioli.
First performance: Venice (Teatro Sant' Angelo) Autumn 1727.

Notes:
Vivaldi had two shots at the Orlando subject, though the operas, separated by 13 years, have nothing in common bar the loosest link of theme. *Orlando finto pazzo* failed when it was produced in Venice in 1714, and when Vivaldi returned to the subject in 1727 he took a quite different line, though using the same librettist, Grazio Braccioli. *Orlando* was originally named *Orlando furioso* (the title on the MS in Turin), but subsequently Vivaldi dropped the *'furioso'*. The text is taken from Ariosto's poem which fed so many Baroque operas, including two by Handel » (*Alcina* and *Orlando*) and Haydn ». Though *Orlando* has virtually nothing to do with its predecessors some use is made of the same recitatives. It is the arias which carry the musical burden. Even so, the recording interpolates a Vivaldi chamber cantata to bolster Orlando's music. Like many Baroque opera plots the storyline is largely incomprehensible.

La Fida Ninfa
Opera in 3 Acts.
Text by Scipione Maffei.
First performance: Verona (Teatro Filarmonico) January 6, 1732.

Notes:
This is the only Vivaldi opera in print; the MS is in Turin. It is not a particularly attractive work, containing few musical plums. The recording (no longer available) is heavily cut, containing *da capo* arias, duet, trio and choral finale, plus the overture. The conventional plot concerns pirates and lovers and reunitings after hard times.

Tito Manlio
Opera in 3 Acts.
Text by Matteo Noris.
First performance: Not known.

Notes:
No dates of composition or performance are on record for this

opera. There are two manuscripts in Turin, on one of which is written in Vivaldi's own hand *'fatta in 5 giorni'* (written in 5 days). It is now thought that the work dates from around 1719 and was written in Mantua. Like many of Vivaldi's works some parts are borrowed from other compositions. Thus the final chorus is appropriated from Vivaldi's oratorio *Juditha triumphans devicta Holofernis barbarie* with a text of Jacopo Cassetti, which was sung at the Pietà in 1716 and has been recorded. The text of *Tito Manlio* concerns the usual squabble between factions (in this case the Romans and the Italians and their allies) and the usual love entanglements. Vivaldi, the master of the concerto, can be discerned behind several of the arias where the instrumental texture and *obligati* are more interesting than the vocal line.

Above: *Antonio Vivaldi, nicknamed 'il prete rosso', a pioneer in the orchestral, particularly the concerto field, but whose operas have not remained in circulation.*

Above: *Wagner founded a theatre for his operas at Bayreuth in 1872.*

RICHARD WAGNER
(b. Leipzig 22.5.1813; d. Venice 13.2.1883)

More books have probably been written about Wagner and more controversy aroused by him than by any other composer. His legal father died when he was six months old and his mother married a Jewish actor named Ludwig Geyer, who may have been his true father. Although as a child he moved in artistic circles he did not decide to become a composer until he was 15 years old, when he was shaken into activity by hearing Beethoven's » *Choral* symphony and *Fidelio*; the Ninth Symphony especially remained his musical ideal and model and he described it as "the redemption of music from out of her peculiar element into the realm of universal art". From then on, he saw himself as a musical Messiah. Totally self-centred, like many men of short stature, he had a frighteningly powerful personality, and behaved as one who knew he was a supreme genius; selfish, arrogant and full of prejudices, demanding that the world should support him — "I can't live on a miserable organist's pittance like Bach . . . the world owes me what I need . . . brilliance, beauty and light!" He worked with unrelenting dedication, wrote volumes about himself and his music and established at Bayreuth a theatre where his music could be worshipped. All this would have been ludicrous in a man of lesser ability; fortunately his genius was as great as he presumed it was, and his music was a tremendously powerful influence on those who followed. After his life and work, opera could never be the same again. His first operas were comparatively conventional and not very successful. The tremendous effort he put into works like *Rienzi*, *Der fliegende Holländer* and *Lohengrin* left him impoverished and his life in a turmoil. In various conducting posts that he held he antagonised those with whom he worked, and those whom he played for. But gradually the operas made their mark, forever arousing extremes of hostility and devotion. With *Tristan und Isolde* and the great *Ring* cycle he found his true form, matching words, music and imagination in a glory of sound and olympian drama.

Die Feen

Opera in 3 Acts.
Text based on Gozzi's 'La donna serpente'.
First performance: Munich, June 29, 1888.

Notes:

Wagner's second opera (the first, *Die Hochzeit*, was never completed) was not produced until after his death. It declares its allegiances to the German Romantic operas of Weber » and Marschner.

Das Liebesverbot, oder Die Novize von Palermo

Opera in 2 Acts.
Text by Wagner based on Shakespeare's 'Measure for Measure'.
First performance: Magdeburg, March 29, 1836.

Notes:

Das Liebesverbot is quite unlike anything else that Wagner wrote: he seemed to go against all his professional ideals and wrote in a simulation of the Italian style of Donizetti ». The overture, which is really all that survives, has castanets and tambourines, and is full of Latin gaieties. But then the whole work was written in a spirit of youthful hedonism through which it is necessary for spirited young men—even Wagner— to pass.

Rienzi, der letze der Tribunen

Opera in 5 Acts.
Text by Wagner based on the novel by Bulwer-Lytton.
First performance: Dresden (Court Opera) October 20, 1842. New York 1878; London 1879.

Notes:

Rienzi was written as a Grand Opera for Paris, with all the trappings of fashionable Parisian opera. It was an attempt to out-Meyerbeer Meyerbeer », and asserted the firm Wagnerian principle that if you can't join them, beat them. He suffered humiliations in Paris, and *Rienzi* was produced eventually in Dresden. There are many hints in the score of the Wagner to come, as well as a good deal of noisy theatrical emptiness.

Der fliegende Holländer (The Flying Dutchman)

Opera in 3 Acts.
Text by Wagner based on an episode in Heine's 'Memoiren des von Schnabelewopski'.
First performance: Dresden (Court Opera) January 2, 1843. London (Drury Lane) 1870; Philadelphia 1876.

Notes:

The Flying Dutchman was the first opera in which Wagner found his true voice. It is a work of passionate genius; and if it still has its immaturities, it tingles with life. Both dramatically and musically it spreads out both ways from its pivot point, Senta's ballad. The sea music, so vividly created, came to Wagner while he was on a small ship on his journey from Riga to Paris, and was caught in a violent storm and forced into port, where the sailors' songs gave him his clue for the sailors' chorus.

Tannhäuser und der Sängerkrieg auf Wartburg

Opera in 3 Acts.
Text by Wagner.
First performance: Dresden (Court Opera) October 19, 1845. New York 1859; London (Covent Garden) 1876; Paris (revised version) 1861.

Notes:

In *Tannhäuser* Wagner made further progress in pursuit of his artistic ideal and objective. It has probably more of the faults of crudeness and banality of which Wagner is frequently accused than any other of his works. But no doubt they had to be worked through anyway; and he recognised it. When he came to prepare a production for Paris in 1861, he substantially revised the score. Wagner, at this stage, was a more mature composer altogether, with the first two sections of *The Ring* and *Tristan und Isolde* behind him. Evidences of this can be seen in *Tannhäuser's* rewritten parts, with their greater flexibility and freedom. Some say the later version shows too many creative seams; but these days it is the preferred edition. Tannhäuser himself was a historical character from the 13th century, as were the minnesingers.

Lohengrin

Opera in 3 Acts.
Text by Wagner.
First performance: Weimar (Court Opera) August 28, 1850. London (Covent Garden) 1875; New York 1871.

Notes:

In *Lohengrin*, following *Tannhäuser*, Wagner approached the evolving of his mature style from the opposite end. Whereas *Tannhäuser* with its central theme of the contest of song and the minnesingers looks forward to *Die Meistersinger von Nürnberg*, so *Lohengrin* with its Holy Grail motif can be seen, in the retrospect of Wagner's total life and achievement, to have thrown a rainbow bridge across the years to *Parsifal*. Each opera in its way prepares the ground for what is to come; for the fully fledged music drama. Because of his political involvements and consequent banishment, Wagner himself did not hear *Lohengrin* until 1861, and it was first produced in Germany at the insistence of Liszt, who staged it at Weimar.

Der Ring des Nibelungen (The Ring of the Nibelungs)

A Stage Festival Play for Three Days and a Preliminary Evening.
Text by Wagner based on the Nibelung Saga.
First performance (complete): Bayreuth, August 13, 14, 16 and 17, 1878.

Notes:

The *Ring* tetralogy is so vast, so complex in motive and meaning that no synopsis can do more than follow out the main story line. In 1848 Wagner finished a libretto for an opera *The Death of Siegfried*. He decided that it was necessary to go back to tell the story of Siegfried himself, then back again to his origins, then back once again to explain the overall context. Thus it came out as four complete works. The complete libretti were published in 1853, and Wagner set to work on the music. He wrote *Das Rheingold*, *Die Walküre*, and the first two-and-a-half acts of *Siegfried*. He then broke off for 12 years, during which he wrote *Tristan und Isolde* and *Die Meistersinger*, before completing *Siegfried* and *Götterdämmerung*. *Rheingold* and *Walküre* were produced independently in Munich, but the whole cycle was first presented in Wagner's own festival opera house at Bayreuth in south Germany, in 1876. The first half of the *Ring* cycle represents Wagner's technique of music drama with its complex of *leitmotiven* at its strictest and most 'pure'; when he returned to it after the 12-year break, he was a composer with the experience of *Tristan* behind him. Thus, the latter part of the

Ring contains new subtleties of harmony and melody added to the earlier style and in several respects modifying it.

Das Rheingold
Prologue in 1 Act.
Text by Wagner.
First performance: Munich, September 22, 1869.

Die Walküre
Music drama in 3 Acts.
Text by Wagner.
First performance: Munich, June 26, 1870.

Siegfried
Music drama in 3 Acts.
Text by Wagner.
First performance: Bayreuth, August 16, 1876.

Götterdämmerung
Music drama in Prologue and 3 Acts.
Text by Wagner.
First performance: Bayreuth, August 17, 1876.

Tristan und Isolde
Music drama in 3 Acts.
Text by Wagner.
First performance: Munich (Court Opera) June 19, 1865. London (Drury Lane) 1882; New York (Metropolitan) 1886.

Notes:
Tristan is music's great testament to sexual love. Wagner himself was perfectly clear about it. It is also perhaps the most perfectly realised music drama, in which subtlety of leading motif, of chromatic harmony and of 'endless melody' are so closely interwoven that it is virtually impossible to tell them apart. Wagner wrote *Tristan* while staying near Zürich, at the house of his friend, Otto Wesendonck. At the time he was having an affair with Wesendonck's wife, Mathilde—a union which also produced the five *Wesendonck Lieder*.

Die Meistersinger von Nürnberg
Music drama in 3 Acts.
Text by Wagner.
First performance: Munich (Court Opera) June 21, 1868. London (Drury Lane) 1882; New York (Metropolitan) 1886.

Notes:
Die Meistersinger von Nürnberg is as different from *Tristan und Isolde* as day is from night. Indeed, as *Tristan* celebrates the

Above: Die Meistersinger von Nürnberg *at Covent Garden.*

enfolding powers of night so *Meistersinger* extols the colour and luminosity of day. Between them they reveal and inhabit the dark and light sides of Wagner's genius, and are complementary; the saturated chromatic tragedy of *Tristan* being the obverse of the diatonic comedy of *Meistersinger*. But *Meistersinger* is not all and only comedy; originally the opera was intended as a frontal attack on crabbed criticism; Beckmesser being called Hans Lick (a direct jibe at Wagner's sworn enemy, the powerful Viennese critic Eduard Hanslick). But from such crude beginnings, warmth and humanity took over and triumphed. Hans Sachs was a historical figure, like Tannhäuser; and just as that earlier opera dealt with the aristocratic minstrels, known as the minnesingers, so the later opera deals with the essentially bourgeois, but also historical, Guild of Masters.

Parsifal
Sacred music drama in 3 Acts.
Text by Wagner based on the legends of the Holy Grail.
First performance: Bayreuth, July 26, 1882. New York (Metropolitan) 1903;
London (Covent Garden) 1914.

Notes:
Parsifal was a subject long in Wagner's mind: it appears in *Lohengrin* (who is Parsifal's son) and he saw at one time the 'sin' of Tannhäuser passing through Tristan to rest in Amfortas. When he came finally to write *Parsifal*, Wagner was old and exhausted. Despite the opera's musical subtleties and the stamp of genius on its best pages, some saw signs that Wagner was worn out and defeated. Wagner called *Parsifal* a Sacred Festival Play, and he wanted it played only at Bayreuth; a wish his widow Cosima obstinately tried to carry out. But inevitably the opera went out into the world. It is perhaps the most controversial of Wagner's mature works: there is a religioso

atmosphere about which frequently offends, but for many it represents Wagner at his most subtle and profound.

(Note: The origins and historical background to all Wagner's operas are both complex and important. They are brilliantly uncovered and analysed in Ernest Newman's *Wagner Nights* (Putnam, London), a book that is essential for a full understanding of Wagner's mind and work.)

VINCENT WALLACE
(b. Waterford 11.3.1812; d. Château de Haget, Haut-Pyrénées, 12.10.1865)

Son of an Irish Army bandmaster, Wallace lived an adventurous life. As well as being a prolific composer, he was a travelling virtuoso of the violin and had many escapades around the world, including encounters with cannibals, a tiger and an exploding steamer. In 1831 he went to Australia, became involved in a number of enterprises, lost money, and left 'in a clandestine manner'. He married one of his piano pupils, Isabella Kelly, in Dublin, then lived with and later married (bigamously) another pianist, American Hélène Stoepel. Wallace had gone to America in 1850, intending to become an American citizen, but returned to Europe and finally settled in France. He wrote many operas, for London and Paris, of which *Maritana* is the only one significantly remembered.

Maritana
Opera in 3 Acts.
Text by Edward Fitzball based on Adolphe d'Ennery's play 'Don César de Bazan'.
First performance: London (Drury Lane) November 15, 1845 Philadelphia 1846; Vienna 1848.

(Sir) WILLIAM WALTON
(b. Oldham 29.3.1902)

The senior and one of the most important of the 'middle generation' of English music's 'renaissance' began his musical life at home and at the age of 10 went to Christ Church Cathedral Choir School in Oxford where, among other benefits, he was introduced to Sir Hugh Allen. It is said that Walton is largely self-taught, but there is no doubt he had a thorough grounding in music upon which he was able to build his highly individual talent. He began composing early; but most of his youthful compositions were destroyed, and thereafter he composed and published only at longish intervals and after much deep thought. A major event in Walton's life was his meeting with the Sitwell family at Oxford which led to a long association and the inspiration for several works, the most

notable being *Façade*, an Entertainment for speaker and small orchestra to poems by Edith Sitwell. Like that other, older and very different genius of English music, Sir Thomas Beecham, Walton was born and has remained a Lancastrian, with the typical Lancashire directness and honesty of speech and attitude. Walton has written two operas, the full scale *Troilus and Cressida* and the one-act comedy *The Bear*.

Troilus and Cressida
Opera in 3 Acts.
Text by Christopher Hassall based on Chaucer.
First performance: London (Covent Garden) December 3, 1954. San Francisco 1954.

Notes:
The text is not from Shakespeare (or the *Iliad*) but Chaucer — though with some changes of emphasis. The opera is written in a kind of post-19th century style, with the major operatic conventions observed, and re-charged. Walton's lineage in English music is via Elgar rather than Vaughan Williams ». Although he was a provocative 'modernist' in his early works, he later evolved a personal style which could be called typical English compromise: making use of serial techniques from a wholly individual standpoint, yet giving an overall traditional impression. So it is with *Troilus and Cressida*. There was a very successful 1976 revival of the opera.

The Bear
Comic opera (Extravaganza) in 1 Act
Text by Paul Dehn based on Chekhov.
First performance: Aldeburgh Festival, June 3, 1967.

Notes:
The plot is taken from the most successful of the five short 1-Act plays Chekhov issued under the name 'vaudevilles'. It concerns the fortunes and misfortunes of Madam Popova, still mourning the death of her dear departed husband, and the wealthy landowner who comes to collect an outstanding debt. They quarrel, but in the end, things sort themselves out and the bereaved lady capitulates to the insistent and rich, if boorish, suitor.

CARL MARIA VON WEBER
(b. Eutin, Lübeck 18.11.1786; d. London 5.6.1826)

Weber played a major part in the establishment of German Romantic opera. He was the link between Mozart » (*The Magic Flute*), Beethoven » (*Fidelio*) and the massive achievement of Wagner ». He took opera into enchanted fields first explored by Schubert » in symphony and song, yet he remained a composer with a distinctive voice of his own, in instrumental music as well as opera. The son of a travelling musician, he learnt his first music from his father, and at the age of 10 began to study with Michael Haydn. His operatic career began with *Peter Schmoll und seine Nachbarn* in 1803. After that he held a number of appointments in Germany (including the conductorship of the German theatre in Prague in 1813) and in 1816 took over directorship of the Dresden Court Opera, where he did much to consolidate the emergent German opera. *Der Freischütz* was produced in Berlin in 1821 and *Euryanthe* in Vienna in 1823. He was commissioned by Covent Garden to produce an opera in English and he studied the language closely before undertaking the task. The result was *Oberon*, which appeared in 1826, but by then he was already in declining health and he died in London at the house of his friend Sir George Smart.

Abu Hassan
Singspiel in 1 Act.
Text by Franz Carl Heimer.
First performance: Munich, June 4, 1811.

Der Freischütz
Opera in 3 Acts.
Text by Friedrich Kind based on Apel and Laun's 'Gespensterbuch'.
First performance: Berlin (Schauspielhaus) June 18, 1821.

Notes:
This is the most famous German Romantic opera before Wagner ». In it are several innovations: the first, the overture which not only introduces the principal melodies of the opera but is carefully fashioned into a complete tone poem in a way Wagner was to follow up in *The Flying Dutchman*, *Tannhäuser* and *Die Meistersinger*. Secondly, it introduces that note of magic, the supernatural and the fantastic-mysterious that was also to be a Wagnerian leading motif. It is the early German Romantic opera *par excellence*.

Euryanthe
Opera in 3 Acts.
Text by Helmine von Chézy.
First performance: Vienna (Kärntnertor Theatre) October 25, 1823. London (Covent Garden) 1833; New York (Metropolitan) 1887.

Notes:
This is one of those operas which are alleged to be unstageable

Above: *Carl Maria von Weber, whose works helped to establish German national opera.*

because of the lunacies of the plot. But the music of *Euryanthe* is quite good enough to keep it going. The subject of medieval romance and ladies in distress was near to the heart of the Romantic generations.

Oberon, or The Elf King's Oath

Opera in 3 Acts.
Text by James Robinson Planché based on Sotheby's translation of Wieland's 'Oberon' and earlier French sources.
First performance: London (Covent Garden) April 12, 1826. New York 1828.

Notes:
The libretto of *Oberon* is even more complicated than usual; but again Weber poured into the opera some of his finest and most eloquent music, beginning with another magical overture. Much of the trouble lies in the way the music is continually interrupted by pantomime spoken dialogue. The opera was, of course, originally in English, but *Oberon's* proper place is in the German Romantic theatre and that is where it now abides, in the German translation.

CARL MARIA von WEBER

Die drei Pintos
Opera (unfinished by Weber, completed by Gustav Mahler).
Text by Theodor Hell, based on Carl Ludwig Seidel's 'Der Brautkampf'.
First performance: Leipzig (Municipal Theatre) January 20, 1888.

Notes:
This is something of a curiosity. Weber began it in 1820 but for
some reason never adequately explained, abandoned it in 1821.
After his death his widow handed the sketches to Meyerbeer »,
who kept them for a number of years and left them untouched.
In 1852, after trying to interest the young Wagner » in the task
of completion, she reclaimed them. In the end they came into
Gustav Mahler's hands, and he worked out a 'completion' using
Weber's original sketches, which consisted of a first Act and the

initial part of a second, plus other material from Weber's works. Thus it is hardly a Weber opera in any full sense; but it is still worth attention. The plot, such as it is, concerns Don Gaston Viratos who decides to impersonate Don Pinto de Fonesca who is travelling to Madrid to claim Clarissa as his bride. Don Pinto himself also goes along—and the third Pinto is Clarissa's lover Don Gomez de Freiros. All pretty preposterous.

Peter Schmoll und seine Nachtbarn
  (1803)
Silvana (1810)

Below: *Weber's* Der Freischütz *was first performed in Berlin in 1821, and by 1884 had been performed there over 500 times.*

KURT WEILL
(b. Dessau 2.3.1900; d. New York 3.4.1950)

Like many composers caught in the confusing cross-currents of 20th century music, Weill seemed to follow many paths. Like many young intellectual musicians, following musical studies with Humperdinck » and Busoni », he might well have continued to write the rather serious Germanic music, represented by works like his early Violin Concerto, written for Szigeti. The strains of Stravinsky » and Hindemith » found here were always with Weill's work but, as he turned to the stage, and wrote his first opera *Der Protagonist*, he was becoming aware of the universal call of folk-music, popular music and jazz. By the time he wrote his first great success *Die Dreigroschenoper* in 1928, these popular elements had been absorbed and intermingled with the academic German strains to produce a unique style — a strange mixture of the humorous, sardonic, sentimental and the sinister. His association with Bertolt Brecht confirmed his socialist beliefs and his duty to write music for the people. In their modernisation of *The Beggar's Opera* story, exactly the right libretto emerged to bring out the best of Weill's music. In the morally and politically slanted operas that followed, he continued to mix the ingredients into a product that was romantic entirely in the contemporary terms of a world torn by one World War and preparing for the next. He found in the voice of Lotte Lenya, whom he married in 1926, the perfect interpreter of his music. After 1933, Weill's works were banned in Germany, and he and his wife fled first to Paris and then to New York where he settled for life. So sensitive to contemporary life, it was impossible for him to write the same music in America that a German background had produced. Many have been disappointed that another *Dreisgroschenoper* did not materialise. Instead we must accept that Weill was not a one-work composer and discover the width of his achievement and the unique qualities that have left their mark on the contemporary musical theatre.

Der Protagonist
Opera in 1 Act.
Text by Georg Kaiser, based on his tragedy of the same title.
First performance: Dresden, March 27, 1926.

Mahagonny-Songspiel
Songspiel in 1 Act.
Text by Bertolt Brecht.
First performance: Baden-Baden (Deutsche Kammermusikfest) July 18, 1927.

Notes:
Weill was commissioned to produce a short opera for a festival of modern German chamber music. His first idea was to set a scene from *King Lear* or *Antigone*, but as he and Bertolt Brecht were already working on the *Mahagonny* opera they decided to compile the songspiel, a 'style study' of the work of an incidental

Above: *David Atherton directs Kurt Weill's* Happy End.

nature which gave Weill an opportunity to try his hand at writing for opera singers.

Die Dreigroschenoper

Opera in a Prologue and Eight Scenes (later in 3 Acts).
Text by Bertolt Brecht, based on Hauptmann's translation of 'The Beggar's Opera'.
First performance: Berlin (Theater um Schiffbauerdamm) August 31, 1928. New York 1933. American version by Marc Blitzstein, New York, 1954 (The Threepenny Opera); London 1956.

Notes:

The opera is broadly based on Gay's » piece but spends far more time moralising in long vocal sections as opposed to the short snippets of folksong used by Gay. In view of the pervading gloom that precedes it the pardon comes as a curious ending and less effective than Gay's (see *The Beggar's Opera*).

Happy End

Play with music.
Text by Bertolt Brecht.
First performance: Berlin (Theater am Schiffbauerdamm) September 2, 1929.

Notes:

Not strictly an opera but so close in style to *Die Dreigroschenoper* and not far removed from it in form that it is worth mentioning in the list of Weill's vocal works. The song *Surabya Johnny* is a remarkably close relative to the earlier *Moritat*, and the musical score is a substantial part of the entertainment.

Aufstieg und Fall der Stadt Mahagonny

Opera in 3 Acts.
Text by Bertolt Brecht.
First performance: Leipzig, March 9, 1930. London 1963.

Na und? (1926)
Royal Palace (1927)
Der Zar lässt sich photographieren (1928)
Die Bürgschaft (1932)
Der Silbersee (1933)
Marie galante (1933)

A Kingdom for a Cow (1935)
Knickerbocker Holiday (1938)
Lady in the Dark (1941)
Down in the Valley (1948)
Lost in the Stars (1949)
etc.

ERMANNO WOLF-FERRARI
(b. Venice 12.1.1876; d. Venice 21.1.1948)

The son of a German father and an Italian mother, Wolf-Ferrari was first apprenticed, in Rome, as a painter: his father's profession. But his musical proclivities soon became apparent, and he studied in Munich with Rheinberger. On his return to his native Venice in 1899, he was sufficiently proficient in composition to have an oratorio produced by the Philharmonic Society. He wrote a number of instrumental works, but it was his operas that brought him principal fame. His first was produced in 1900 on the familiar Cinderella theme (*Cenerentola*); but it failed to impress in Venice and made a better showing in Bremen in 1902. Henceforward many of his operas were given first in Germany—the last of all being presented in Hanover in June, 1943. His most lasting opera is his little masterpiece *Il Segreto di Susanna*. Apart from this work it is the sparkling overtures to the others that claim our principal attention.

I Quattro Rusteghi (The Four Rustics)
Opera buffa in 3 Acts.
Text by Giuseppe Pizzolato based on Goldoni's comedy.
First performance: Munich (as 'Die vier Grobiane') March 19, 1906. Milan (La Scala) 1914.

Notes:
A production of this opera was presented by Sadler's Wells, London, in 1946, under the title *The School for Fathers* in a translation by the late Edward J. Dent.

Il Segreto di Susanna (Susanna's Secret)
Comedy in 1 Act.
Text by Enrico Golisciani.
First performance: Munich (as 'Susannens Geheirnnis') December 4, 1909. New York 1911; London (Covent Garden) 1911.

Notes:
This little work could be seen as a linear successor to Bach's 'Coffee' Cantata, which has a go at the then new coffee craze rather than the smoking habit. But there, the connection ends.

I Gioielli della Madonna (The Jewels of the Madonna)
Opera in 3 Acts.
Text by Golisciani and Carlo Zangarini.
First performance: Berlin (Kurfürsten-Oper) (as 'Der Schmuck der Madonna') December 23, 1911. London (Covent Garden) 1912.

Il Campiello
Opera in 3 Acts.
Text by Mario Ghisalberti based on a comedy by Goldoni.
First performance: Milan (La Scala) February 12, 1936.

La Dama Boba
Opera in 3 Acts.
Text by Ghisalberti based on a comedy by Lope de Vega.
First performance: Milan (La Scala) February 1, 1939.

224

*L'amore medico (1913)
Gli amanti sposi (1925)
Das himmelskleid (1927)
Sly (1927)*

*La vedova scaltra (1931)
Gli dei a Tebe (1943)
etc.*

RICCARDO ZANDONAI

(b. Sacco, Trentino, 28.5.1883; d. Pesaro 5.6.1944)

Another Italian opera composer in the *verismo* line of post-Puccini », Zandonai studied under Mascagni » at the Liceo Musicale de Pesaro where he took his diploma in 1902. Thirty-seven years later he became the Liceo's director, and remained so until his death. He had an individual lyric vein of melody but only a nominal dramatic gift. But his operas make good theatre and are a positive contribution to Italian music. His non-operatic music is unimpressive and infrequently heard. Of his ten operas the most successful were *Francesca da Rimini* and *Giulietta e Romeo*.

Francesca da Rimini

*Opera in 4 Acts.
Text by Tito Ricordi based on D'Annunzio's tragedy drawn from Dante.
First performance: Turin (Teatro Regio) February 19, 1914. London (Covent Garden) 1914; New York (Metropolitan) 1916.*

225

Index to composers, musicians and works.

231

234

237